The Democratic Tradition and the Evolution of Schooling in Norway

Recent Titles in
Contributions to the Study of Education

The Democratic Tradition and the Evolution of Schooling in Norway

Val D. Rust

Contributions to the Study of Education, Number 34

GREENWOOD PRESS
New York • Westport, Connecticut • London

Library of Congress Cataloging-in-Publication Data

Rust, Val Dean.
  The democratic tradition and the evolution of
schooling in Norway.

  (Contributions to the study of education, 0196-707X ;
no. 34)
    Bibliography: p.
    Includes index.
    1. Education—Norway—History. 2. Education and state
—Norway. 3. Educational equalization—Norway. I. Title.
II. Series.
LA891.R87 1989   370'.9481   89-11847
ISBN 0-313-26849-5 (lib. bdg. : alk. paper)

British Library Cataloguing in Publication Data is available.

Library of Congress Catalog Card Number: 89-11847
ISBN: 0-313-26849-5
ISSN: 0196-707X

First published in 1989

Greenwood Press, Inc.
88 Post Road West, Westport, Connecticut 06881

Printed in the United States of America

The paper used in this book complies with the
Permanent Paper Standard issued by the National
Information Standards Organization (Z39.48-1984).

10 9 8 7 6 5 4 3 2 1

370.9481
R971d

243099

Dedicated to

Jonathan, who attended Korsvoll Elementary School, Joshua, who attended Sogn Nursery School, and Daniel Erik, who was born in Ullevål Hospital.

Contents

Tables

Preface

The casual observer might find it curious that an American historian has chosen to engage in a study of Norwegian school reform. As I was doing field work in Norway, well informed Norwegians would often pose the question, "Why do you want to write about us?" Even they were rarely aware of the uniqueness and importance of the Norwegian social and educational evolution. Their story must be told, if a clear perspective of the entire school reform process in Europe in the past two centuries is to be gained.

Seeking to isolate the relevant historical forces and factors which have come into play in Norwegian school reform since that country gained independence from Denmark in 1814, I discuss the story of structural reform in Norway. No comprehensive historical study of the Norwegian educational reform process has yet appeared in the English language. Although Norwegian scholars have written extensively and competently about their own reform activities, very little of this material is available to the outside world. It is crucial to understand the Norwegian school reforms if a general understanding of the European educational reform process is to be gained. Scholars, having little awareness of events that characterize Norwegian developments, continue to make mistaken comments about the European reform process. Theses comments are based on an understanding of the major countries of Europe, such as France, Germany, and Great Britain, and are made without realizing that the Norwegian reforms have been, in many respects, either quite different or far in advance of these major countries.

In one major respect, the educational reform process in Norway has been quite similar to that existing in other European countries. Its focus has been on structural change, involving the establishment of a unified school catering to the entire population of learners. However, the ends that these reforms were intended to serve would be quite different.

In most of Europe, a major purpose of structural reforms has been to help bring about social amelioration by creating a common school structure. In other words, the belief of liberal reformers has held firm that a common school would increase the "democratization of educational opportunities and social mobility."[1] In Germany, for example, the school reformers of the past century have attempted to create an educational institution that would be used as an instrument "to bring about a change in German social and political life." School reform in Germany was not conceived as an attempt to create an institution that would extend and support the existing form of social life, but to create an institution that would effect social change.[2]

I began my inquiry conjecturing that the Norwegians did not intend to alter their basic social fabric through their reforms. In fact, I suspected that Norwegians believed their society was already highly democratic long before the school reform process was initiated, and I suspected that the Norwegians actually intended to create schools that would better reflect social life and serve its aims more appropriately. In relative terms, I suspected that Norway's social structure was in advance of its schools at the time of independence and was probably making greater progress toward social unity than were its schools. If its social structure was more democratic and egalitarian than the schools, it is unlikely that school reform could have acted as an intervention agent in social amelioration. This situation also helps to explain why Norway could have succeeded in its structural reform endeavors. The task of this study is to assess the evolving relationship between school and society in this regard.

A conceptual framework often used to assess relationships between various facets of life is the so-called "mobilization model," popularized by Karl Deutsch and used extensively by social scientists in past decades.[3] The basic notion of this model is that a number of specific processes are bracketed together as a society develops. Social scientists usually operationalize terms such as social mobilization, political mobilization, economic development, and political democratization in such a way that they can easily be quantified. Consequently, social mobilization typically refers to such factors as urban/rural shifts, radio audiences, newspaper readers, and literacy rates, while political mobilization may refer to the number of specialized political institutions, the rate of enfranchisement, and the number of political parties. A crucial improvement in the model was developed in by B.G. Peters, who extended the model to include the development of public policy.[4] The model has been somewhat discredited, because it fails to place operational variables in a broader social and structural context that actually explains their meaning and relationship to each other. In spite of its limitations, the model is conceptually useful in suggesting interactive relationships between certain broad phenomena that form the major focus of inquiry in the study.

I suggest that school reform at the national level is one type of public policy formation, and public policy formation is an outgrowth of the interaction of social mobilization, political mobilization, political democratization as well as economic development. Of course, public policy is often intended to play back on the various elements of social, political and economic development so that there is reciprocal influence, but it rarely has the capacity to redefine the nature of society as proponents of structural change in education hope it will. In fact, the degree of success in structural reform in education is probably a clear reflection of the degree of integration already achieved in any given society, and typically explains much of the success or failure experienced by proponents of structural reform in various European countries.[5]

In a study of this complexity, a number of themes come forth in the story of educational reform. Of course, the major focus shall be on structural changes that occured within primary and secondary schools, but other themes must accompany this analysis.

One implicit theme throughout the study will be on "equality of educational opportunity," although the term is rarely used in the discussion because the term is quite contemporary. The most prominent scholars using this term are social or behavioral scientists possessing a sociology, economics or psychology background.[6] Certain historical claims have been postulated by these social scientists, who suggest that the concept of equality of educational opportunity has undergone a number of historical mutations. These mutations have provided various current day interpretations of the concept, such as equal access to schools, equal participation in educational programs, equal achievement, and equal educational effects on life chances. A major task will be to assess, if the historical stages within the Norwegian case, which are postulated by social scientists, are historically grounded. In fact, Chapter Eighteen is devoted to the issue.

Another theme in the discussion shall be on control. Who runs the schools? Is education centrally determined or locally run? Are there great historical shifts in terms of control that take place in Norway? This issue is so central that Chapter Nineteen is devoted to it.

The book is organized in six major sections. In Section I, the social and educational context surrounding the time when Norway declared independence in 1814 is provided. One of the most important periods in Norway's social and educational history is dealt with in Section II. With the rise of romantic nationalism in the 1830s, Norway began to chart its own educational path that led to educational reforms at the primary and lower secondary school levels. The building of a comprehensive school that would begin to include large segments of the population, such that by the end of the century the country had constructed one of the most progressive educational systems in the world, is charted in Section III. Norway is one of the few countries of the world that achieved some form of common schooling prior to the turn of this century. In Section IV, a third major educational reform movement which began shortly after Norway broke away from Sweden in 1905 and ended in the 1950s is outlined. In Section V, which focuses on the period from the 1950s until the mid-1970s, a fourth major educational reform movement which culminated in the comprehensive school system as it exists today is outlined. By the mid-1970s, Norway had essentially completed its quest for a unified school system by providing all children with an integrated schooling program from seven through nineteen years of age.

Three chapters are included in the final section. First, the degree to which Norway has accomplished its goals for equality of educational opportunity is focused upon. Then the radical move to change the locus of control from the central government to local entities is discussed. In the final chapter, the reader is reminded of the original aim in the book and certain tentative conclusions about the findings are drawn.

Acknowledgments

Three institutions were helpful in my work with this book. The University of California, Los Angeles and the Norwegian Department of Church and Education provided financial support for the project. IMTEC was particularly helpful at all stages of the work. IMTEC has become a focal point for international educators, who take an interest in Norway and education, and it provides an invaluable service to those educators. I was also gratified to find that all Norwegian scholars were willing to give me every assistance I requested. Their support, warmth, and intellectual depth is indicative of the kind of climate that has drawn me to devote so much time and energy to the Norwegian culture.

Section I

Social and Educational Foundations in Norway

1 Democracy and Education in Pre-Independent Norway

On May 17, 1814, Norway declared independence from foreign domination. This declaration was made possible as a result of external factors. Denmark, which had ruled Norway for some four hundred years, had made the mistake of aligning itself with Napoleon, who was defeated in Germany in 1813 by the combined forces of Russia, Prussia, and Sweden. The Swedes then forced the Danes to cede Norway to Sweden.

The Norwegian response to being bartered from one nation to another inspired defiant and quick reaction. A constitutional assembly was quickly called, which quickly drew up and enacted the most democratic constitution in the world. In the subsequent struggle with Sweden she managed to retain her constitution and only be subject to Sweden in terms of foreign affairs.

That constitution has stood the test of time, remaining essentially intact with amendments supporting the spirit of the original document. It insured the Norwegians the distinction of having established the first modern parliamentary system in Scandinavia,[1] of being among the first nations to abolish all future hereditary titles and privileges,[2] and of being one of the earliest nations in the world to have franchised a substantial portion of the population with the right to vote.[3]

The claim to being democratic is always somewhat relative and events subsequent to 1814 would see Norway become even more democratic. At the time it declared independence, the country was actually ruled by a small, elite, official class of people.[4] Clearly, a society which is stratified into separate and distinct classes is fatal for democratic values to flourish. Democracies must have the capacity to bridge differences and

maintain a broad community of interest.[5] Norway could lay claim to a
long, sturdy, and early democratic tradition,[6] but it had suffered the pains
and degradation of being "a nation in eclipse,"[7] a country "in the
shade,"[8] a mere "province of Denmark"[9] for four centuries. The events of
those years had catastrophic consequences not only for Norway's political
identity, but also for its cultural life. The whole country was in a seeming
condition of acquiescence and dependence when it suddenly awakened
and declared independence.

In spite of the fact that it had been a mere appendage of Denmark
for so many centuries, there is compelling reason to believe that Norway
had retained a spark of the democratic spirit and that certain factors came
together at the time of independence that allowed the country to step forth
prepared to be counted among the world's leading democracies.

NORWEGIAN SOCIAL STRUCTURE

Some of these factors are attitudinal in nature. For example, we
shall see that Norwegians retained a fierce sense of personal independence
throughout their long state of political dependence on Denmark. In
addition, Norwegians have traditionally been law-abiding people, holding
firm to the idea of a legal order and the obligations which public officials
and the common people should have toward it. Even the king was required
to obey the law.[10] The Norwegians have also possessed a sense of national
identity. Centuries before their independence was taken from them in the
fifteenth century, Norwegians were already "in possession of that strong
fellow-feeling and mutual acknowledgment of homogeneity which constitute the essence of nationality."[11]

In addition to attitudinal factors, important structural elements of
society also contributed to Norway's democratic birth. Socially, at the
time of independence Norway could have been divided into four major
groups: an official class, a burgher estate, a farmer estate, and an
underprivileged group, which were quite unique in their historical evolution and relationships with one another.

The Official Class

In Norway the official class consisted mainly of a small upper
class of foreign nobility, civil servants, and clerics, who politically
controlled the country. At the time of independence this class represented
less than two percent of the electorate. In contrast to most countries of
Europe, which were maintained by an indigenous nobility, the Norwegian

nobility was largely foreign born, being Danish and representing, therefore, an alien element in Norwegian culture. Without question, the clergy had long held a revered position in Norwegian society, but because they had been appointed from Denmark, they also constituted a separate group, without a firm Norwegian identity. If we were to speak of a "ruling class" in Norway at the time of independence, it would have been those civil servants in the upper levels of the bureaucracy. The common people complained little about their power and probably respected the official class sufficiently to have allowed them to retain constitutional power without resentment. It is to their credit that the official class contributed mightily to the democratization process, though they retained the major political power for some years. Even as the *Storting* (Parliament) began to meet, the new nation's representatives were heavily skewed toward the "better class." During the first six sessions of the *Storting* almost half of all representatives were from the official class, although the number dropped off rapidly so that it had been reduced to almost nothing by the time Norway broke away from Sweden in 1905.[12]

The Burgher Class

At the time of independence, the burgher class represented a crucial element in the democratic equation, but it was still not overwhelming in terms of numbers, because Norway had remained rural. By 1799 the largest city in Norway was Bergen, with only 16,000 inhabitants; Oslo had barely 10,000 and Trondheim 8,000 inhabitants.[13] In spite of this, one fifth of all representatives to the first *Stortings* were from the commercial and industrial sectors[14] and they dominated the representation coming from the towns and cities.[15]

The Free Farmers

Norwegian mythology claims that it was the farmer who retained the real identity of the Norwegians during the time the country was a province of Denmark, while other power groups tended to undermine the cultural foundations of the country. The farmer formed the backbone of Norwegian culture and nationality. A major structural feature of Norway was the low level of development of villages and towns and the extensive existence of self-sufficient, independent farmers who owned their estates. The household of these farmers transcended even the nuclear family and constituted the fundamental social unit of Norwegian society; it was the focus of food and manufactured products, religious life, child rearing and education.

6   Social and Educational Foundations in Norway

The farmer lived a life of special independence and leadership over his household; however, he also served as the link for interdependent activities in the economy, religion, and politics. The skills for initiative and adaptability, so crucial for democratic conduct, were a part of his everyday life. So fundamental was the farm household that the king himself has been depicted in Norwegian mythology as little more than a fellow ruler over his household, a "fat, genial farmer who could be approached as an equal."[16]

During the century prior to independence, the number of farmers increased greatly. In times when large estates were maintained by nobles and others, the farmer was relatively insignificant. However, because of economic shifts and changes in royal policies, the number of farmers quadrupled between the mid-1600s and the mid-1700s, when more than half of all land came to be controlled by the farmers themselves. However, the farmer typically held ownership over a relatively small parcel of land, less than one seventh the size of the typical Swedish farm.[17]

Neither a landed aristocracy nor even a large middle class farming community existed at the time of independence. In fact, only modest differences existed between the typical free farmer and those tenants and crofters who rented the land and worked the soil.[18]

The Underprivileged

The final social class category, the underprivileged group, is as crucial as any in assessing the degree to which Norwegian society was democratic. Norway was one of the few places in Europe that escaped a feudal phase in its history. While the Danish nobility gained control over the peasants of their own country and consumed their resources, that nobility was unable to reduce the Norwegian peasant to a condition of serfdom. In fact, the cotters eventually gained the right to buy their own land and they then fiercely laid claim to that which they held.[19] There was rarely any sense of subservience and certainly no feudal mentality.

The implication this holds is monumental. The feudal stage of European history colored and shaped much of that continent's development. Social class differences have been defined largely in terms of the historical groups formed in the feudal period.[20] Political relationships between the feudal lord and serf constituted the antagonistic class struggle of the period. But Norway had skipped that stage so typical for European development.

The conclusion we must come to is that Norway has been unique in Europe in terms of its various social class alignments. Those elements of feudalism and capitalism that have formed our historical view of Europe simply did not exist to a significant degree in Norway. Even at the time of independence, Norway possessed few sharp antagonisms and unapproachable social groups, and it was already well on its way to forming a consensual democracy in which the various groups were able to resolve political conflicts and work harmoniously with one another more easily than in other European countries.[21]

Norway was democratic in outlook, even though there were distinctions in the status of these groups, but there was healthy competition between them for recognition and for a political voice. The constitution they drew up and ratified allowed these various voices to be expressed in the formal political arena.

This is nowhere better illustrated than in accounts of estimates of the total number of people franchised to participate in the first regular election to the *Storting* in 1815. In contrast to Great Britain, where between 2-3% of the people were in the electorate in 1832, Rokkan[22] estimates that 11% of those in the cities and 10% of those in the rural districts were able to vote in the initial Norwegian election. Kuhnle[23] estimates that 45% of all men 25 years of age and older were enfranchised at this time, including all free farmers. Denmark did not move toward broad suffrage until 1849 and Sweden maintained its four estate regime until 1866, but even then less than 6% of the population was given the right to vote for candidates to the Lower Chamber and approximately 11% to vote in the municipal elections for the Upper Chamber. We must agree with Rokkan, that "by the standards of 1815 Norway was a remarkably democratic country."[24]

At the time of independence Norway's formal school system was inferior to much of Europe. It certainly could not account for the intellectual strength and democratic fibre being manifest in the country at the time of its independence. Was it only from a small patrician class that any intellectual vitality was shown? What was the educational vitality that existed in the country at the time it declared independence? The answers to these questions become our next task.

CONVENTIONAL SCHOOLING

It is no easy task to give a tightly bound description of "the Norwegian education system" that accounts for the training of Norwegian leaders. We shall describe, for illustrative purposes, the education of a single individual: Niels Treschow, the highly regarded professor at the University of Oslo and the first Minister of Church and Education in the independent state of Norway.[25]

Born in Drammen in 1751, Treschow was sent, at the age of five, to the country where an old retired ship's captain was living on a farm called Gjøkepp teaching school. Treschow remained at this farm for over three years before returning to Drammen. Niels' father was deeply involved with a movement known as the Moravian Brethren Movement (herrnhutiske bevegelse) and a decision was made that Niels would receive a "learned school" education. One of the supporters of the Moravian Brethren Movement, H. Peder Nyborg Hesselberg, had come to Drammen in 1749 to be the private tutor of the "best folks" children in town."[26] Hesselberg eventually created a type of private school for a small number of children. That school has been described as a burgher-Latin school and differed from the conventional Latin school in that it offered a modern curriculum of science and certain practical subjects. It was here that Treschow began learning Latin.

At the age of fourteen Treschow left Hesselberg's school and went to live with his uncle by marriage, Johannes Green, who was the priest of Aker. Here Treschow received private tutoring and began to polish his Latin. At the conclusion of that year he took his secondary school leaving examination and passing it with honors was admitted to the University of Copenhagen. He remained only one year in Copenhagen before returning to Drammen because of economic hardships. In the year at home he came under the influence of Hans Hammond, a parish priest known for his historical studies of missions, who tutored him in theological studies. His father's close friend, Nicolai Arbo, also gave him extensive private help in the natural sciences so that he became conversant with physics, chemistry, and medical science. At the end of 1768, at the age of seventeen, he traveled to visit his ten year old brother, who had been sent to school in Zeist, Holland, where a strong element of the Moravian movement was located. That visit resulted in extensive exposure to the new philosophical impulses of the time, which greatly influenced his academic disposition when he returned for further study at Copenhagen University.

We could trace his further progression as a student, teacher, and professor, but our primary aim has been to hint at the difficulty in providing a sense of the educational options Norwegians faced. On a superficial level, we find a dualistic schooling structure not unlike that found throughout the continent. There were higher schooling opportunities for the elite classes, albeit very limited in number, and there were minimal schooling programs for the undistinguished classes run by the local parishes. In Chapter Two, we shall discuss a wide range of other educational options.

The Latin Schools

At the time of independence, Norway could boast of only four higher Latin schools having a total of less than 200 students.[27] In this respect Norway had not progressed beyond the situation that existed in the twelfth century, when the arch-bishop domain was established at Nidaros. It was common practice, at that time, for each bishop in a domain to found a school in connection with his cathedral. The schools at Oslo, Nidaros, and Bergen could have been established as early as 1153, while the cathedral schools at Stavanger and Hamar appear to have been established somewhat later.

The purpose of these schools was strictly religious in nature. In fact, the purpose of all book learning was for religious purposes.[28] The schools were professional training grounds for the priesthood, and young boys, including some poor boys, were gathered under the direction of the bishop to prepare themselves to become priests within the realm. In this early period the children of nobles rarely participated in the cathedral schools, but were educated in the medieval apprenticeship manner, first serving as a page, then as a squire to some aristocratic kinsman or friend, then finally as a gentleman-in-waiting at the royal court.[29]

Norway did not possess any institution of higher learning prior to 1811, so those few people desiring to obtain extended education were obliged to travel to foreign countries to do so. Some pre-Reformation references can be found of Norwegian priests having extensive learning and of having studied at institutions of higher learning at St. Victor in Paris, at Bologna, Orleans, Cambridge and St. Andrews.[30]

The Reformation not only represented a difficult time for Norway in general, but it represented a trying time for all Norwegian schools. The Cathedral School at Hamar was even discontinued in 1602, because the lands that had been used to provide revenues for the school and its scholars were diverted to pay for Danish courtiers and ecclesiastics.[31] While the other cathedral schools suffered enormous financial problems they did survive the Reformation, although those schools were also forced to close their doors from time to time.[32]

At the time of the Reformation the cathedral schools were transformed into so-called Latin schools, although the old name never disappeared. In fact, it was retained so that the cathedral schools could be distinguished from the lower Latin schools that were established at certain churches, serving as preparatory schools for the "higher" Latin schools at the cathedrals. The Danish church ordinance of 1539 had stipulated that each free city (*kjøpstad*) have a Latin school to prepare church and state officers who would insure that sound Christian piety was given to the population. It was at this time that the scholarly pattern of Latin school and university education began to predominate among the aristocracy.[33] The purpose of the school had expanded beyond the church itself and now included the education of those preparing for roles in the government.

A full Latin school would have five levels, the first class being devoted to the teaching of Latin. The pupils would move through the curriculum, set out mainly by Melancthon, so that in the highest class Hebrew, logic, metaphysics, and rhetoric would be studied. Denmark witnessed a rapid expansion of Latin schools, most of which offered only the first levels of instruction. Willis Dixon[34] estimates that about 60 of these schools existed in Denmark as a consequence of the new church ordinance. Norway would never be able to boast of such wide-spread Latin schooling, mainly because there were so few free cities.

Lower Latin schools could only be found at cities such as Båhuslensbyene, Tønsberg, and Skien. The old free city of Sarpsborg, for example, opened a lower Latin school in the sixteenth century, with a curriculum of Latin and Christianity, but there were so few pupils that one teacher handled all duties.[35] Things had not changed much over the next two centuries. For example, in 1730, Rector Christian Molbech could barely maintain a single class and it could only focus on writing and calculating.[36] Christiansand actually established a cathedral school as a consequence of the burning of Stavanger and its temporary loss of free city status. That school graduated some 287 pupils from 1683-1813.[37]

In 1600, a general rule was set that cathedral school students from Norway continue their studies at the University of Copenhagen, and during a period of strict orthodoxy in the Lutheran Church in the 1600s, the formalization of credentials based on examinations became a reality. In 1629 the theology degree (*teologisk embetseksamen*) from Copenhagen University was instituted, which became the major credential necessary not only to function as a priest but to be recognized as a member of the official class. In 1650 an examination was instituted, signifying that a student was eligible to be admitted to the university. This *examen artium* was defined as the school leaving examination from the Latin school. In 1675 a middle level exam (*anneneksamen*) was instituted which was an alternative examination for those at the university wishing to teach at the lower levels of the Latin school.[38]

As the purpose of the school gradually shifted to include not only professional preparation for the church but preparation for civil service, the actual program for the young students remained classical and mainly in the Latin language, although Pietism and realism forced some change in that world.

The most significant school regulations of this period came in 1739, which reaffirmed that religious and moral education shall be the main goal of general education.[39] One of the main outcomes of the regulation was that the mother tongue, geography, and history were introduced as compulsory subjects in school; however, these subjects dealt little with Norway. The mother tongue was Danish. It was even decreed that the mother tongue be used as a support language to Latin instruction, but that language was, once again, Danish.

It is little wonder that at the beginning of the nineteenth century the cathedral school was of almost no consequence to the intellectual life of the Norwegian as a Norwegian. The Latin school played such a small role in the typical Norwegian's life, that it was serving approximately one person in every 5,000 in the population at the time of independence. The number of pupils sitting for the *examen artium*, the school leaving examination, each year at the time of independence was only 16 young scholars.[40]

As long as Norway was in a state of dependency on Denmark little would happen in terms of defining the Latin school as a Norwegian Latin school. However, the Danish Latin school reforms at the beginning of the nineteenth century did have a fundamental impact on the nature of the school in the next half century in Norway. In 1806 two new teaching positions were declared: *overlærer* and *adjunkt*. These were civil servant titles, with all the prestige and honor that comes with such status.

Also, the old class teacher organizational structure was abolished and replaced by subject matter specialists. This was made necessary because of the introduction of a wide range of subjects to be taught. Danish, Latin, religion, geography, history, and arithmetic would be taught in each of the four levels of a full Latin school, while Greek and French would be introduced at the second level, German and elementary geometry at the third level, and Hebrew (for theology students) at the top level. The 1809 law also allowed the addition of school subjects of physics, anthropology, English, drawing, singing, and gymnastics.[41] With all of these new subjects being introduced, the unity that had characterized the Latin school from its inception was finally voided. Even though there had been subject divisions in Latin schools from the beginning, these subjects had always been a part of a unified, coherent program focussed ultimately on God and the church. The breakdown in the Latin school as an agent of the church was formally recognized in the 1809 law. From that date they were recognized as institutions "having their own life," even taking on a new, more secular name of learned school (*lærde skole*).[42] Even the old mandate that scholars must sing in the church was abolished. The major argument for this move was that the scholars no longer had the time because of the new curricular demands, but it was symptomatic of a continuing secularization of the Latin school, not only in content but in purpose.

At the time of independence there were approximately 2,200 inhabitants for every priest in Norway and the Latin schools were easily able to satisfy the clerical needs of the country.[43] However, their additional role had become the preparation of increasing numbers of young men for government service. For example, of the thirty three pupils who passed the secondary school leaving examination at Christiansand between the turn of the century and independence in 1814, at least ten would eventually become government officials.[44] At the time of independence, the Latin schools would soon be hard pressed to satisfy both the clerical and civil service needs of the country.

The Lower School

General schooling was available for the less privileged classes in Norway at the time of independence. This took place in an institution quite separate from the school for the official class. While the Latin school can trace its roots back to the Middle Ages, the lower school is a creature of the Reformation. Salvation rather than vocation became the aim. Children in Lutheran Norway would learn to read so they could gain access to the word of God as revealed in the scriptures. The Danish church ordinances of 1537, 1539, and 1629 gave support to Luther's plea for schooling, but the first substantial move in furthering general education came in the mid-1730s. Bishop Peder Hersleb, of Akershus, introduced the rite of confirmation into Norway in 1734, which required young persons to demonstrate certain knowledge and skills before they were allowed to take communion for the first time. This was generally extended throughout Norway in the next two years. Confirmation represented the rite of passage into adulthood, and failure to be confirmed was seen as a great disgrace and carried with it heavy penalties. Parents were subject to fines if they did not see to it that their children were confirmed. The children were also subject to strict sanctions, such as not being able to be married until they were confirmed.

1739 School Ordinance. In 1739, a royal decree went forth, which required all young people in the countryside, regardless of social station or position, to attend school for the purpose of gaining a foundation of Christian faith and turning toward salvation. All children would be expected to attend school from the age of seven years and remain at least until they were ten to twelve years old,[45] or until they could read and undergo confirmation in Christianity, at about the age of fourteen.[46] This represents a relatively early compulsory education program in Europe, replicating a document that had been passed by the Danish parliament in the same year. It predated regulations coming out of most of the German states, such as the 1763 decree of Frederick the Great, that all Prussian children in rural areas attend school. In fact, most European nations would postpone such mandates until the end of the next century. In Great Britain, for example, elementary education would not be made universally compulsory until 1880, and in France, compulsory primary education would not be established until 1882. Even in Sweden, where home teaching was more deeply embedded in the culture than in Norway and Denmark, compulsory schooling was not introduced until 1842.[47]

Unfortunately, the initial plan for Norwegian schooling had been worked out for the Danes by Germans, who knew next to nothing about the conditions in Norway. Consequently, the decree dictated that permanent schools be established wherever possible, and that the bell ringer in each parish be responsible for conducting school. It was simply not possible to establish permanent schools in a country where over 90% of the population lived in isolated farming households. There were additional problems. The schools were to be administered centrally by the official class, but the local districts would be required to raise the funds to pay for the schools.

The decree encountered great resistance, so in 1741 adjustments were made which dictated that each local parish become responsible for setting up its own type of common schools.[48] The energetic work of priests and officials led to creative schooling solutions. For example, priest Niels Winding, took the initiative to try and organize the people in the parishes along the Søffjord. There were 360 farmers in the parishes of Odda, Ullensvang and Kinsarvik, and it would take a teacher in each parish to carry the task through. School would run from the end of September until the first of April, and teachers would move from location to location, with each session lasting from six to eight weeks with 22-24 children in each group. Odda being more compact would receive 12 weeks of schooling. It would take two years to circulate through the districts to reach all the children.[49]

The parishes along Aurlandsfjord just north of Søffjord also decided to establish travelling schools in their sparsely populated area. Vangen parish established five catchment areas where the children would meet at farms until a school could be set up at Vangen. Flåm and Undredal were each divided up into three catchment areas, with four or five farms in each area. Instruction would take place for eight weeks in each location. The main teacher would be bell ringer, Christen Jørgensen, and he would have an assistant teacher.[50] The typical daily expectation of the teachers was that they carry with them a prayer book and the *Psalms*, that they work at least a bit on spelling and a great deal with reading practice, that they help the children master and be able to explain the catechism, and that they examine the children in what they know and understand.[51]

The early schools rarely taught the children to write. In Scandinavia the purpose of lower schooling was to teach children religion and reading. Writing had little connection with these needs and so it was almost totally neglected. With this restricted aim, the number of schools quickly expanded after 1741. Tveit has found that by 1745 approximately 90% of the diocese of Akershus had schools in place and operating, and schooling had become essentially universal by mid-century.[52]

The 1739 School Ordinance actually pertained only to countryside schooling, because the towns remained self-governing corporations. Actually, common schooling had been much easier to establish in most towns, and a general schooling process was well under way by the time the 1739 School Ordinance came into being. For example, Christiansand had established a school for poor youth as early as 1656 and a second one in 1722.[53] Even in the smaller towns some general schooling was taking place long before the 1739 ordinance. Kragerø, for example, records the existence of "bell ringers and school masters" from 1667 onwards.[54] In fact, by 1720, a number of permanent town schools were being established, including those at Lier, Bærum, Sandsvær and Opdal (Sør-Trøndelag) and Strinda (Trondheim).[55] The content of these schools was not unlike that occurring in the countryside, although the town children usually attended school longer.

The larger towns were able to make claim to a number of lower schools. By the time of independence the free-cities had an abundance of lower schools. Christiansand maintained five such institutions: a "free-school" for girls, an "industrial school" for girls, two "free-schools for single boys (apprentices)," and a "reading school." Most of these schools were connected with some work establishment, so that the children would be in school for a part of the day, then work and learn a trade or skill for the other part of the day. The free school for girls allowed half of the working girls half a day to study writing, reading and other subjects, then they would trade with the other girls, who would leave work and engage in studies.[56]

As can be seen from the Christiansand example, some of the schools addressed themselves to the girls. At Drammen, for example, the local priest prevailed upon his relatives who owned a factory, to set up a school where the girls could learn the catechism for a portion of the day, then learn to make hats, weave, and crochet socks for another portion of the day.[57]

SUMMARY

We must conclude that at the time of independence Norwegian schooling was rather widespread in the towns and cities, but it remained undeveloped in an absolute sense. There were few elite schools and there was no higher education institution in the country until just prior to independence. It had long been Danish policy to compel those who qualified for advanced study to go to Copenhagen, not only "to spend their money," but to "return injured in their principles and in their health."[58]

One consistent value orientation was universal in pre-independent Protestant Norway: all God's children were capable of leading equally holy lives. In this respect, Norwegians were committed to a type of equal educational opportunity advocated by Luther, who considered all men equally capable of spiritual life, repentance and ultimate salvation. People differed in terms of worldly standing, but these came from "human laws and inventions." God's law dictated that all were capable of being "equally

Christian." The only difference in man was in "office and work" but not of "estate."[59]

In spite of this, the level of general schooling, though almost universal, was also minimal, as most of the young people attended travelling schools for brief and sporadic periods of time.

2 Educational Alternatives at the Time of Independence

The conventional dualistic school system characterizing most of Europe existed in Norway; however, educational options extended far beyond the schools that fell within that framework. In this chapter we take a closer look at a variety of educational alternatives that existed at the time Norway declared independence. From time to time, attention is given to the alternative educational experiences of the delegates to the constitutional convention to explore the varied educational experiences represented at the convention and to suggest the richness of educational alternatives available at the time.[1]

NONFORMAL EDUCATION

Literacy and General Enlightenment

Even prior to independence, Norwegians generally prided themselves in being literate and well read, but until recently, little objective data has been available pertaining to the level of general knowledge or literacy of the Norwegians, although some impressionistic evidence has been available. As early as the sixteenth century the Lutheran Church efficiently promoted literacy by conducting periodic general examinations in reading.[2] The junior clergy and anyone else who could read were simply expected to help those who could not read. This process took place in a strictly nonformal educational sense, but outside the confines of a place called school. As early as 1631, Anders Bure, in his political and geographical description of the north countries, would exclaim that the inhabitants of *Norrland* "are so fond of letters, that, although public schools are very few, nevertheless the literate instruct the others with such enthusiasm that the greatest part of the common people and even the peasants are literate."[3]

Even the farmers laid great store in reading. Jacob Aall, an Eidsvoll representative, had traveled through Telemark finding people possessing and discussing Peder Claussøn's translation of Snorre, a book on philosophy for the unlettered by Bastholm, and other books.[4] It is not uncommon to find reports such as that made by the Scottish Evangelist, John Patterson, writing in 1807/08, after a visit to Scandinavia, exclaimed that "it was a pleasing circumstance that all could read," even though there was no "provision for the education of the people by means of parochial schools," because "the parents were the teachers of their children."[5]

We find striking examples of young people who grew up in difficult peasant circumstances, who became competent scholars and leaders. The eighteenth century revivalist, Hans Nielsen Hauge, the "modest farmer's son," whose formal schooling was limited to a travelling school, gained an impressive reading experience, including the writings of Luther, Pontoppidan, Johann Arendt, Heinrich Müller, and others. As a youth he had in his possession Kingo's hymnal, a prayer book, and the *New Testament,* which he diligently studied while working during the day.[6]

Literacy is a vague term open to various interpretations. Scholars usually resort to operational definitions, such as the ability to sign one's name on a bill of sale, will, or other document.[7] More recently, specific criteria have been applied both to reading and writing in Scandinavia. Two levels of reading have been identified: the ability to read (a) familiar texts, and (b) unfamiliar texts.[8] Three levels of writing have been identified: the ability (a) to write one's own name, (b) to write letters and words, and (c) to express oneself in written form.[9]

Scandinavians in general laid great stress on reading at a relatively early period of time, but they did not deem it important to write. The purpose of reading was to facilitate religious learning. One of the important early figures, responsible for the development of universal reading ability among the Norwegians, is Peder Hersleb, Bishop of Akershus from 1731-37. He had over 10,000 copies of a prayer book printed and distributed to the people under his jurisdiction,[10] which amounted to one prayer book for every 26 residents.[11] It is also to Hersleb's credit that the so-called "register of souls" (*sjeleregister*) was more fully activated in Norway. Priests were directed to visit the households in their parishes and determine the level of "enlightenment" that had been attained. Unfortunately, only a few of these registers remain in existence, but they provide the best record of reading ability in that century.[12]

One conscientious priest in Nannestad reported in 1730 that of 900 unmarried people in his parish, only 18 were illiterate. Such a claim is somewhat tempered by his further claim that 600 of them could actually "read a book."[13] The parish of Sandar reported in 1736 that 219 (59%) of 371 single persons above the age of 7 could read very well/properly/ without fault, while only 18 (5%) could not read at all. The others at least knew the alphabet (10%), how to read but poorly (18%), or how to read fairly well (8%).[14]

If these registers are to be taken at face value, one must conclude that reading ability was widespread even before common schooling became popular in the 1740s. Knut Tveit cautions against such conclusions and suggests that the registers of souls that have been preserved are not representative of the total population. The information was obviously collected and preserved by some priests because it was a source of pride to those who were particularly committed to literacy and schooling, while other priests did not fill the register out.[15]

In spite of these reservations, it is clear that reading ability was widespread by the middle of the 1700s, though it is unclear when illiteracy in terms of reading ability was eradicated from Norway. Tveit has concluded that by 1800 essentially everyone could read at least at the lowest level, which is remarkable considering the fact that as late as 1850 from 45-50% of the adult population of Europe could not yet read.[16]

We also have some recent information about writing ability in Norway just prior to Eidsvoll. Johannes Helgheim studied 5,265 signatures that have been preserved for the years 1797-1806, which appeared on civil settlements in 28 districts in Norway. A settlement commission in each district consisted of an *embetsmann* and a farmer, and Helgheim found only two farmer commissioners unable to write their names.[17] In other words, a high percentage of those in status positions, even though they were farmers, could write their names. Tveit studied the signatures of school commission members for the years 1816-29 from the various parishes in Akershus diocese, who met once a year, and he found it was seldom that a commission member could not sign his name.[18] Finally, among those delegates to the constitutional convention, only one delegate, Even Thorsen, was unable to sign his name, although he would undoubtedly have undergone confirmation and had demonstrated some ability to read.[19]

Writing was quite a different matter with the general population. In the study by Helgheim, noted above, only 20% of those Norwegians involved in the disagreements could write their names. Vannebo has investigated the "register of souls" for Verdal from 1809 and found that approximately 3% of the 1162 young people between the ages of 7-16 could actually write in any meaningful sense.[20]

Investigations about literacy demonstrate an early pride in literacy and its value among the people long before it had come to the rest of Europe. People of higher station, those selected to represent the people in legal, school, or political capacities had mastered the basics both of reading and writing. A good deal of the credit for this pride must be given to the households, which carried the major burden for learning in pre-independent Norway.

The isolated farm structure of Norway required the household to become the basic institution of Norwegian life, and at the time of independence it was the household that shouldered the burden of most of the education. The mountainous terrain was so isolating that each valley contained and protected its own dialect and culture, and the residents were reluctant to move to other parts of the country. Even today the internal migration rate of Norway is less than half that of the United States,[21] and at the time of independence it was minimal. Consequently, the household was the primary agency of early childhood socialization, and shaped the child's values, attitudes, manners and morals. It introduced the child to the basic forms of civilization.

Home Teaching

The Norwegian household's educational role often extended far beyond basic socialization to include the basic skills and the first steps in vocational preparation. In rural Norway the farmer taught his child all of the vocational training necessary, while the small tradesman also imparted vocational competence.

The Norwegian household also adopted a more formal educational practice. The upper classes of Europe often did not use the schools to educate their children but relied on private tutoring. A young man having high moral and academic credentials was hired by an aristocrat to live with the family and teach the children. Thus, the title of *Hauslehrer* (home teacher) in Germany and *huslærer* in Norway was common. A significant number of the greatest minds of Europe functioned at one time as a home teacher, including Locke, Rousseau, Basedow, Herder,

Harnisch, Diesterweg, Schleiermacher and Herbart.[22] In Norway, Eidsvoll representatives such as Christopher Frimann Omsen,[23] and Jonas Rein[24] had also served as *huslærer* at the beginning of their careers. Differences in home teaching styles existed from country to country. In Germany, home teaching was often the first step taken toward an academic post. Consequently, the brightest young men in that country entered home teaching service. In England the quality of tutors was not always the best, inspiring observations that men in England usually take greater care in selecting a trainer for their horse than for their children.[25]

Scandinavian home teaching stands apart from most of Europe in that it was not the exclusive domain of the aristocracy. The very nature of the isolated farming population required such a process, if the young were to remain at home. In Sweden as many as 40% of all youth were educated by home teachers at the time of Eidsvoll,[26] and while the figures are certainly not as high as in Norway a fair percentage of Norwegians were likewise educated.

Of course, people of modest means would not be able to hire the best, so one finds a striking variety of backgrounds in the home teachers. Some families would simply arrange for the local priest or chaplain to instruct their child as a part-time activity, or they would hire someone who had not completed his formal education or someone who was somewhat dull. The better families would hire young men whose backgrounds and capacities would rival those home teachers in Germany or Switzerland.

Illustrative of its importance, would be the extensive experiences of the constitutional convention delegates with home teaching experience in their youth. Jacob and Jørgen Aall, the sons of a wealthy merchant in Porsgrund, were instructed at home during their early lives.[27] Jacob was finally sent to Denmark at the age of 15 to prepare for his *examen artium*. At the age of 16 Jørgen went off to England and France to round out his education. Gustav Peter Blom, the son of a wealthy family in Holmsbo and representing Jarlsberg Realm, had a private tutor until he was 14 years old before being sent off to Schleswig for his first taste of school.[28]

A number of representatives had received tutoring from local priests, including Jørgen Sverdrup,[29] Henrik Carstensen,[30] and the son of a small farmer, Tollev Olsen Huvestad.[31] Delegate Anders Rambech had sat with the local district judge, who had read the law to him and prepared him for the Danish law exam at the University of Copenhagen.[32]

Apprenticeship

The household and local business role in vocational training had been extended and formalized as apprenticeship, which was a contractual arrangement that allowed for the exchange of young people for training. A young man would be placed with a master for a period of several years, the time and responsibilities having been carefully defined by laws dating back to the fifteenth and sixteenth centuries. Apprenticeship responsibilities went far beyond the simple skills of a particular craft. The master took over the broader family responsibilities but also provided guidance toward a specific world view, including norms of behavior, an identity with the world of work, and a sense of personal identity. It included gaining a sense of history, a sense of belonging to a long line of competent vocational experts.[33]

If an apprentice was to become a journeyman and then a master, he was expected to spend several years abroad, working in the craft.[34] This was the case with certain of the Eidsvoll representatives, although most of them, including Thomas Bryn,[35] Carl Adolph Dahl,[36] and Alexander Møller,[37] used their foreign experience to shift from a craft orientation to qualify for professions granted only by the university.

Self-Improvement and Libraries

It is difficult to identify the contribution made by public and quasi-public institutions, such as libraries, which are devoted to self-improvement, but they undoubtedly contributed mightily to general enlightenment. Norway was the first of the northern countries to initiate a system of public libraries, the first coming in 1780 with the establishment of the Deichman Library. Thus, Norway predates Denmark's public library beginnings by a full century, and their system was well under way with over 230 libraries when Sweden was just beginning its system around 1840.[38] Of course, libraries existed in earlier periods at schools and in the churches, serving the official class, the owners of property, and the wealthy.[39]

In spite of the Danish policy of not allowing Norwegians to purchase libraries,[40] certain eighteenth century Norwegians such as Benjamin Doss and Gerhard Schøning in Trondheim, Claus Fasting in Bergen, and Carl Deichman in Porsgrund had collections. They willingly loaned books out to those interested in reading. In fact, these private collections formed the basis of the public libraries that emerged. The Deichman library in Oslo possessed 6000 volumes at the time it was given to the city. The Fasting collection formed the beginnings of the Bergen

Public Library in 1793, and the collection of Sivert Knudsen Aareflot became the foundation of the National Library in 1800.[41] Even though the official class made great use of the materials being collected in these institutions, the documents also contributed to the general enlightenment necessary for democracy to take root at the time of independence.

Societies and Associations

One of the major nonformal educational instruments of the eighteenth century was the widespread development of scientific and philosophical organizations. We recall the Royal Society of London for the Promotion of Natural Knowledge, established in 1662, the *Academie des Sciences*, established in France in 1666, and the *Deutsche Academie der Wissenschaft*, established in 1700. Because Norway possessed no institution of higher learning, such groups were of vital importance in helping those in Norway keep abreast of new ideas and concepts. The first scientific society in the country was The Trondheim Scientific Society (*Det trondhjemske videnskabs-selskab*), which dated from 1760 and featured historical studies, agricultural papers, and even calls to redress the neglect of higher education on the part of the Danish king.[42] The oldest farm associations were established in 1771, and called themselves Countryside House-Holders Societies (*Landhusholdningsselskaper*). They concentrated on informing the house-holders of new farming techniques.[43]

One of the peculiar features of Norway's associations was their focus on independence or more nationalistic themes. Eidsvoll representative Peder Jørgen Cloumann, of Bratsberg Amt, had organized a "patriotic association" in 1790 for the purpose of increasing the general knowledge of those living in his area.[44] Probably the most famous of the political groups was the Society for Norway's Welfare (*Selskab for Norges vel*), set up in 1809 by Eidsvoll representative Count Wedel-Jarlsberg, who advocated separating from Denmark and uniting with Sweden. The stated purposes of this group was to promote agriculture and the different branches of industry, but its hidden curriculum was to promote a new political order in Norway. In the first year over 2000 members had joined together in various chapters.[45]

The activities of this group led directly to the establishment of a university in Oslo.[46] Rumors were circulated in Denmark that Wedel-Jarlsberg had become a traitor, and he was summoned by the king. Wedel-Jarlsberg demanded to know why he had been summoned, and the king, having no evidence that he was a traitor, covered himself by suggesting that he had been called to discuss the establishment of a university in Norway. The rescript of March 1, 1811, instructed the directors of the University of Copenhagen to enter into the planning. The Norwegian association started a subscription among the wealthier people to support such a movement and within two years the university was a reality.[47]

In terms of general enlightenment, one of the most influential groups was the Norwegian Bible Society, organized in 1814, and made possible by a generous grant from Karl Johan. In subsequent years thousands upon thousands of *Bibles* were made available to the population, which could be said to have made the greatest advancement to enlightenment through the scriptures.

ALTERNATIVE SCHOOLING ARRANGEMENTS

At the time of independence, a number of formal schooling arrangements were available beyond the Latin schools and the lower schools. These emerged, in part to satisfy specific needs of special groups, including the burgher school, the vocational school, and the military school.

The Burgher School

In the towns, common formal education was conducted in so-called poor schools (*fattigskoler*), but with the rising middle class of merchants and commercial interests, the towns became populated with people who considered it beneath themselves to enter the poor schools. They were often not wealthy enough to pay for instruction in the Latin schools with the consequence that they were not schooled at all. Eventually, a new schooling form began to emerge, known generally as the burgher school,[48] which was modelled generally after Basedow's *Philanthropinum* in Germany, which came into being in 1774 and featured a program of practical studies. One of the features of the burgher school was its national flavor. It catered to the local merchants and officials with the claim that their children would not have to be sent outside the country where they would "take on the foreign nation's character."[49]

Burgher schools were largely private, although some were run by a city. The oldest Norwegian school of this type, the *Trondheim borgerlige realskole*, was initiated for boys and girls through the endowment of a local merchant in 1783.[50] The term "Real" had been borrowed from German schools with that name and suggested a "real" or "concrete" orientation toward scientific and modern subjects. In Trondheim, the boys began their studies in religion, recitation, history, geography, calculating, reading and drawing, followed by German, English, French, mathematics, letter writing, book keeping, and navigation. The girls began with the same studies but then graduated on to "studies suited to women."[51]

Just prior to independence Christiansand was operating a burgher school in a so-called Didactic Institute for Youth, which contained a Latin school, burgher school, and a poor school in a single facility.[52] The Christiania Burgher School, begun in 1806, served mainly as a preparatory school for the Cathedral School during its first six years of existence, but it quickly moved beyond that role and began to rival the Latin school.[53] Kongsberg opened a school for 40 pupils in 1797, which was also attended by children of the official class, while Risør divided its old lower school, retaining one part for the poor children and the other part, for the so-called "Risør Alternative School" (annen skole).[54]

Vocational and Technical School

The industrial revolution was occurring at the time of Norwegian independence and with it came the notion that special schools ought to be set up to train young people for special kinds of tasks. The old guild system was dying and the tradition of a master craftsman teaching the neophyte the skills of the trade was dying with it. Some mechanism was necessary to reach those who would engage in the more practical vocations of life. Schools began to spring forth in Norway addressing the specific vocational needs of the country, including seamanship and handwork. In addition, drafting and architecture crafts were beginning to be taught in formal educational institutions.

In the eighteenth century, Pietism brought another thrust toward practical learning. Pietism focused, of course, on a renewed inner life, a new commitment to spirituality. What this meant for the youth was an elimination of that carefree, joyous stream of activities known in play and recreation. The youth was expected to be engaged in work, in useful activities and in production.

The vocational school seemed a worthy model to satisfy the two above needs. Seaman schools are probably the earliest vocational schools in the country. It was necessary for a shipmaster to satisfy specific qualifying requirements. The use of the compass, sailing techniques, the used of the quadrant, map reading, record keeping, etc., required extensive basic skills. Even in the introduction of the earliest known book in

Norway instructing about sailing, written in the 1530s, the author admonishes his readers that the most important skills for a ship's mate (*styrmand*) are the abilities to read and write.[55]

In these early times, navigation was learned from tutors and from self help manuals. Eventually seaman schools were set up, initially in Copenhagen, then in towns such as Christiansand (1666), Bergen (approximately 1690), and Trondheim (1686).[56] In the next century public appointments of so-called *navigation informators* were made in the various towns to insure some standard of instruction and skills of seamen. Besides the above mentioned towns, appointments were also made in Arendal (1771), Langesund (1790), Tønsberg (1791) and Christiania (1786), where seaman schools were also established.[57] Instruction would take place during the quiet months in a seaman's life, from October until April, when the sea was not in a condition to sail.

These schools undoubtedly played a major role in extending the education, both general and professional, of those whose life was connected with the sea. The first vocational school that actually included a more general, theoretical foundation in its program was probably the Harmonious Academic Drafting School, established in Bergen in 1772.[58] It provided a sound basis for building design, though it unfortunately lasted only 14 years.

In 1802 Sunday schools came into existence in Christiania and Bergen. A year later, the priest at Trondheim urged all journeymen and craftmasters to attend the Sunday school that was established in that town, and within ten years other Sunday schools were found in Christiansand, Fredrikshald, and Stavanger. Evening schools were also popping up here and there, shortly after the turn of the century, where bakers, businessmen, woodworkers, and brushmasters received instruction. In 1815 two priests in Christiania exclaiming distress that bookbinders could barely write and calculate, also began an evening school. In fact, one of the main purposes of these institutions was to provide instruction in reading and calculating, skills that had not been adequately taught in the common school.[59]

Norway was emerging as a mineral producing nation, and we find rich opportunities to learn about that world. At Kongsberg, a mining academy had been set up in 1757, and at the time of independence the children of miners were studying two hours a day two days a week in mineralogy, chemistry, physics, mathematics, and other branches of science, without cost.[60] One of the three professors in the academy, Professor Esmark, was known throughout the world. It was so advanced that people, such as Eidsvoll representatives Hieronymus Heyerdahl[61] and Paul Steenstrup,[62] had engaged in post-university training at Kongsberg. There were, of course, other mining programs, such as that which Captain Richard Floer, representative of Røros, had attended as a mining cadet at the Røros copper mine as a young man.[63]

Still another type of vocational school emerged in Christiania in 1811, and it emulated the Copenhagen Art Academy, although it provided elementary drawing and drafting exercises for the children of the crafts and working classes. The school was sponsored by The Society for Norway's Welfare, and represented one its great ambitions in providing a beginning step in Norway's higher educational aspirations.[64]

Military School

Young military men, most of whom had joined the service in their teens or early twenties, had gone through the lower school of the day and were somewhat literate. The army recruits of the Austrian Empire, France, and the Russian Empire were largely illiterate at the time of Norwegian independence, but because of the high level of literacy in Norway, we must conclude that the Norwegian military men were more nearly like the Prussian army recruits, who were, by and large, literate.[65]

As was the custom, the sons of military officers and other officials would regularly be sent to military training very early in life. Several years of such schooling were required in order to receive a commission.[66] Even though the Copenhagen military institutes had been the source of most training of officers, who were in their prime at the time of independence, including Eidsvoll delegates Thomas Konow,[67] Peter Motzfeldt,[68] and Valentin Christian Wilhelm Sibbern,[69] the Norwegian War Academy was coming on strong. Delegate First Lieutenant Frederik Wilhelm Bruenech Stabell, joined the infantry regiment at the age of fourteen, and went on to the Christiania Mathematics School at the age of seventeen, where he remained for three years.[70]

The war academy of Norway was called the Mathematics School and was somewhat similar to the National Cadet Academy in Denmark. One of the representatives at Eidsvoll, Diderik Hegerman, had been sent to Norway in 1790 as an officer of the Mathematics School after having served as a cadet in Copenhagen. His mission had been to upgrade the school and in 1798 he changed its name to the Royal Norwegian Cadet Corps.[71] It was well known and maintained a high visibility among the military as well as public figures.

FOREIGN EDUCATIONAL EXPERIENCES

A substantial number of young men and even certain young women from the better families of Norway had lived in another country as a youth or travelled there to study. The form of the experiences is extremely varied and includes almost all of the educational forms we have mentioned so far.

Formal Schooling in Foreign Parts

A number of young people were sent to Denmark to attend a Latin school, burgher school, military academy, or vocational institute, but foreign schooling was not at all restricted to that country. This would, of course, include many Eidsvoll representatives. Approximately one third of the representatives held a degree from Copenhagen University, and while Nicolai Wergeland, Hans Jacob Grøgaard, Hieronymus Heyerdahl, Lars Oftedahl, Wilhelm Frimann Koren Christie, and many others had gone through the conventional Latin grammar school training in Norway, about 40% of the representatives, who had attended Latin school had done so in Denmark. That would be predictable because Norway had been a province of Denmark and had long relied on Copenhagen for its intellectual nourishment.

However, the delegates to Eidsvoll had been in a number of other countries. Gustav Peter Blom, representative of Count Jarlsberg's domain, had attended Pastor Forschammers Institute in Schleswig before travelling to Kiel and finally to the University of Copenhagen.[72] Severin Løvenskiold had lived with aristocratic families in Germany while he attended schools, including the *Gymnasium* and a mining institute, before moving on to the University of Copenhagen to study law.[73] Peder Valentin Rosenkilde went to school in Hamburg before becoming a businessman.[74]

France and England were the countries where representatives such as Frederik Meltzer, Johan Casper Herman Wedel Jarlsberg, Jørgen Aall, and Anders Hansen Grønneberg attended school. After passing his theology examination at the University of Copenhagen, Gabriel Lund spent several years in France where he distinguished himself as being a most sophisticated and erudite individual. He brought these talents with him to Eidsvoll, as the representative of Lister-Amt.[75]

The Grand Tour

The so-called Grand Tour was still a major educational experience for many young men in Europe, and certain Norwegians took advantage of that opportunity. Originally, the Grand Tour was intended to provide a general cultural and intellectual experience, but by the nineteenth century, it had taken on vocational dimensions, as sons were gaining useful and practical experience about foreign peoples, about languages, and resources in countries. These experiences assisted the young in their diplomatic, business and political careers.[76] Carsten Tank Anker would serve as a good example. He spent six years traveling in Europe establishing relations with important figures, particularly in England, that served him well throughout his career, which included working in London with the Danish-Asian Company as the middle man for the English East India Co.[77]

SUMMARY

Norway, at the time of independence, neither possessed a national system of education nor a national educational policy. Rather, it possessed fragmented policies and systems, each serving a particular segment of the population. While the conventional definition of a national system was wanting, the actual programs available to Norwegians were rich and extensive, and the attainments of a wide spectrum of Norwegians were impressive. Even the general population was widely literate and had access to reading materials, although they were somewhat narrow in scope, focusing mainly on religious matters.

Within this context, equality of educational opportunity had little relevance. Structural divisions between schools coincided, by and large, with the divisions that existed in society. The family carried the major responsibility for providing the kind of education that was appropriate for the child. There was little consideration for equity, within the context that we usually discuss it today, although there are striking examples of individual Norwegians who break out of their station in life, who become "mobile" within Norwegian society, who rely on education, both formal and nonformal, to establish a new social identity.

At the time of independence, Norway had already evolved a diverse number of educational options. The problem facing the new nation would be to make some sense out of the diversity, but that would wait for a later period as the immediate needs and the policies established to address these needs, only further diversified the educational options open to Norwegians.

3 Educational Imperatives in Independent Norway

The new state of Norway began with gigantic challenges. Its population of less than one million was spread over a vast territory averaging one person in every eight square miles. It was exhausted from a brief but debilitating conflict with Sweden, and its government, which had been centered in Copenhagen, was now without resources and almost bankrupt.[1]

It was without any national system of education, and it would be many years before one would emerge. A good deal of consternation has been expressed by educational scholars about the first half of the nineteenth century in Norway. Both Dokka and Myhre describe its educational condition as a period of "stagnation,"[2] because the country did not immediately move to adopt a school system that reflected its democratic constitution. In comparative perspective such a lament might have some justification in that certain other countries seem to have moved more energetically than did Norway toward a national system in the first half of the nineteenth century.

Prussia had been the first to establish a comprehensive educational system in the first two decades of the century. The French proclaimed as early as 1791 that a system of public instruction shall be created and established, which is common to all, without cost, and indispensable to all men.[3] Even in Denmark the school act of 1814 laid the basis for the modern Danish school system. However, the circumstances surrounding these national revitalization activities were somewhat peculiar. The Prussians had suffered a humiliating defeat at the hands of Napoleon at Jena in 1806, and the state had attempted to revitalize itself through educational reforms. French educational reforms had grown out of the violent French revolution and its conservative aftermath. Denmark was undergoing enormous social and economic reforms including moves to abolish the feudal-type laws binding the peasant to his birthplace.[4]

Few of the above conditions held in Norway. Its military defeat in 1814 did not have the trauma attached to it that came with the fall of the mighty Prussian army. Its revolution was not social and internal as had been the case in France. Its perceived social condition was actually rather stable and satisfactory to the Norwegians. Samuel Laing, writing about Norway in the 1830s, made the perceptive observation that "there is not probably in the history of mankind another instance of a free constitution, not erected amidst ruins and revolution, not cemented in blood, but taken from the closet of the philosopher and quietly reared and set to work, and found suitable without alteration to all the ends of good government."[5]

We have seen that the ingredients of a democratic state were already in place as Norway declared independence. If we must compare Norway to another country seeking revolutionary change, it would most likely be the United States, which was revolutionary only in that it threw the colonialists out, but the temper of actual social change which it inspired was rather moderate. Such was also the case in Norway. Neither newly independent Norway nor the United States saw the necessity of reforming their educational heritage. That would come at a time when unrest of some sort in the political, economic or social arena emerged. The common school movement in both countries would wait for several decades before it would appear as a national imperative.

At the time of independence, Norway not only lacked a social crisis, its leading figures, members of the official class, were by and large committed to an educational program that was much like the one they were exposed to as young men. The three most vital figures in the national education at the time were Professor Georg Sverdrup, Bishop Frederik Julius Bech, and Professor Niels Treschow.

Bech had been reared and educated in Denmark and had studied theology. He had been appointed Bishop of Akershus in 1805 and had been the leading force in a Norwegian school commission appointed in 1811. He believed that each class of people required quite a different educational experience, a notion quite consistent with the existing order of things.[6] Sverdrup had attended the Latin school at Trondheim before studying philology at Copenhagen and Göttingen. He had served as Professor of Greek at Copenhagen from 1805 until 1813, when he came to Oslo as

Professor of Greek Philology. Educationally, he was clearly committed to classical philological studies.

Treschow was Professor of Philosophy at Oslo, having spent several years in a professorship at Copenhagen before coming to Oslo when its university was opened. While he was a strong advocate of general enlightenment, including the incorporation of modern subjects into the *lærde skole* program, he was a Platonist, believing that a productive society requires an intellectual elite.[7]

Treschow was selected to chair the first committee to oversee education: the *Kirke- og undervisningskomite*. The government would upgrade the Church and Instruction Committee to the Church and Education Department in 1818, with Treschow remaining as the minister.

CIVIL SERVANT IMPERATIVES

Among the questions facing the Church and Instruction Committee was the issue of how to satisfy the need for new civil servants. Because it had been so dependent on Denmark for its intellectual nourishment, Norway was not geared to meet its own needs for high government officials. There was little thought of changing the intellectual route of becoming an official via the *lærde skole*, with its *examen artium*, and the university, with its *embetseksamen*.

In spite of Treschow's positive attitudes about modern subjects, there was little serious consideration in these first years of diluting the Latin focus of the *lærde skoler*, as had been done in Denmark in 1809. The Latin schools remained classically oriented in the spirit of Wilhelm von Humboldt's "Königsberger Plan" in Prussia.[8] In fact, Sverdrup proposed a *lærde skole* law in 1818 that would have increased the time devoted to the classical studies of Greek and Latin while reducing the time devoted to the Norwegian language, whatever that meant, and deleting altogether the natural sciences and gymnastics. That plan was highly criticized and never adopted.[9]

He was more successful instituting university policy pertaining to the Latin School. A *lærde skole* teachers examination was established in 1820 at Oslo University. It became the national *embetseksamen* for teachers in 1824 and consisted of a purely philological examination, being called the *store philologicum*. It was divided into six sections, including Latin, Greek, Hebrew, history, philosophy, and mathematics. All answers were written in Latin. Such attempts to retain such purely classical studies probably contributed as much as anything to its rapid demise in Norway. Steen notes that barely one student each year opted for that "purgatory."[10]

These activities were secondary compared with the real issue facing the leaders of newly independent Norway. Their major problem centered on how to train enough officials. An immediate solution came with the return of Norwegian students from Copenhagen. Of the twenty-eight students who came to Copenhagen in 1811, all but two chose to return to Norway and 19 ultimately became *embetsmenn*;[11] however, alternative mechanisms were necessary.

An average of only 16 school leavers qualified to enter the university each year at the time of independence.[12] Consequently, in 1816, the *examen artium* was reluctantly lifted as the exclusive qualifying examination for university study.[13] A so-called "preliminary examination" was added, which gave those not having the *examen artium* the privilege of engaging in university studies. The exam concentrated on Norwegian and calculating plus a little Latin, history, geography and religion. Granted, it was deemed an emergency measure, but the law remained in force until 1845.[14] This measure was a contributing factor in breaking the hold of classical studies in the minds of those aspiring for higher educational studies.

A second step taken was to increase the number of Latin schools. In 1817, Drammen became the first town not having a bishop's seat to establish a new higher Latin school. Frederikshald and Stavanger followed in 1822 and 1824, respectively. Smaller towns also moved to establish lower Latin schools, which came to be called middle schools, with Larvik, Kongsberg, and Skien taking such a step in 1823, Arendal in 1824, Molde in 1832, and Tromsø in 1833. In an effort to bolster the attendance at some of these schools, burgher and *real* school curricula were added to their programs. Even so, it was difficult even to call some of these programs "schools" in a conventional sense. For example, at Skien only four pupils were enrolled during the first year. Such an assessment is by no means meant to demean the educational programs in these institutions. In fact, there was strong argument from some scholars of the day that large national schooling programs would actually be detrimental to the educational enterprise. In Germany, Johann Friedrich Herbart, for example, had argued in 1810, that universal home teaching become the mode of education rather than mass schooling.[15] He might have used the Skien Latin school program as a model to emulate, because two of those four pupils in 1823, Anton Martin Schweigaard and Peter Andreas Munch, would eventually become potent leaders of Norwegian nationalism. Schweigaard had lived for six years in Germany receiving private tutoring

from a pastor, before he was enrolled at the school at the age of 16. Munch
was tutored in several foreign languages as a young boy by his father, who
was a pastor. He was already involved in reading Old Norse, when he
enrolled in the Latin school at the age of thirteen.[16] Both these boys would
eventually take faculty positions at Oslo University.

The endeavors for expansion began to pay dividends by the early
1820s, when the number of *examen artium* candidates had quadrupled.
Significantly, One third of these candidates were "private," having not
attended a "recognized school," and their success ratio, at least in those
first few years, matched that of the candidates from the recognized
schools.[17] By the early 1830s the number of *examen artium* candidates
each year had doubled once again. In Table 3.1,[18] we find that most of the
candidates were coming out of Oslo, but a total of 616 candidates had
successfully completed Latin School studies between 1813-1837.

Table 3.1

The Number of School Leavers from the Full Latin Schools of
Norway between 1813 and 1837.

Trondheim	91
Oslo	234
Bergen	90
Kristiansand	115
Drammen	91

In spite of these optimistic comments, it is necessary to put this
type of schooling in comparative perspective. At the time the first school
census was taken in 1837, only about a dozen Norwegian towns maintained Latin schools of any type. In 1837 a little more than ten percent of
the population were living in the forty-two towns that possessed the right
to maintain their own system of schooling. According to the census
figures, less than three percent (approximately 600 students) of the school
aged youth in the towns were then attending a Latin school. Of course, the
alternative schooling options (burgher, vocational, military schools) mentioned in the last chapter were almost exclusively found in the towns. For
example, nineteen of the forty-two free towns possessed at least one
burgher school where six to seven percent of school aged youth in the
towns were attending.[19]

This would not amount to a great number of students, when calculated on a national scale, but we must keep in mind that over 1600 young people in the countryside were receiving private tutoring,[20] which was about the only way possible for them to engage in Latin school type of instruction. Substantial numbers of those youth attending school in the towns were from the countryside. In other words, the population in the countryside was relatively active in contributing to the numbers of youth attending Latin, burgher, and other types of schools. When we look at attendance on a national scale, approximately two percent of the school aged youth were attending a school that was not a poor or common school. This is a remarkable achievement in view of the fact that such schooling options were so limited at the time of independence. In comparative terms, Norway was already becoming competitive with Prussia and France in the 1830s in what we would today refer to as secondary school enrollments.[21]

GENERAL ENLIGHTENMENT IMPERATIVES

Because popular education in Norway at the time of independence was being determined by Danish law, the major educational imperative was to redefine that education. It was good fortune that a school commission had been set up three years prior to independence to explore schooling issues peculiar to Norway itself. This commission offered a forum for making public various points of view about education; however, it would take the new government thirteen years to design a comprehensive law concerning common schooling.

There was no debate concerning the basic purpose of the common school. It would continue to be devoted to knowledge and virtues necessary to live a good Christian life, although attention was now being given in some schools to skills not directly related to religious training. For example, the children at the poor school in Fredrikstad in 1823 received instruction in "handwriting, reasoning exercises, reading exercises, mental calculating exercises, catechism, *Bible* history, arithmetic and writing.[22] Though more secular skills were melding with religious studies in the instructional program of some schools, they remained, as yet, quite free of a nationalistic tenor. Whereas in Prussia and France the masses were already being instructed not only in the basic skills, but toward the virtues of industry, piety, and patriotism,[23] in Norway little sense of nation building seems to have entered the schools in the first years after independence.

The Danish law of 1739 was generally perceived to have adequately served Norway at the time of independence, and the new government addressed itself only to particular issues related to administrative and budgetary mechanisms of schooling, as well as issues surrounding teachers.

A *Storting* committee was appointed in 1815 to deal with school matters, and its work led to a preliminary school law in 1816. In that law a clear separation was retained in the manner in which countryside and town schools were run. The administrative unit that would be responsible for countryside schools would be the individual parish,[24] which was a church district containing several parishes. However, a public element entered into the picture through the formation of a school steering committee that would be formed in each parish composed of the priests, local administrative officers (*lensmenn*), priest's assistants (*medhjelpere*), and parish elector (*valgmann*).

The main task of the school committees would be to set the annual budget for education within the parish. Without question, the major issue facing the various parishes was finances. There was no standard procedure for paying the bills connected with schooling. Of course, it fell on the parishes to raise the funds through parish income, fines and penalties, attendance fees, and other devices.

At Aurland the new school committee was barely able to put 10-12 of the new national dollars (*spesiedaleren*)[25] in the school fund each of the first five or six years after the Norwegian Bank came into existence in 1816. However, because each of the five teachers, including the bell ringer, was given a salary of three national dollars a year the committee was running short about five national dollars a year, with little prospect of making up the deficit. The situation could only be made more critical between 1822 and 1826, when the salary increased three times. These were very hard times. Aurland was fortunate in one respect because it had been able to maintain a permanent school since 1802, which was held in the home of the bell ringer, Ole Stephaus Olsen.[26]

The more typical condition in the countryside was travelling schools, although some of the travelling teachers were much better off than those at Aurland. The Ullensvang parish was paying each of its six teachers nine national dollars a year in 1818, although their school year was twenty-seven weeks as opposed to a fifteen or sixteen week school year at Aurland.[27]

Obviously, the major financial burden facing the school committee was for teacher salaries. In fact, most of the concerns of the local committee were connected in one way or another with teachers. Teaching was such a poorly paid job that the higher issues of teacher qualifications and competence were secondary. Often, notices of teaching vacancies would simply end up with no applicants or if there were applicants, they might request salaries far in excess of the salary the school committee was able to pay.[28]

Ideally, the teacher would be a person connected with the church, because the school was so closely linked to the purposes of religion. In fact, the 1739 Danish school ordinance had specified that the bell ringer, the person responsible for ringing the church bell and leading the singing be the school teachers. That was not always possible but we find that the bell ringer, if one existed, usually played the role of head teacher in a parish.

Consequently, people of every walk of life, mainly those who were unqualified, could no longer practice their vocations, or needed to have a second income, would hire on as a teacher. Halvor Larsen Foslund describes the teachers in 1825 as being "discharged petty officers, injured seamen, impoverished merchants and small grocers, unsuccessful students and craftsmen, who were unable to practice their craft: in short, people of all classes who sought refuge in the schools as the occupation of last resort."[29] Nicolai Wergeland wrote in 1832 that the salaries of teachers were so bad that "most of them are cripples and disabled workers." He suggested that they actually "could earn more as farm hands."[30]

In spite of such negative assessments, there were some positive accounts. Priest Nils Hertzberg recorded the following report about the teachers he observed during his visit to rural schools in 1818.

> They write fairly well, some even handsomely. Their under-
> standing is sufficient to instruct in the 4 grammar cases, in
> whole numbers and decimals, and the rule of three (in math).
> They are practiced in catechizing.[31]

As yet teacher training was almost entirely unknown at the time, either in Norway or in other areas of Europe. Men such as Bishop Bech had expressed some concern for the situation, in 1810, when he had proposed a plan to the *Selskabet for Norges vel* that a seminar be established in each deanery run by a chaplain and the song leader.

The first such seminar to open, was actually in Øvre Telemark in Sundbygden, which opened with fourteen students in 1819 and admitted a total of 165 students during the next seventeen years. A permanent school was connected with the seminar, where the teachers instructed each day. They would remain, as a rule for half a year receiving training.[32] A seminar for the North country was also opened in 1826, and this had the distinction of being the first with direct state support.[33] Four other seminars came into existence in the next two decades, connected with the various bishoprics of Norway: Asker (in Oslo) in 1834, Klæbu (in Trondheim) in 1838, Stord (in Bergen) and Holt (in Kristiansand) in 1839,[34] these coming as a consequence of the 1827 school law stipulating that one seminar should be set up in each bishopric.

THE 1827 SCHOOL LAW

The 1827 school law not only dealt with teacher training, but it represented the first comprehensive national regulations intending to replace older ordinances and expectations. At that time, towns retained an enormous autonomy. Their status as free cities had been assured at the time the Norwegian legal code had been set in 1688. This meant that they stood outside the law set by the storting concerning general education, and it would be another two decades before a common school law for them would be passed.

The new law stipulated that school administration would continue to be composed of a mixture of religious and secular authorities, and it would remain decentralized in that each parish was directed to establish a school steering committee consisting of the priest, his assistants, the local bailiff and the elector.[35] The committee continued to be charged with the responsibility to set the budget and pay for the schooling services being rendered. In other words, the state was not yet ready to commit itself financially to building up the schools.

Organizationally, each parish was directed to establish at least one permanent school, at least if there were thirty or more youth who were of compulsory attendance age. Otherwise travelling schools were allowed.[36]

A compulsory attendance stipulated that attendance should begin at the age of seven years and continue until the young person had completed confirmation. Some flexibility was allowed in that it might be possible to wait, under certain circumstances, until the age of eight before beginning school, and it would also be possible to be relieved of school attendance the last two or three years prior to confirmation.

The yearly instructional time was set at two-three months, and the content of instruction would be (a) reading with comprehension, (b)

Christian studies with *Bible* history, (c) singing in the hymnal, (d) writing and calculating.[37] It is difficult to assess the impact which the 1827 school law had on Norwegian common schooling, mainly because we have little objective and general information about attendance figures and school support prior to that time. Some subjective data comes in the form of reports of priests, who were required by law to circulate throughout their district and file a report on the state of schooling. The priest of Stord, C. Daae, wrote in 1836, "In spite of all the appeals and admonishments of the previous year, one must complain that so few have learned to write...And with calculating? Not a single one can boast of having mastered the fundamentals thereof." In 1840 Daae's impressions were little changed. "With *Bible* history," he wrote, "poor, poor! — with writing, no better."[38] More typical assessments, however, were not so critical. Bishop Neumann at Aurland, observed in 1832 and 1833 that those confirmation candidates "were especially well informed."[39] We shall see, however, that writing and calculating received little attention until much later in the century.

The first major census in education came in 1837,[40] which affords some opportunity to measure the extent to which the 1827 school law had been implemented. We shall make some references to three provisions in the law: school organization, pupil enrollments, and teacher recruitment and training.

School Organization

The school law implies that there is some advantage to having permanent rather than ambulatory schools. In spite of this value tendency, common schooling in the Norwegian countryside remained largely ambulatory, only four percent of the schools being permanent by 1837. A travelling school was very common in Europe in the seventeenth and eighteenth centuries, but by this time more permanent arrangements were generally being made,[41] so Norway appears to have lagged far behind other countries in its desire and ability to establish permanent schools.

Part of the reason for this can be explained in terms of the dispersed nature of the Norwegian population. In the towns only permanent schools could be found, suggesting that they were established where possible. However, such sentiments were not universal. At the time the law was set, there was little debate over the issue, mainly because the *Storting* was dominated by civil servants, who would retain the more traditional institutional modes.

Three factors account for the lack of debate. First, conditions were such that permanent schools were as yet not even remotely possible, given the dispersed nature of the population. Second, the law did contain a clause allowing these sentiments toward permanent schools to be expressed, but it was stated in such a way that few communities would be bound to establish a permanent school. Third, the voices for ambulatory schools represented the farmers.

However, in the 1830s the farmers became a force in government and began expressing their own sentiments, as a political group, about policies that affected them. Consequently, as we shall see, the major debates only began to surface in the 1840s and 1850s as further legislation about common schools was considered.

Pupil Enrollments

According to the school census of 1837 only 4.8% of the school aged youth in countryside areas were not attending school. This represents an impressive finding in two respects. First, rough estimates available on a world wide scale indicate that attendance rates in the 1830s in Norway were exceeded only by Germany and the United States, and were as high as in Sweden and Denmark. The Netherlands, Belgium, and Switzerland, though lagging behind, were competitive with Norway, but other countries, including England, Canada, Australia, France, Austria, fell far behind in terms of attendance figures, compared with the total population.[42]

Second, a much higher school attendance rate was found in the countryside than in the towns of Norway. Because commercial centers were exempt from the national school law, they were not bound to provide common schooling, and approximately eighteen percent of school aged youth in the towns were not enrolled. Of course, some of the towns were vigorous in attempting to provide adequate educational programs for all youth, but others were very lax. Høigård and Ruge suggest that over half of the 3,630 children who were not attending in the cities would have if there had been places for them. Abuses were particularly flagrant in the larger cities such as Oslo and Bergen, where 300 and 400 young people of school age, respectively, did not attend because there were too few school places.[43]

If we draw the two above factors together, we could easily conclude that the countryside youth of Norway were attending school in the 1830s at a higher percentage rate than anywhere in the world, with the exception, perhaps, of Germany.

It would be misleading to make excessive claims about the schooling the Norwegian children in the countryside were receiving. They were often attending for no more than three months a year while the town youth usually had a thirty-four week school year with two or three days of instruction each week. In other words, the school year for town children was from 70-100 days, while the school year in the countryside rarely exceeded 60 days,[44] and was far short of that in some cases. For example, at Bø and Malnes in 1836, the school year was only four weeks long.[45]

The length of the school year and school size are related with permanent versus travelling schools. Permanent schools in the countryside were run more days and were larger than travelling schools. Whereas the average size of ambulatory schools was 21.8 pupils, it was 90.9 pupils at the permanent schools. In other words, well over fourteen percent of all countryside pupils were actually attending a permanent school even though only 4% of the schools were permanent.[46]

Another cause of concern was attendance, which was not consistent. Almost all of the non-attenders were older children. Dropouts usually left school about the age of ten and by the time of confirmation at age fourteen or fifteen a fair portion of the children were no longer in school.

We do not have any figures on absenteeism rates of children who were enrolled, but data elsewhere indicates that it was much higher in the nineteenth century than today and was near forty percent in some places.[47] In other words, because of travel problems, sickness, farming responsibilities, lack of legal mandates, and lack of interest, enrolled pupils simply did not attend as much as in contemporary times.

Add to this the fact that the qualifications of the teachers in the countryside were also more suspect than in the towns, and we have cause to hesitate about boasting too forcefully of the impressive enrollment figures among rural youth in Norway in 1837.

Teacher Recruitment and Training

The 1,826 full-time teachers that were identified in the census were responsible for instruction in 6,971 travelling schools.[48] Another 318 teachers were working in the 171 permanent countryside schools, 198 teachers working permanent countryside schools and 118 in town common schools. While the average number of teachers per school was larger than one in the permanent schools, each full-time teacher in the travelling schools was responsible for an average of 3.8 schools. The teacher went in a circuit from one school to the next, and it was the duty of every farmer or small proprietor, in his turn, to provide a proper schoolroom in his household, and to give the teacher board and lodging during the time school was kept in his home.

The average size of a class in the permanent schools was seventy-one pupils, which was made possible through an innovative system borrowed from England, called the Bell-Lancaster monitorial system, where the older or brighter children acted as monitors, receiving commands from the teacher and giving commands to small groups of slower pupils. Such innovative methods were unnecessary in the travelling schools, which averaged less than twenty-two students per school.

Even in the larger permanent schools, it is highly unlikely that such innovative methods as the monitorial system were prevalent. Only 17.7% of all permanent school teachers in the countryside had completed a training course at one of the teaching seminars. The situation was worse in the towns where only 14.1% had complete a course.[49]

Impressive strides had been made in terms of salaries by 1837. The average permanent school salary in the countryside was 86.5 national dollars a year, although that included the salary the song leaders earned for their church duties. Town and city salaries for common school teachers were even higher, coming to 108 national dollars a year. Travelling school teacher salaries were much improved, but in contrast to their colleagues at the permanent schools they were poorly paid, receiving an average of 18.5 national dollars a year, which was lower than the minimum salary stipulated by the 1827 law, which was twenty national dollars a year.[50] Approximately ten percent of the teachers were receiving less than ten national dollars a year.[51]

There were many hidden benefits for the travelling teacher. He was guaranteed free board and room while under way, and often had many additional benefits, such as a permanent room, free light fuel, heating oil, a small garden to grow vegetables, and other jobs. For example, 332 of the travelling teachers were church song leaders, who earned an additional 28.5 national dollars a year for discharging those responsibilities.[52] Even so, teachers, by and large, remained poorly trained and poorly paid.

SUMMARY

Independent Norway had, as yet, not recognized that the schooling tradition which it had inherited was antithetical to its incipient political democracy. In fact, the country remained, for a time, highly conservative in terms of its educational policies, and perpetuated those practices carried over from the time of Danish dependence. That was all temporary and short lived, because in the 1830s a new wave swept through the country. National romanticism would soon alter forever the political structure of the country bringing it in line with the cultural structure that was already largely in place.

Section II

First Reform Cycle —
A Norwegian School
Structure Takes Form

4 Educational Overtones in Romantic Nationalism

Because the major challenge facing Norway at the time of independence was the threat of external co-optation, particularly by the Swedes, relatively little attention was given to potential political power realignments within the country. The immediate general imperative was stability and even national survival. Within a generation, however, new imperatives began to surface, including a turning inward toward an understanding of the Norwegian culture, an awakening of a Norwegian consciousness.

Norway would soon undergo a fundamental shift in its political power structure, with the main initial stress point being manifest between the farmer and the official class. At the time of independence, the farmers were not yet ready to avail themselves of the rights and privileges granted to them in the constitution, but in the 1830s the farmers would begin to establish a political power base. By the middle of the century the workers movement would also be underway. These groups would challenge the official class and eventually unseat it as the dominant political force in the country.

It would be misleading to characterize the farmers as the group initially pressing for movement. In fact, in matters pertaining to "religion, social improvement, and intellectual culture, they were as a rule ultra-conservative."[1] The major initial forces toward a shift in the inner mental life of the people actually came from a faction of the intellectuals, mainly children of the official class. The major stress point would best be symbolized in the two leading literary figures of the day: Wergeland and Welhaven.

Johan Sebastian Welhaven was the literary spokesman for the burgher and bureaucrat, who defended traditional high culture in Norway. Of course, cultural continuity and historical roots with the past would have to include a Danish connection. Henrik Wergeland, on the other hand, came originally of peasant stock and spoke for a more indigenous Norwegian culture.[2] He recognized this culture was in its infancy, and it would require space to grow, freedom to develop according to its own imperatives and protection from foreign influences.

Wergeland was the more talented of the two men and represents even today the greatest poetic genius in Norwegian literature and much more. In a brief life spanning only thirty-seven years, his prolific works are compiled in twenty-three large volumes that span an enormous range of writing modes and topics. He is best known as the one who became the symbol of national feeling and political liberty. He was the champion of a broad, living Norwegian democracy among a people who would be free of cultural and political dependence, a people who would possess their own Norwegian language and literature.

Born in 1808 in Christiansand, Wergeland lived in a household rich in the arts and religion. His father, Nicolai, was a lecturer at the local Latin school and became one of the outspoken representatives to Eidsvoll in 1814. The independence movement would play a major role in the orientation of the household where Henrik was growing and learning. In 1817, when Henrik was nine years old, the family moved to Eidsvoll, where his father became the parish priest. At that time Henrik received a home teacher, who worked with him for two years, then he was sent to Christiania to attend the Latin school and live with his cousin, who was an administrator of the school.

While the school immersed him in classical studies, he was of quite a different temperament. He would write smug satirical pieces about his teachers and send them round to his school comrades. During summer vacation time he composed comic theatre pieces. Even at the age of thirteen, one of his *novelle* was published anonymously by *Morgenbladet*, a Christiania newspaper.[3]

As a young man he became the storm center of public life as he united those diverse elements that had slumbered in Norway into agitated, restless, boisterous activity. He represented the new Norway, the center of a current that demanded, not only political independence from Denmark, but intellectual separation. The official class continued to give over-whelming importance to Danish influences and Wergeland recognized that if Norway was to establish its own cultural independence it must break that bond and build the new Norway on a different foundation, a foundation consisting not only of the official class, but of all the people, including the farmer.

Wergeland realized that the common Norwegian was not well educated, and he would have to earn his right to govern; he would have to gain that sense of enlightenment enjoyed by the official class.

In 1830 as a young man of twenty-one he began a series of pamphlets directed to the common people, and sponsored by the *Selskab for Norges vel*. In the first pamphlet he chastised those common people who were satisfied to putter around doing their routine tasks, without learning and reading. "A farmer's burden is more than plowing," he exclaimed, "a thresher's more than threshing." Their full potential required quite another mode. He implored them to join together to establish reading and study groups.[4]

Wergeland published his second pamphlet for the common people later in 1830,[5] encouraging them to continue organizing themselves into societies that would contribute to the nation's economic and industrial progress. In 1832 he published a catechism for Norwegians, and two years later he published a two volume history of Norway, expressly written for the common person.[6] He was tireless in his endeavors to get the common person on the road toward broader enlightenment. "Read and learn," he implored, "and you will not any more feel yourself cast away to a joyless by-place, even if you are sitting in a cottage behind snow and mountains and barren moor! You will follow your plow as an enlightened and free individual."[7]

He recognized that one of the surest ways to general enlightenment was through books, but that the common Norwegian was nowhere near reaching his potential. Studies of the period would confirm this impression. Eilert Sundt, for example, surveyed 288 families in one region and found them to possess only those books used in school and church. Over half possessed the hymnal, 41 the *Bible*, 134 the *New Testament*, 23 the pamphlet "For Fattig og Rig" (For Rich and Poor), and an assortment of 93 copies of 30 other book titles, making a total of 558 books. None possessed the materials Wergeland had written for the common people. The average family possessed approximately 2 books, and 15 had no books at all. Less than half subscribed to a newspaper.[8]

Ole Vig suggested that he would have been satisfied to have found a half or even a third of the common folk who could read fluently and with comprehension.[9] One of the better present day students of that period, Hans-Jørgen Dokka, maintains that the whole social life of the common people was so limited, geographically and socially, that they did not even have a desire for more learning. They were satisfied with learning how to work their plot of land or to do their handwork and went with reluctance to school.[10]

Wergeland possessed quite another vision of the common people. He believed they would take advantage of the opportunity to grow and change if given the chance. At the time he was working on the earliest pamphlets for common people, he began his campaign for public libraries, where free books would be made available. Libraries were in existence, but previously they had been intended mainly for those of the official class. For example, at Stord, priest Eric Olsen had given a collection of his books in order to establish a "church library for my civil servant brothers (embetsbrør)."[11] In contrast to such endeavors, Wergeland proposed that the *Selskabet for Norges vel* assist him in getting local parishes to set up libraries for the common people, relying on donors who would contribute from twenty to forty books each.[12] Through his initial example at Eidsvoll, where his efforts led to the establishment of a library, many parishes soon came to possess a collection of books for general use.[13] The initiative for each library usually came from the local priest or an influential community member, such as the fictitious, Knud Aakre, described in the novel, *The Railroad and the Churchyard*, by Bjørnstjerne Bjørnson.[14]

By the end of 1833 no less than 86 common people's libraries had come into existence.[15] The number had risen to 185 by 1837.[16] The situation had reached the point that the *Selskabet for Norges vel* felt compelled in 1838 to issue a booklet designed to advise the parishes about the most appropriate books to place in their collections.[17] Such suggestions were probably valuable because another 45 common peoples libraries came into existence in the next two years, making a total of 230. In 1841 the Department of Church and Education began making state grants for libraries, supplementing the private subscriptions. Norway has the distinction of being the first country to adopt a policy of state support for libraries.

The cities could also make claim to an expanding number of libraries, made available to the various populations in them. At Fredrikstad, for example, a reading association had existed for many years having its own collection of novels. A deanery library had also existed for many years, and in the early 1820s the church helped establish another library at the local *realskole*. In 1848 the garrison was able to use some funds, supplemented by officers subscriptions, for a library so that soldiers could not only receive "moral influences," but they could free themselves from "boredom and idleness in the long winter evenings." The library possessed 94 volumes by 1854 and 240 volumes by 1860. In addition, two poor people's libraries also existed in the city showing evidence that Wergeland's work was having an impact on the cities as well.[18]

Wergeland's educational work was not restricted to libraries. He recognized the value of higher schools but demanded that they be of service to all the people. Even the university at Christiania, "with all four faculties, with a library, museums, lecturers, tutors, surrounded by the whole scientific apparatus" was inadequate to the task. That life, so isolated from the broader world, "must penetrate public, private, and family life until every member of society, man and woman is found devoting his/her spare time, as long as possible into the night, with some scientific pursuit."[19]

All of this seems, in retrospect, to have been constructive and positive, but Wergeland soon found himself the center of a great intellectual battle that would be waged until his premature death in 1845. Not only would he find detractors raging against what he was writing and doing, but they would speak out against the way he was doing it.

The major antagonist and adversary would be Johan Sebastian Welhaven, who represented quite a different side of Norwegian culture. His heritage was urban and partly foreign. One grandfather on his father's side was German and his mother possessed Danish blood. He thrived on the training of his classical philology teacher at the Bergen Cathedral School, Lyder Sagen. He was a year older than Wergeland, but because of difficulties in mathematics at school he actually entered the University of Christiania at the same time in 1825. Welhaven detested what he saw as the crude power play of Wergeland's national movement. He maintained that it lacked form, possessed no standards, and revealed no order. It was all noise and thunder. What the nation needed was more refinement, harmony, and high culture, probably best exemplified in the classic harmony of the Danish poetry of his day.

To Welhaven, Norwegian intellectual life was destitute when separated from the Danish. Its literature was next to nothing and that which existed was immature, clumsy, narrow, provincial. Wergeland epitomized for Welhaven what would occur if the Danish connection were severed. Wergeland's incessant productivity represented a river of writing often without form and literary laws. There might be some good but there was undoubtedly more bad. It was unbridled and chaotic, lacking style, grace, and other poetic qualities that were demanded by genuine artists.[20]

At the time the conflict between Welhaven and Wergeland began, they were both students at Christiania University. Other students quickly became involved in the controversy with the most talented and able rallying around Welhaven, not so much because he was the more engaging of the two, but because he represented the tradition of the academic world toward which most of them were aspiring. They included students such as Anton Martin Schweigaard, Fredrik Stang, and Ulrich Anton Motzfeld, who would all eventually be invited to join the law faculty at the University of Christiania upon graduation. Bernhard Dunker would also become a lawyer active in politics and scholarship. Peter Andreas Munch was destined to become a professor of history at Christiania University.

The split between the two student groups constituted the origins of the two great political parties that would one day come into existence. On the one hand, Welhaven thought that political leadership would be catastrophic if lost to the masses. The farmer lacked every sense of political maturity, and any thoughtful person would recognize they did not have the right to participate in the leadership of the country, because the most intelligent, better trained segment of society was only to be found in the official class. They arrogantly identified themselves as members of the "Intelligence Party."

On the other hand, Wergeland, who was joined by a few literary friends, campaigned vigorously for a new political force to emerge in the country. Of course, Welhaven rejected Wergeland's travels through the country campaigning for the farmers to become politically active, and when forty-five of the ninety-six *Storting* seats were won by farmers in 1833, Welhaven and his colleagues reacted by suggesting that it signaled "the triumph of ignorance," and was "the forerunner of barbarism."[21]

Welhaven was not hostile to the farmers but he maintained that people must earn the right to govern. They must become educated and achieve a sense of high culture before they would be allowed to assume responsible positions. In his polemic work *Norges dæmring*, he characterizes Norway as becoming like a wrecked ship, that could only be restored through education in its finest, academic sense.[22]

It may have been fortuitous that such a storm raged between the proponents of independence and those for continuity, because it heightened the tensions, directed and consumed the energies of the brightest young minds in the country, and more clearly defined the national agenda. In actuality, both camps were necessary for the new Norway and both camps had the same ultimate objective: a strong and resourceful Norway. Even Welhaven loved the national elements of his culture and ultimately contributed his share to national romanticism by drawing from the folk songs and ballads of the country in his poetry.

Norway needed to become spiritually independent and establish a separate national identity, but it would have impeded the process to have become overly isolated. It was the Welhaven oriented students, for example, who followed the lead of the rest of Europe in moving toward the adoption of science and modern languages in the *lærde skole*. Further, the brothers Grimm, who had published the folk songs and folk tales in Germany between 1812-22, provided the model for Andreas Faye's *Norwegian Legends and Myths*.[23]

By the end of the 1840s the entire country was engaged in the flowering of a national romanticism, which permeated every facet of intellectual and artistic endeavor. The intellectual foundation of that movement was laid by historical investigations begun by Rudolf Keyser and P. A. Munch. Keyser, a theology student at Christiania, had come to concentrate his energies on Northern history and had become a history professor at Christiania, writing almost exclusively on medieval Norwegian history. P. A. Munch, the stanch defender of Welhaven during student days, was tutored by Keyser in Old Norse and history and soon became a central figure in studying the origins and early history of Norwegians. His eight volume *History of the Norwegian People*[24] traced that history down until the Union of Kalmar in 1387 providing a distinct theory of Norwegian origins, a unique early Norwegian-Icelandic literature, and evidence of a great medieval culture.

Their historical documents were supplemented by Old Norse legends, myths and sagas, which began to divert attention away from the classical studies so central in the elite grammar schools toward the study of Norwegian antiquity. In fact, the classical school teachers examination began permitting, in 1848, a candidate to substitute Old Norse for the customary Hebrew.[25]

Patriotic fervor could only be enhanced by those Norwegians out in the country collecting folk tales. Faye had quite a different intent than patriotism, but his intentions were soon lost, especially with the appearance of the collections of Christen Asbjørnsen and Jørgen Moe.[26]

Beginning with the assumption that old folk tales sprang from the innermost life of the people, they began building folklore studies as a scientific endeavor, by systematically collecting many variants of the same tale and through comparative analysis attempted to throw light on the nature and relationships of the early peoples of Norway. The University of Christiania has the distinction of being the first institution of higher learning in the world to appoint a lecturer in folklore studies, that coming to Moe in 1849.

It was also in this era that M. B. Landstad and Olea Crøger were independently engaged in gathering together an impressive collection of Norwegian ballads, which had sprung from the romance and chivalry of past ages. Landstad was particularly anxious to help his people see the connections between ancient works and more contemporary ballads.[27]

Ballad collectors were joined by Ludwig M. Lindeman, who sought out and published folk music over a period of several decades. These ballads and folk songs served as sources of inspiration for the common people and for some of the greatest artistic geniuses Norway would ever produce, including Ibsen and Grieg. In fact, the man most instrumental in enhancing the reputation of Norway as a land of unique culture in the early days of independence was Ole Bull, who travelled the Western world as a violin virtuoso. His programs inevitably included variations and fantasies based on Norwegian folk tunes.[28]

Pictorial art was also closely connected with romantic nationalism. Artist Adolph Tidemand depicted an idealic peasant life in his paintings and he was joined by Hans Gude in producing numerous peasant portraits. Johan Christian Dahl, although living abroad, exposed the world to the wonders of the Norwegian landscape and Norwegian folk life.

The most controversial element of romantic nationalism was that of language. The written language of Norway was Danish, but a movement gained ground to "Norwegianize" it; the first actual written form coming out of the work of Henrik Wergeland, who consciously deviated from the Danish language rules.[29] The most radical early transformation in literary language came through the works of Asbjørnsen and Moe as they attempted to capture the essence of the ancient folk tales. It proved to be impossible simply to translate them into Danish, so they began to create new written words and expressions, reshape sentences according to the demands of the rules of living Norwegian. In the process the foundation for a new language was being set.

It was left to a self-taught farm boy by the name of Ivar Aasen to undertake the painstaking task of collecting from various parts of the country the local dialects, joining them into one, and building a new language, which was a composite of the local languages, although he gave decided preference to the more "perfect" Western dialects.[30]

Aasen was, at first, not particularly interested in replacing Danish by his so-called *landsmaal* (countryside speech). Such agitation came mainly from a schoolmaster, Knud Knudsen, who, in the early 1850s, began a campaign directed toward national policy that the written language form be brought into conformity with its spoken form.

Aasmund Vinje must also be counted as one of the greater moving forces in the language movement. Vinje is probably best known as a journalist and has the distinction of having initiated the first journal in *landsmaal*.[31] In 1857 he even proposed to the *Storting* that Old Norse become a language of study on an equal footing as Latin, Greek, and newer languages.[32]

The efforts of Knudsen, Aasen, and Vinje would constitute the main forces about language that went to the core of the Wergeland-Welhaven debate two decades earlier. All three had been reared in circumstances which those in the "Intelligence Party" had claimed were unworthy to assume a role of leadership in the culture. They were all sons of very poor cotters and had little more than an ambulatory school experience to initiate their personal development. Obviously, this was very limited material to help lead a national awakening.

The main defender of the *status quo* was the old Welhaven university companion, P.A. Munch, who argued that Norway would be set back to the 13th century if it did away with the language forms of the day and tried to build a nation on an extinct language that had no currency in the broader European culture. Besides, he felt that language had such an inner integrity that men should not tamper with it. The debate centered on two questions. Should Norway break so completely from its Danish roots? Could the country actually build a meaningful high culture from its peasant roots? The answers to these questions have not, to this day, been completely resolved.

SCHOOL TEACHERS AND ROMANTIC NATIONALISM

We recall that in 1814 members of the official class were almost exclusively responsible for the democratic definition of the constitution. The romantic nationalist spirit appearing through various modes of literary and artistic expression, was a much broader effort representing gifted contributions from all strata and all spheres of society. Of course, the major contribution, at least in numbers of contributors, remained those in the official class, most of these having clerical and Latin school connections. Faye and Landstad were clergymen, while Moe and Munch had been theology students. More significantly, a larger number were children of clergymen, including Wergeland, Welhaven, Landstad, Munch, Schwach and Crøger. Falnes speculates that the clerical profession led these people to take a natural interest in the "beliefs and traditions" that formed the core of the romantic movement.[33]

However, there were many with no classical educated or clerical background who participated in the movement. Asbjørnsen's father was a master glazer in Christiania; Bjerregaard and Unger came from families connected with the military; Ole Bull's father was a pharmacist in the port city of Bergen, while J.C.C. Dahl's father was a fish handler.

Many had a direct connection with the common school and witnessed a major breakthrough. New options were opening up to those previously limited to a common school experience. One of these options was the establishment of a number of agricultural schools. The first such school was actually private and was founded in 1825 by Jacob Sverdrup, the estate manager of Count Wedel Jarlsberg. Since 1819, Sverdrup had played an active role publishing an impressive series of pamphlets on ways to improve farming,[34] but the government quickly became involved in the establishment of county agricultural schools, and by the 1850s up to 18 such schools were operating, providing bright young people of humble means an opportunity to advance themselves.[35] Young Øyvind, in Bjørnson's *The Happy Boy* typifies the advantages this could bring to a modest cotter's son.[36]

More significantly for romanticism was the enhanced condition of the rural schoolmaster, in part because of the influence of the teacher training seminars that had grown up around the bishoprics of the country. Whereas, in 1840, only 49 teachers could be found who had passed through the teaching seminar, that figure had risen to 275 by 1852.[37] The year 1848 is usually noted as the time the common school teachers began to organize themselves into associations and to take a direct interest in politics. In 1850 a priest in Molde began publishing a journal for them called *Norsk Almueskole-Tidende*. The rural teacher had previously occupied one of the humblest occupational positions in the country, but he was beginning to take on a growing influence in the rural society.[38]

Many of the most significant contributions to national romanticism came directly from people whose initial exposure to learning was in the common school in remote areas of Norway. Ivar Aasen is the classic example. Born of very meagre means in the wild fjord region of Sundmøre, Aasen was orphaned at age twelve. He left the common school as early as possible to work for five years as a farmhand, relying almost exclusively on the *Bible* for his personal education before becoming a schoolmaster and beginning his lifelong struggle at self-education. He eventually left common school teaching to serve as a home teaching tutor for several years while engaged in personal study, mainly of linguistics and natural history.

Knud Knudsen's father was a cotter who had also done some common school teaching and Knud followed his father into common school teaching before qualifying for higher studies. Vinje also came from poor cotter stock in an isolated valley in Telemark. He educated himself enough to get into a teachers seminar and became a common school teacher. After taking several jobs, none of which worked out, he engaged in a crash preparatory course, which helped him qualify for university studies at the age of thirty-two.

All of these people worked directly to improve the lot of the common people and enhance the image of the common school. Knudsen was a main force in the establishment of the Association for National Enlightenment, and Vinje's works are filled with materials relevant to common school education. In fact, the third edition of *Dølen* is devoted completely to issues surrounding the common school teacher.[39]

A final example might be Ole Vig, the son of a poor cotter in Stjørdalen. In 1841, at the age of seventeen, he was sent to the teachers seminar at Klæbo for two years after which he became a home teacher at the parish in Aafjorden, then a teacher at the common school and later at the burgher school in Christiansund. In 1851 Vig took a trip to Denmark where he met Grundvig, and returned to Norway to become a disciple of Grundvigian thinking.

Grundvig was a Danish bishop and poet and founder of a theological movement that exercised great influence on church thinking as well as a general awakening of the masses. He maintained that Christianity was being treated as a theological and philosophical notion when it was a living, historical revelation that lived through acts such as baptism and communion. In educational terms Grundvig denounced Latin and the classics as abstract, distant elements separated from and unintelligible to the ordinary people. He stressed the importance of the mother tongue and the possibility of a national awakening tied to the historical realities of the nation and the people. Rome and its culture represented oppression and destruction while Danish language, literature, history and mythology represented liberation, sympathy, and solidarity.

These ideas were taken up in the folk high school movement that began in 1844 in Denmark. The most important educational activists of the period, including Vig, carried Grundvigian ideas into their national movement. Eventually a series of folk high schools would be established in Norway, their purpose being to provide the rural population with lectures, discussions, poetry readings, and other general education, mainly in residential courses. The first such school of this type came into existence in 1864 at Sagaun, near Hamar.

Vig is best known in educational circles for his work in organizing teachers and holding meetings intending to enlighten the people through historical studies, singing, and expounding "the living word," to use a Grundvigian concept. One of Vig's greatest achievements came through the publication of a journal, *Den norske folkeskole* (The Norwegian Peoples' School), which he published with Knud Knudsen between 1852-58. The journal was infused with an aim to inspire, to enhance, to move the teacher in the common school to participate in the national awakening. Its very name suggested a new mission for the school, whose basic purpose had been toward basic skills, toward God and church, even toward some general enlightenment. Now, it would be a school devoted to the development of a sense of national feeling, an awakened Norwegian culture.

The local schoolmaster would soon take on an idealized form, typified by the old school master portrayed in Bjørnson's *The Happy Boy*, who "grew to be almost a supernatural being," as he awakened the young children not just to basic skills but beautiful verses, songs, and moral passages,[40] helping them gain a sense of stature, love, faith and promise.

TROUBLE IN THE LATIN SCHOOL

A curiosity of Norwegian romanticism was the lack of participation and educational response on the part of the Latin schools. To be sure, certain people supportive of aspects of the movement were also central figures in the Latin school. For example, Fr. M. Bugge, the Rector of the Trondheim Latin School, served as head of the Scientific Association (*Videnskabsselskabet*) in Trondheim, when it became the initial sponsor of Ivar Aasen. Because of the encouragement of Bugge, the Association provided Aasen with the first financial award to collect the remnants of Norway's ancient language and "work out a grammatical dissertation on the dialects."[41] However, the schools themselves remained, at first, strangely silent with regard to the entire movement and then turned defensive and even reactionary.

Such a reaction would ultimately contribute to their downfall. At least four major sources of tension between the Latin schools and the romantic movement might be mentioned. First, the higher studies could hardly ignore the importance of adopting Norwegian classics to accompany those from Greece and Rome. Old Norse was crucial in building the notion that Norwegian culture was built on a long, advanced cultural tradition. It would be necessary to know this tradition as a companion area of study to the more standard classical languages. Important inroads were made at the University of Christiania in this regard, but the Latin schools seemed impervious to its importance.

Second, the romantic movement placed a high value on the language of the common people. To insist on the continuation of formal and classical language forms in church and meeting places was a sign of insensitivity, self-glorification, and self-righteousness on the part of the classically oriented scholars. The language of the day was folksy and simple, it was grounded in daily experience, and it implicitly rejected the pretentious, flowery language being taught at Latin school.

Third, It was elitist to the extreme. The Latin schools, for whatever reasons, had failed to become more inclusive. The number of students from the recognized Latin schools qualifying to take the *examen artium* between 1826 and 1850 was extremely constant, as seen in Table 4.1.[42]

Table 4.1

The Average Number of Pupils Each Year from Recognized Latin Schools, Who Qualified for the Examen Artium between 1826 and 1850

1826-30	31
1831-35	32
1836-40	32
1841-45	26
1846-50	34

The Latin schools continued to serve but a small portion of the population and inevitably fostered a sense of superiority, where a sense of commonality and unity characterized the romantic spirit of Norwegian nationality.

Finally, the Latin schools were largely irrelevant. They had already lost their hold as gate-holders of social privilege and status. The stopgap attempts of independence leaders to satisfy higher civil servant needs had broken the floodgates. As a consequence, between 1826 and 1850 less than 800 of the 2500 students who had applied to take the *examen artium* had followed an ordinary Latin school program. As would be expected, those who had gone through Latin school had a much better success ratio (96.8% vs. 81.5%) than did those who had taken the alternate routes. Even so, only 35% of all those who passed the examination had gone through the Latin school. Because most of the university trained leaders of the country had never gone through the Latin school itself,[43] their level of commitment to the Latin school would be understandably low.

According to Halvdan Koht, many of those aspiring to qualify for university study were really not interested in knowledge and their studies as an end in itself. They viewed the *examen artium* as a hurdle to get over rather than a reflection of some intellectual or humanistic attainment, and they took advantage of every possible alternative open to them, including the alternatives mentioned in Chapter 3, such as home teaching, self-study, and foreign travel. In addition, new alternatives had become available to them, the most prominent being privately run cramming mills, whose major purpose was to prepare students to pass the examination. Some of these schools paralleled the recognized Latin schools in that they admitted young people of all ages. We have previously made mention of Støren Preparatory School, but the most prominent institution of this type was Møllers Institute, run by Ulrik M. Møller, which had opened its doors in 1822 and had remained open for the next 28 years.

As a young man Møller had attended Trondheim Latin School before going on to the university at Copenhagen in 1811 to study theology. The events of 1814 broke off his formal studies so he returned to Christiania where he taught Norwegian, history, and geography at the Military Academy before initiating his private schooling venture.

One of Møller's teachers from 1838 to 1843 was a man named Henrik Heltberg. He was a sickly but brilliant man who struck on the idea of setting up a two year private program to help young adults who had been deprived of Latin schooling because of lack of funds, or other reasons. His preparatory school became affectionately known as the "student factory," and the names of the students passing through the program include Theodor Abildgaard and Paul Botten-Hansen, now identified with the early years of the labor movement. It also includes names that almost represent a "who's who" of the greatest literary artists in Norwegian history, Aasmund Vinje, Bjørnstjerne Bjørnson, Henrik Ibsen, and Jonas Lie.

These people would form the most distinguished group of literary figures that Norway would ever produce. While the early work of the romantics provided the data and the sentiment, it was left to this later group to capture the essence of Norwegian life in its literary form. They would draw from the sagas, the folk tales, the history and contemporary Norwegian culture in providing the world with a creative genius rarely matched.

These artists would also communicate an educational message more loudly than any political proclamation. Their genius was not drawn out of them by the Latin school. Their talent was not a product of classical studies. Their contribution was from a Norway far distant from that world of schooling that had been so defended by Welhaven and his fellow students so many years earlier. The new Norway was strong and vital and its strength and vitality came from a source far removed from the sterile program of the Latin school of the day.

SUMMARY

National romanticism in Norway came out of the lively activities of young university students at Christiania in the 1830s, but it quickly penetrated the broader society. Even though the classical schools remained immune to the movement, the idea of general enlightenment led to the establishment of an extensive network of libraries and other educational outlets. Common schools, teacher seminars, and vocational schools provided the means for the common person to become a part of and awakened Norwegian spirit.

There remained during the initial stages of the movement, little sentiment to alter the existing school structure. However, a new sense of educational opportunity took firm hold in the country. Equality of educational opportunity now included the notion that each person was capable of enlightenment, rationality, and learning. Earlier impulses for the general learning had been largely other-worldly, while this new impulse was toward more worldly, human spheres. However, it reflected something internal rather than something social. As yet, there was little inclination to do away with social differences, but each person, regardless of his place or social station, possessed the right to enlightenment.

5 The Winds of Educational Reform

ECONOMIC AND POLITICAL CONDITIONS

Economically, Norway did not fare well during those first decades after independence. The currency system was a shambles, and the economy struggled terribly as the lumber industry suffered an initial depression, due to the attraction of the British to the new forests in Canada. Iron and Copper mining suffered a decided drop in output.

In spite of these difficulties, some advances were being made. Farming, which continued to dominate the economy, was expanding because new farms were being registered as land was cleared. In the 1820s alone over 25,000 acres were opened up for farming, and another 40,000 acres became available in the 1830s. In addition, church lands became available for private purchase, which allowed cotters the opportunity to gain a piece of property. The total output of farming doubled in the two decades following independence.[1]

Politically, farmers began to become a major force with the surge of influence among the farmers in the *Storting* in 1833. Their presence in Christiania was initially looked upon with great suspicion and was considered by some, even many farmers, to be illegal, which curbed their effectiveness. However, they were able to influence legislation that established local government on a completely different form. Whereas local government had been seen as an organ doing the bidding of the civil servant class, an 1837 law allowed local officials to be elected. Such a shift in political power not only affected the nature of schools, welfare agencies, etc., but it provided a political school for the farmers, who needed direct experience with political life.[2]

The farmer was only one of many coalescing forces that signaled the advent of a modernized economy, as the countries moved toward mid-century. Contrary to much of Europe, that experienced political upheavals in the second quarter of the century, Norway remained politically stable. In addition, government policy itself laid much of the groundwork, in large measure because of the efforts of those young intellectuals, such as Schweigaard and Stang, who had moved into the political arena as members of the *Storting*. They advocated a free trade policy and were successful in 1842 in reforming the monetary system of the country, both of which stimulated private enterprise.

Shipping and merchant marine activities grew rapidly, and that period is now referred to as the "golden age of the windjammer," as Norway relied mainly on wind driven ships. By 1870, Norway had outstripped all other countries, save Great Britain and the United States, in merchant marine capacity.

Whereas industry had previously consisted of small crafts production, by mid-century Norway was beginning to experience an urbanization process that allowed the towns to become major production centers. The population living in towns had never exceeded 10% until just prior to mid-century, but a strong upswing in the percentage of urban residents occurred, as the population reached 15.6% in 1865, 18.3% in 1875, 23.7% in 1890, and 28.0% by 1900.[3] Whereas only about 5% of the population had been involved in industry of any kind at the beginning of the century, that figure had risen to 15.5% by 1865 and continued to climb.[4] England, which had experienced its industrial revolution a century earlier, became the model for many young men eager to learn. They travelled to their neighboring country and brought back an understanding of how textiles were being manufactured, how alcohol was brewed, how factories were constructed.

Fishing, which had consisted of a part-time activity by farmers along the West coast, quickly grew into a major industry as gill nets for cod and seining techniques for herring were introduced along with new preservation techniques for the fish.

None of this would have been possible if a modern communications system had not been developed, including a modern road system with an extensive number of bridges and reasonable grade ratios. In 1851 the first railway was introduced and after 1855 the telegraph system expanded rapidly. Postal reform brought postal rates low enough so that common people could take advantage of the service.

As Norway modernized economically, social welfare issues began to surface and educational reform imperatives became evident. The initial educational impulses were related to curricular matters at the Latin school, but they soon spilled over to considerations about a comprehensive Norwegian school system.

REALISM VS. CLASSICISM

The advent of a modern economy would require a sophisticated understanding of technical processes as well as business people able to interact with the major trading centers of the world. While some attention had been given to modern school subjects such as science, technical subjects, and modern languages at the burgher school, vocational schools and other outlets, the schools intended for the official class had consciously considered them to be peripheral to the main focus of the program. Some attention had been given, but these courses were treated in the same form as the classics.

It was the young budding members of the official class itself that put forward the first major proposals to change this. Significantly, the initial thrust for change came from Anton Martin Schweigaard, the student companion to Welhaven, who would eventually become one of the great conservative statesmen and jurists of the country. Welhaven and his companions had established a periodical called *Vidar* in 1832, which was intended to act as an outlet for the views of the intellectuals. In its very first issue, Schweigaard launched a direct attack on the dominance of Latin and Greek in the *lærde skole*.[5] He maintained that the schools must exist on a cultural-philosophical basis. The Latin schools were but a "shadow of bygone days" that had little relevance to the contemporary world. They must shed themselves of their closed and irrelevant formalities and become involved in the vital realities of the day, including both scientific and social issues. They must provide the student, not just with dead languages, but living modern languages, including the study of the mother tongue.

Schweigaard's challenge could not go unheeded by his colleagues in the Intelligence Party.[6] Frederick Stang responded in issues 5-8 of the *Vidar* with a long and thorough argument for retaining the classics as the foundation of the *lærde skole*.[7] Even Stang agreed that the natural sciences have a place in the elite schools, but he maintained that language study was more appropriate, psychologically, for the young at school than was science.

The difference in perspective of these two University of Christiania companions highlights the influence that alternative schooling arrangements were having on those experiencing the alternative arrangements. Whereas Stang had taken almost all his schooling at the Bergen Latin School and had little else to compare his experience against, Schweigaard's experience was rich and varied. His father had intended him to become a seaman or a businessman, as himself. He was, consequently, placed in a burgher school as a young boy, but at the age of ten both parents died, and he was placed on a ship to learn the shipping business. He could not adjust to this life, so at the age of fourteen his family sent him to Germany where a local pastor tutored him in German, French and Latin. The pastor, J.A.D.C. Koeppen, also opened his substantial library to the young man, and he took advantage of it to read and study. Koeppen was so impressed with the Schweigaard that he prevailed upon the family to allow this gifted young man to prepare for university studies.

And so, at age sixteen, Schweigaard was enrolled in a Latin school for the first time, but the school at Skien was unlike the more established schools. The school was just getting started and of necessity engaged the boys in a semi-tutorial experience. In addition, Schweigaard was much more mature than the other boys, so he could judge his experience from a perspective of criticism and comparative value.[8] Finally, rector Orn challenged his students to read beyond the compulsory subject matter and included questions on each school examination that allowed the students to elaborate on their outside readings.[9]

The *Vidar* debate took place essentially in academic circles. The young men were at the time neither a part of the professional education establishment nor of the political community, and it was left to others to bring the issue into the educational and political forum. That occurred in 1833 when the official class, including the academic personnel, attempted to rescind the preliminary examination for medicine, which allowed those who had not passed the *examen artium* to enter the university. Their argument was that enough candidates were now qualifying for university study through conventional routes and the alternative mechanism was no longer needed.

The major spokesman in defense of retaining the preliminary examination was Hermann Foss, an artillery officer, who had first come into the *Storting* in 1827. Foss had received military academy training, which was not Latin language dominated but focused on modern subjects.

His sophisticated and precise stature stood as evidence that Latin was not the only means to such stature. Through his leadership the *Storting* refused to repeal the preliminary examination, which signified a turning point in the whole attitude toward the classics.[10]

Previously it had been taken for granted that the classics were crucial in awakening the inner spirit and creative energies of the young, and convey more perfectly than any other medium that essence which liberalizes and humanizes, and any alternative would be a second-rate stopgap measure. Now, it was being claimed that other routes could be just as legitimate as Latin and Greek.

As the debate became a public affair, it fell on the shoulders of Frederik M. Bugge, the young rector of Trondheim Cathedral School, to make the case of the classics. Bugge had gone through that school as a young boy, had studied classical philology under Georg Sverdrup at the University of Christiania, then had received an appointment as a teacher at the Stavanger Latin School before he had returned to Trondheim.[11] Having known little else, Bugge feared the unstable circumstances that had arisen through political events such as the July Revolution in France, but he was especially concerned about the unsettling influences of naturalistic thinking. It had become a hydra that slithered its cold body over the lives of the people and threatened their very existence. The only hope for salvation and stability was to hold fast to traditional ideals, to return to classical studies.

In 1836 Bugge received a stipend from the *Storting* to spend a year abroad, particularly in the German states, studying exemplary schooling programs. As might have been expected, he devoted most of his time in those areas where programs were in harmony with his own point of view.[12] Friedrich Thiersch, in Bavaria, had himself been involved in a study of German states as well as France, Holland, and Belgium,[13] and had judged them harshly. For example, he was critical of the French because its system had been dampened by a "free spirit," and only after physics, chemistry, natural history, intensive historical studies, and higher mathematics were eliminated and neo-humanism restored, would the young cease to be suppressed and fragmented.[14] Such a point of view would reinforce Bugge's conviction that he was on the right track in playing down the importance of natural science and modern languages as useful educational media.

The outcome of Bugge's study tour was a monumental three volume work.[15] Central to his recommendations was the notion that schooling must be an organic system, not a segmented conglomeration of little bits and pieces. This comprehensive view did not imply a comprehensive school structure, but it did bring into focus the necessity of looking at all the components and justifying their various roles in a system.[16] Each institution would have its designated place in that system, with the *lærde skole* standing at its pinnacle, representing the life beacon casting its light over the state. In Bugge's plan the system remained decidedly dualistic, with the folk school standing separate from the rest of the system. Remaining consistent with the German tradition, he recommended that the folk school provide an eight year program of studies.[17]

The rest of the structure would be integrated in the earlier stages in that the burgher school and the Latin school would be joined together. That integrated school would consist of three phases. The first phase would last four years and would stress classical studies, particularly Latin.[18] The second phase would also last four years but consist of two tracks. In the one track, called the *alminnelige borgerskole*, modern studies would be given to young people destined to small commercial enterprises and skilled crafts. At the end of this period, formal studies would cease. The second track, named the middle level, would also consist of a four year program of a conventional classical course, and it would be attended by members of the official class and the better children from the burgher class.[19] The third phase would build on the middle level program, and the youth would go on either to a two year higher burgher school or a four year *lærde skole*, that would qualify the students for university study.[20] Bugge's recommendations served as the focal point of a government commission, organized in 1839 to consider broad questions relating to education.

THE GREAT EDUCATION COMMISSION

The so-called Great Education Commission (*Den store undervisningskommisjonen*), came as a direct response to Bugge's proposals, and its charge was to look at all issues connected with education in Norway. Consequently, is was particularly active in trying to arrive at a comprehensive proposal on all aspects of some future educational system. Within its purview came town and countryside folk schools, the burgher schools, the Latin schools, the university and military schools.

The original composition of the Commission, headed by Count Wedel-Jarlsberg, consisted of men of the official class, although Hermann

Foss, a son of a businessman, was appointed to the group in 1840.[21] Only Bugge was intimately connected with schooling.

In spite of the fact that this was the first major school commission, it was destined for difficulties from the outset. Wedel-Jarlsberg died in 1840 and was succeed by a seventy five year old priest, Bishop Sørensen, who was too old to move the Commission. School was certainly not the highest priority of the Commission members, all of whom were preoccupied with conflicting responsibilities. Even Bugge considered his role to be outside his major sphere of professional activity; he continued to serve in a full-time capacity as the head of his Latin School in Trondheim for the greater period of time he sat on the Commission. Sharp differences also existed between the members. The realism vs. classicism controversy played itself out all over With Bugge and others defending classicism with Schweigaard and Foss leading the arguments for the newer studies.

Another major difficulty facing the Commission was the fact that the boundaries of their task were simply undefined. Because no system of schooling existed, it was difficult to determine what central questions and issues to address.[22] In addition, even though Bugge's major contribution was the notion that a comprehensive system of schooling should be set up, it remained frozen in outdated notions. Bugge's school system retained a dualistic framework and a traditional allegiance to Latin language study.

Norway was quickly entering the modern world and romantic nationalism was taking the country in quite a different direction than the classical Greek and Roman world. Schoolmen such as Bugge were not entirely in touch with the flow of their own culture and economy. The period actually represented a genuine turning point away from all that the elite schools represented, because the Latin language entered into a state of decline and erosion until it disappeared altogether from the school scene.

The Commission completed its work in 1844,[23] and the outcome was not very positive. The proposals on the Latin and burgher schools were buried in the Department and *Storting* committee structure. Some minor curricular and examination changes were made at the university. The most direct substantial consequence of their work had to do with the folk schools, where a school law relating to towns was eventually enacted in 1848.

Even their folk school recommendations were compromised. The Great Education Commission had drafted its proposal to pertain not only to the folk schools in the trading centers but in the countryside. The countryside schools were simply not providing a well-rounded program. In 1837 only 22% of the travelling schools were teaching writing and 11% were teaching calculating.[24] None of them had regular singing exercises.

The proposed folk school law originally framed by the government in 1845, pertained both to the towns and the countryside. The proposal for folk schools in the countryside raised enormous protests on the part of the farmers, who recognized that such a law would represent a great financial burden, which the local parishes would have to carry. The two farmer representatives of the *Storting*, who would carry the voice of the farmers for many years, Ole Gabriel Ueland and Søren Pedersen Jaabæk argued strongly that the measure was inappropriate, especially in those poor districts in the West, which had little income. Jaabæk was especially vexed that the state would support the education of the official class while requiring the local communities to finance the education of the folk people.[25]

Financial responsibility on the part of the state for folk schooling was beginning to take on greater importance and served as the major obstacle in obtaining a law for all folk schools in the countryside. The fact that the farmer representatives, Ueland and Jaabæk, worked against a folk school law for the countryside had little to do with their commitment to education as such. In fact, as a young man, Jaabæk had served as a folk school teacher for thirteen years. However, he was a model of the self-made man that was so characteristic of the period. He had already set his goal to be in the *Storting* as early as 1836.[26]

The efforts of the farmer representatives would ultimately contribute to the decision that the state participate in financing education, but in the 1840s, there was little favorable sentiment. Central financing of schools would be restricted to an array of educational institutions that were providing educational services to the better classes of people. At any rate, the major outcome of The Great Education Commission was the recommendation that the poor schools in the towns become folk schools.

THE 1848 FOLK SCHOOL LAW

The folk school law for towns, passed in 1848, provided a hint of educational developments to come, although its aims remained largely lodged in the past. Education was not yet viewed as the responsibility of the state. The home was still the primary educational agent with the school providing a supplemental service to the home.[27] We find that in Norway, unlike the larger countries of Europe such as France or Prussia, state ends had not become more important than family and religious ends,[28] although there was some reference to the fact that schooling would now serve both Christian and social interests.[29]

Norway mandated that at least one permanent folk school exist in a town, that teachers be teacher seminar qualified, that they instruct no more than 60 pupils in a single day, and that children attend from the age of seven years until confirmation. Each town was bound to provide enough schools so that every child could receive two days instruction each week throughout the year, allowing for the usual vacation periods.[30] It was expected that each school typically be provided with a single teacher, who usually alternate classes if the group was large and needed to be divided. In those cases the child would attend every other day, and the number of days each year that a child would attend ranged between 84 and 126 days,[31] which compared generally with attendance standards in countries such as Great Britain and the United States.[32]

The law also mandated that each town have a school commission consisting of the priest, the residing curate, a representative of the magistrate, and other representatives determined by the town council.[33] The towns and parishes were also administratively under the county (amt), of which there were 18 in the country. The county and the bishop played some inspection role in the running of the schools for the people.

The course of study, which had focussed mainly on reading and religion in the past, was also expanded to include other basic subjects. Because there had been no mandate to teach anything but reading and religion, other subjects had not been universally taught even in the permanent schools, as the survey of 1837 had revealed. For example, only 71% of the poor schools in the towns had taught writing, 63% had taught calculating, and 29% had taught singing.[34] The new law was to have a dramatic effect on the situation as singing, writing, and calculating were to be taught in all schools.[35] It is heartening to note that by 1853, 91% of the town schools were teaching writing, 82% calculating, 29% spelling, 10% geography, and 8% history. Significantly, there remained almost no attention given to civic training and other patriotic oriented endeavors. The focus remained on religious studies, music, basic skills, as well as handwork for the girls and gymnastics for the boys.

SUMMARY

In the decades just prior to the middle of the century, a number of social, political and economic changes had taken place that contributed to a growing crisis in education that eventuated in the establishment of a major commission to look at the entire schooling situation. The beginnings of a long process of educational reform began to unfold that led to some initial educational reforms. As additional social welfare issues began to emerge, educational reform became even more imperative. In the next chapter, we shall look at a limited number of these issues.

6 Social Reform Impulses at Mid-Century

The economic changes occurring in Norway were accompanied by a growing sense of social discontent. This discontent found expression in a number of ways, both liberal and conservative. Attention is given here to three movements. First, a religious reawakening took place that exhibited a heightened tension between conservative and liberal forces. Second, a labor movement suddenly sprang forth. Third, the question of the woman's place in society appeared.

THE RELIGIOUS REVIVAL

Toward mid-century, a religious revival rolled across the land, although it did not represent a unified movement. On the one hand were those so-called Grundtvigians, who "fostered a blessed, kindly, cheerful life, rich in praise, with an open eye for all God's works in human life."[1] The focus of the young clergy in this camp was toward a new sense of devotion to the people and to the inner life. They tried to help bring the clergy into closer touch with the people and democratize the church itself.

This movement was violently opposed from several sources, probably the most important being Professor Gisle Johnson, who became identified as one of the most powerful preachers in Norwegian church history. Johnson led an oppressive conservative revival in the 1850s, introducing a somber Pietism that engulfed the country.

The impact of the religious ferment on education was considerable. Grundtvigian influences had been felt since the 1820s and by the 1840s most of the teacher seminars were Grundtvigian in orientation, which meant that an entire generation of teachers, filled with

Grundtvigian ideas, flooded the schools. In addition the major educational reformers, such as Hartvig Nissen and Ole Vig, were declared Grundtvigians.

At midcentury, these and other reformers began an energetic fight for the betterment of the common people. In 1850, in a somewhat paternalistic move, Nissen organized a group of twenty-six members of the cultured classes including Eilert Sundt, Rudolf Keyser, and P.A. Munch, into The Society for the Promotion of Popular Enlightenment (*Selskabet til folkeoplysningens fremme*), with the following motto: "Our aim should be to develop self consciousness and to stimulate national feeling."[2]

The most successful aspect of this venture was the publication of an organ with the telling name, *Folkevennen* (The People's Friend), which would remain in publication almost until the turn of the next century (1850-99). Nissen was able to attract Ole Vig to be the journal's first editor, its purpose being to be broadly instructive, and to impart a sense of enlightenment, national consciousness, a love of the fatherland, its mother tongue, and a respect for the folk heritage. The second editor, serving from 1857 to 1866, was Eilert Sundt, who not only was committed to Grundtvigian ideas, but had been heavily influenced by Henrik Wergeland and Markus Thrane. Sundt is known to have been one of the pioneer sociologists not just in Norway but in the entire world.[3] He filled the pages of the *Folkevennen* with articles on the plight of the poor and their need for greater enlightenment than they were then receiving.

On the Pietist side of the religious revival, the most direct link with schooling had to do with Christian studies. Since the time of the educational decree in 1739 and the Conventicle Ordinance of 1741, the most influential Christian studies materials in the schools had been those written by the Pietist theologian, Erik Pontoppidan, especially his *Explanation to Luther's Catechism*, written in 1737.[4] Pontoppidan had explained Luther's *Small Catechism* through a series of 759 questions and answers, and laid out a Pietist interpretation of the Christian faith, which had served as a standard text for religious instruction for over 100 years.[5]

The leading Grundtvigian pastor in Norway during the 1830s and 1840s, Wilhelm Andreas Wexels, revised Pontoppidan's *Explanation to Luther's Catechism* and in 1843 that revision was authorized by Royal decree. Those lay people who had grown up with the old version immediately recognized that Wexels had distorted many of the teachings they considered to be fundamental. The children no longer learned, for example, that novels, dancing, and theatre were a sin, or that people must repent of their sins in this life.[6]

The laymen reacted with indignation against the Royal decree and the clergy who symbolized these changes. In 1852, the government reversed itself and restored the original *Explanation*. According to Molland, the decision represented "a victory for the Pietist orthodoxy of the laymen over Grundtvigian ecclesiasticism, a victory for the lay movement over the clergy, and a victory for the farmers over the official class."[7]

This occurrence is one of several Pietist instances that contributed to a breakdown between the social classes. The common man was learning it was not necessary to defer automatically to the official class, even to the clergy. He possessed the same access as the clergy to God's word. An awakened lay people quickly took the lead in organizing themselves in the 1850s building prayer houses, organizing *Bible* classes and scheduling devotionals, completely outside the framework of the traditional church. A major consequence was the development of an independent lay movement, with lay preaching, church associations devoted to missionary work, and a political organization based on religion.[8]

This movement provided important forces for change in education. First, the independent lay movement would contribute in a marked way toward the secularization of folk schooling. It was based, in part, on the belief that the organized state church was lifeless. Indeed, all state institutions were lifeless and could only be revitalized by moving away from this bureaucratic structure. That reasoning would lead to the conclusion that the state-church connection was doubly deadly. Of course, church dominated public schools could not escape this sentiment, and there was pressure to move the clergy away from public school involvement. The void would ultimately be filled by the secular state itself.

Second, a rejuvenated interest in missionary work came about, including missionary work to the Lapps in the far North. Efforts to Christianize the Lapps had been undertaken probably since the 11th century, and a major step had been taken in the seventeenth century when the Lapps gave up much of their traditional animistic religion. The Lapps were often lauded for their willingness to study the scriptures and for being receptive to learning, and as early as 1706, one missionary had recommended, among other things, that six schools for the Lapps be organized.[9] The most striking figure in that earlier period was the Pietist "Apostle to the Lapps," Thomas von Westen, who was appointed in 1716 and worked for eleven full years proclaiming that the Lapps enjoyed an opportunity for salvation equivalent to all others. He was the first missionary to speak with them and read to them in their own language. Christianity flourished, many churches were built and schools were opened. At the Trondheim Cathedral School, a teachers seminary was opened to prepare teachers and missionaries for the Lapps.[10]

As with all revival activities, the missionary efforts subsided and were only revived again in the middle of the 1800s. In 1845, a powerful Pietist preacher, Lars Levi Læstadius, came on the scene and inspired the development of a new revivalist cult that appealed to "the cathartic group ecstasy of the old religion as well as inspiring a moral rebirth" among the people.[11] This led to frenzied group activities, including the fatal riots in Kautokeino in 1852. The new doctrine was quickly moderated in order to bring the Lapps into a mainstream of Lutheran thinking.

In concert with the rising feelings of romantic nationalism, these moderated missionary efforts were directed against much of the indigenous culture. While a steady improvement of schooling was found after the 1850s, this improvement was accompanied by a decline in the use of the Lapp language, until it was actually banned from all use except for religious instruction by the Tromsø County Council in 1880, and banned by the *Storting* in 1886.[12] The Lapps were, however, beginning to be recognized as members of the Norwegian state, with the same rights to enlightenment as others.

THE LABOR MOVEMENT

A remarkable labor movement sprang up in 1848, based not so much on working conditions of the laborer as on a better world for the common man.[13] The social ferment was initiated by a young student, Markus Thrane, the son of a bank director, who became the editor of a small newspaper in Drammen and immediately set forth using the paper to espouse socialist ideas coming out of France.

Thrane's efforts so alarmed the owners of the paper that he was dismissed, so he established his own newspaper, called the *Arbeider-foreningernes blad* (Labor Associations News). Taking advantage of his new unemployed status, he began touring neighboring counties engaging in organizing efforts, and by the summer of 1850, 273 unions had been established with more than 20,000 members. The members were not just laborers in the towns. Thrane recognized that the labor class in Norway was too small to have much impact; most of the underprivileged were cotters in the rural areas, approximately 90,000 having been identified in the 1844 census as opposed to less than 20,000 in the labor class in the towns.[14] Thrane's program was outlined in a petition to the Crown calling for such provisions as manhood suffrage, the reduction of a cotter's minimum work requirements to an eleven hour a day, four day a week schedule, greater opportunity for cotters to obtain land, and free trade in corn.[15]

Education played a major role in the labor platform. Thrane had served as a home teacher while a student and eventually he began a Sunday school at Lillehammer in 1845, where he taught adults how to write. As he organized labor associations he gave them the specific task of instituting writing schools and a type of "people's academies" (folkeakademier).[16] Whereas the home and religion had represented the major purpose of folk schooling, Thrane made the first major appeal to the folk school as a civic institution. For him, education could not serve both the state and the church; it could not be both under the direction of the clergy and the civil authorities. The workers movement was clear that the school must be a social-political organ, whose task would be to awaken the citizens to their responsibility and their rights in the social and political sphere. In one of the remarkable expressions of solidarity during that period, a petition, signed by 13,000 handworkers, small farmers, and cotters, was sent to the king requesting, among other things, an improved folk school.[17]

Their petition was rejected. Subsequently, the organization tried to exercise some influence through contacts in the *Storting*, but with little success. Government officials saw Thrane as a threat to their hold on political power and consolidated their position in the early 1850s. Judges gave out no fewer than 117 prison sentences to followers of Thrane. In fact, Thrane served a brief prison term and later emigrated to the United States where he continued publishing his ideas until his death.[18] By 1851 the movement went into eclipse.

Thrane was unable to sustain the movement for a number of reasons. First, the number of urban workers was relatively small. Second, it would be impossible to build an active movement of cotters. They were simply too dispersed at Thrane's time to act as a political force. Third, many of Thrane's followers failed to use restraint in putting into practice the ideas of socialism that Thrane was advocating.

Attempts have been made by some educational historians to emphasize the influence of labor on the educational reforms of the nineteenth century, mainly by attaching it to the Grundtvigian thrust for general enlightenment.[19] Indeed, there is common ground between the two. Both called into question the value of the official class in providing for the general welfare. Both held to the belief that the common man could be a positive influence in the political sphere. And there were individuals who participated in both spheres. One such individual was Eilert Sundt.

Sundt came from rather good circumstances, and as a young man he had progressed through a conventional schooling process and ultimately prepared himself for the priesthood at the University of Christiania. While teaching a Sunday school in Christiania, Sundt came across a gypsy who had been assigned to a House of Correction. Intrigued with this destitute man, Sundt obtained permission and funds to undertake a study of the gypsies, and thus began a life dedicated in many ways to the study of the underprivileged. During the 1850s Sundt would publish a number of studies on the life of the poor as well as topics dealing with death, marriage, sexual behavior, and drinking habits.[20] In the process he helped raise the consciousness of the nation toward the poor, and their plight, needs, and potential.

In spite of the contributions of people such as Sundt, it would be difficult to link this movement too closely with the labor movement of the next century. It appears to have been a temporary aberration in Norwegian politics of the time. The present Labor Party actually began as a small political sect in 1887 and did not elect its first representative to the *Storting* until 1898, and it did not begin to dominate the political sphere in Norway until the 1930s. The educational reforms of the nineteenth century must be counted as something other than labor inspired, even though it helped to instill some sense of the potential of the common person, male and female.

THE WOMEN'S MOVEMENT

A third reform impulse during mid-century came with the publication of a novel, *Amtmandens døtre* (The Governor's Daughters),[21] by the sister of Henrik Wergeland, Camilla Collett. The novel pictured young girls being ruined because they were being reared to be passive, docile servants of men, having no other means for survival except marriage.[22]

Even though the role of the Norwegian woman at the time was believed to be in the family and home, it would be unfair to suggest that the talents of girls were not developed. Girls had always either accompanied boys in the folk schools and poor schools, or they had attended schools specifically for girls.[23] As early as 1736 one Lene Aagaard had received permission to give instruction to poor girls in her home at Stavanger, and by 1740 a hand-crafts school for girls was attached to the *Domsoknets* School. In Christiansand, Ulrich Schnell appears to have set up the first permanent school for girls in 1738, having the aim of teaching girls reading and training them in sewing and related hand-crafts.

Some towns even passed ordinances concerning training for girls. About 1770, the *Nykirken* School in Bergen was directed to hire women teachers to do hand-crafts, as was the folk school in Trondheim in 1790. In Christiania, a number of schools came into existence in the early part of the nineteenth century, including Ankerløkken School (1827) and the school at Grønlands Asyl (1839). Unfortunately, the school law of 1848 did not mandate schools for girls, although it did specify hand-crafts schools for girls as having some value.[24]

The girls of better families had often received a rather rich basic education. Camilla Collet herself could serve as a good example. Although she showed few intellectual interests, Camilla's mother was reputed to have a number of artistic gifts, and her father, Nicolai, was a true son of the Age of Enlightenment. Attracted to Rousseau's principles of child rearing, he gave all four children enormous freedoms. They were not put under tight constraints and were allowed to unfold their talents and gifts in a natural and open manner. Their surroundings were rich with animals and open spaces, and their lives were filled with "songs and ditties, known and unknown, old and new."[25]

Instruction was given to the children by home teachers, many of whom were not the best, but Nicolai was always attending to his children's development and even tutored them in some of the subjects. He was a gifted teacher and taught them both knowledge and appropriate behavior. After the boys left for school, the tutors left as well, but Camilla continued to study selected subjects with her father. Possessing a passion for reading, her greatest advantage was having ready access to the generous library of her father.

In 1827, at the age of fourteen, her father determined that she needed some regular school learning with girls her own age, so he sent her to Jomfru Pharos Girls School in Christiania, where she spent a time experiencing the "purgatory of the boarding school."[26] There were a small number of girls schools for the better classes in Norway at the time. In fact, some of these had been in existence for some years. The first such school had been established in 1783 in Trondheim, and had existed along side a boys school having a similar orientation. The director of the girls school had been tutored in the classics, but it did not provide the kind of classical training available to young boys. It would best be classified as burgher school, giving a good sampling of basic, religious, and modern subjects.

The first girls' burgher school in Christiania was set up in 1793 by a German maiden named Hober, who operated an *Institut for pigebørn*. In Bergen Agathe Scholtz's school was opened in 1817 alongside a school for boys operated by a church singer named Thorstein Hallager.[27] One of the reasons burgher schools for girls came into existence at the time was the desire of such schools to keep girls out of boys classes, because that "represented a great disadvantage, when burgher and real schools admitted girls to the boys classes."[28]

In 1849, Hartvig Nissen would enter the picture of female education with the publication of an important pamphlet on the issue and with the establishment of *Nissens Pikeskole* (girls school) in Christiania. In his pamphlet, he pointed out that the development of education beyond the folk school had been most one sided. Communities had left the higher education of girls entirely to the private world, while the world had taken an active interest in higher schools for boys.[29]

In *Nissens Pikeskole*, he not only provided an additional outlet for girls schooling, but a revolutionary notion of what its program should be. While girls possessed their own unique nature and would require some attention to that nature, Nissen believed their basic education should not differ from that for boys. It would include, as did the boys school, religion, history, language and literature (primarily in the mother tongue), plus other subjects such as German (and perhaps even French and English), geography, natural history (especially botany), calculating, writing, as well as cultivating activities like song, drawing, and needlecraft.[30]

Camilla Collet certainly did not have this type of experience at her school in Norway, which was actually quite oppressive, so her father sent her on to a Moravian institute in Schleswig, where the daughters of many other *embetsmenn* were being training in modern languages, history, writing and music.[31] After returning home, Camilla was given confirmation in the church before beginning a long period of isolation at Eidsvoll. It would not be possible for her to go on to higher studies. Almost three decades would pass before a law was instituted allowing women to participate in the upper level of secondary school (1882), or before they would be allowed to qualify for university study (1884).[32]

However, her education did not cease. Most young women in families of good standing were expected to engage in refining studies as a part of their daily chores. Inger-Johanna, in Jonas Lie's *The Family at Gilje*, typifies what this meant when she exclaimed: "The French is done in a twinkling. I am always ready with that before breakfast, and aunt," who acted as supervisor over her development, "is so contented with my pronunciations; but then the piano comes from nine to eleven. Ugh! only exercises; and then aunt receives calls."[33]

When *The Governor's Daughters* appeared in 1855, it caused quite a stir, but the public was not quite ready to respond as positively as it might have, in part, because her call for social reform attracted people to the cause who were not able to present themselves ably before the public and partly because other social movements implicitly lent support to *Old Testament* and Pauline doctrines that women were inferior.

SUMMARY

While romantic nationalism was the major factor in moving the Norwegians to initiate broad reforms in education, a number of specific reform activities accompanied that movement. Three of these forces and factors were a religious revival, the labor movement, and a women's awakening, that created a climate of innovation and change. The ferment for change, whether from labor, women's advocates, religion, or economic shifts, provided the necessary background for the emergence of someone who could coalesce their forces into a meaningful educational agenda for reform. In the next chapter, we shall concentrate on a single individual, Hartvig Nissen, who would play a major role in helping to define exactly what that change, in the educational sphere, would look like.

7 Hartvig Nissen and the Foundation of Modern Schooling

Ole Hartvig Nissen is generally given credit for being the major school reformer of the nineteenth century in Norway.[1] In a span of over three decades he would participate in the formation of some of the most influential laws and government ordinances in Norway's history. The three most important are the 1848 school ordinance on higher schools, the 1860 countryside folk school law, and the 1869 higher common school law.

As a young boy, Nissen had received a firm classical education, part of which came under Fr. M. Bugge at the Trondheim Cathedral School. He left Trondheim in 1835, the only student that year to qualify for university study, and travelled to Christiania to pursue the study of philology. His classical training had not blinded him from other perspectives, however, as he soon became a staunch supporter of the Wergeland faction of the student movement. Prior to completing his studies, he spent three semesters at Copenhagen, where he engaged in comparative philological studies, including the learning of Sanskrit.[2]

His mentor at Copenhagen was J. N. Madvig, the most distinguished classical philologist in Scandinavia at the time. Even though Madvig was a classicist, he was also politically active and participated as a liberalizing influence in the debate between classicism and realism, that was capturing the attention of journals, school programs, and the daily press. Madvig exclaimed that the school must not only be dedicated to the old, but it must be multifaceted in that it include in its program an introduction to a group's own culture and the natural world.[3]

Nissen was undoubtedly influenced by his mentor's political activities but also came to be captivated by his pedagogical and schooling participation. These impulses were reinforced by personal experiences coming out of the realities of economic life, which forced him to hire himself out as a tutor. While in Denmark Nissen also came under the influence of Grundtvig, who detested what the Roman world symbolized and called for a revision of the focus of schooling toward an inner, living religion, the mother tongue, and history.

In 1843, a year before he had taken his *embetseksamen*, Nissen took a decisive step by opening, with a mathematics student, Ole Jacob Broch, a new private school at Christiania called *Nissens Latin og realskole*. The two young men intended the school to represent the best in pedagogical thinking and practice. Broch had just returned from a two year stay in France and Germany, where he had been inspired by the intense educational reform discussions. However, the thrust of the school was mainly from Nissen, who borrowed the ideas from his neighboring lands, but actually put them into practice two years before Madvig's provisional plans were put forth in Denmark and four years before the Swedish cabinet proposed similar reforms to the Swedish parliament.[4]

The school was built on a foundation of three common elementary classes after which the students separated into a Latin stream, which prepared for university studies, a modern stream, which prepared pupils for admission to military school or commercial studies, which prepared pupils for the business world. The school possessed a number of novel characteristics, including parent conferences, a reading room where parents could send children to do homework, boarding facilities at Nissen's home, literature studies in the mother tongue, and the study of Old Norse. We must give Nissen credit for having probably been the first schoolmaster actually to adopt the study "of our Old Language" as an optional subject.[5]

Nissen's school quickly became a dominant institution in Christiania, not only because of its unique form and because of its size. Beginning with 33 pupils, it numbered 78 by the end of the first year. As the second year began 93 were enrolled and by the end of that year 159 were on the roles. Ten years later the student number stood at 378, and later it reached a remarkable 672 students, including the children of some of the most important statesmen in the country.[6] With the recognition which Nissen received through his school activities, he began to receive various appointments to policy-making groups dealing with education.

The first major appointment came in 1845, which would lead to an 1848 government ordinance on higher schools.

1848 ORDINANCE ON HIGHER SCHOOLS

In 1845 the government, wishing to explore issues related to modernizing the financing of the higher schools in Norway, named a three man committee, consisting of Ole Hartvig Nissen and two classical language professors. The committee was charged to deal with financial principles, but Nissen recognized that some important pedagogical issues were necessary to resolve before any meaningful change could be addressed. Following up on the Bugge's notion that the schools ought to constitute a comprehensive educational system, Nissen maintained that some definition of higher schools receiving funds from the government was necessary.

These schools generally fell under into two major categories: *lærde skoler* and burgher schools. At the time, approximately twenty burgher schools were being run in the towns, some having public and some private endowments. The most completely endowed of these schools had taken on the name *realskole*, after the German *Realschule*. In about half the towns a state-run *realskole* existed in conjunction with a *lærde skole*. The major funding issue centered on the types of programs these schools ought to maintain in order to qualify for funds.

While Latin instruction had previously been necessary to qualify for support, Nissen argued that both types of schools were committed to language instruction of some kind, including modern languages, the mother tongue, and Latin. He also argued that language instruction ought to proceed from the simple to the complex, and that the mother tongue should constitute the earliest stages of language learning followed by modern languages and Latin. He was, of course, standing in direct opposition to his old school master, Fr. M. Bugge, as well as many of the school people involved in *lærde skoler*, including the rector of Skien *lærde skole*, who would suggest it was "absurd" to begin language instruction with the mother tongue, noting that Quintilian had even begun instruction with Latin.[7]

Mainly through Nissen's influence, the committee declared that it would be financially and pedagogically sounder if the lower trunk of these jointly run schools would form a four year common program until the young people reached the age of about twelve years. The common program would concentrate on the mother tongue, the basic skills, German and French, singing, gymnastics, religion, geography, history, and natural history. After four years the pupils would then separate into a five year Latin branch and a three year *real* branch. Pupils in the Latin branch would focus on Latin from the first year and add Greek in the second,[8] an arrangement that paralleled Nissen's own private school.

The traditional cathedral schools were exempted from the ordinance. Consequently, these institutions retained the old standard of teaching Latin from the beginning of schooling and they quickly fell out of step with the rest of education in the country, particularly as social reform impulses began to surface.

THE 1860 FOLK SCHOOL LAW

The *Storting* had passed a folk school law for town schools in 1848, and it became Nissen's task to push for a comparable law for the countryside. In 1850 Nissen was appointed as a permanent consultant to the Department of Church and Education, where he remained for a period of four years. Already in 1850 he was publishing suggestions for changes in the folk schools in the countryside.[9]

Nissen soon turned to the popular press in publicizing the cause of the folk schools. For example, the *Morgenbladet* published a series of eight articles by Nissen in 1852, entitled "About Common Schools and the Peoples Enlightenment."[10] In this series Nissen pointed out that little progress had been made in terms of schooling for the folk people in the countryside. Echoing the sentiments of those in the Grundtvig and labor movements, he suggested that the common people had placed their trust in the official class, assuming that men of high station such as the wealthy, the civil servants, the statesmen, and the clergy in their districts were working in the people's best interests, but he argued that they were engaged in self interest more often than not.

The conditions that had been set in 1814 to entitle persons to vote had changed very little. In fact, a smaller percentage of the male population was entitled to vote in 1848 than in 1814, and women would not be given the franchise until the turn of the next century. In spite of this, the number of official class representatives had declined from 47% to 32%, but it remained the dominant force in the *Storting*,[11] and Nissen argued that the people had received almost no benefits in terms of legislative provisions for general enlightenment. The law of 1827 had accomplished little more than the 1739 provisions set up by a foreign ruler.

If the people were to gain any benefits from their government, Nissen explained that it would be necessary for the people themselves to begin exercising the rights and responsibilities granted to them in the constitution and in the provisions for local control from 1837. The government had put off doing anything substantial. The recommendations of the 1839 Great Educational Commission had never been adopted. In fact, the Department of Church and Education had even diluted many of its recommendations before they came before the *Storting*. The city schools had now surpassed the countryside schools in quality.

In 1853 Nissen received a stipend from the Department of Church and Education to visit Scotland to study their common school system, and again in 1854 he was sent to London to attend a school exhibition. His account of Scotland was published in book form and filled over 482 pages.[12] It represents, along with Bugge's 1839 study, one of the important documents in Norwegian educational history.

In the study, he outlined a broad reform program of the entire system of schools including administrative and economic provisions. Proposing that all youth attend a folk school until they are ten years old, he advocated that the folk school should become the domain of the higher social classes as well as the lower.[13] If this were the case, all would see to it that the school's quality would be high. Having a vision far in advance of his time, he proclaimed that the time would come that public schools would be common to all, with the *realskole* serving as an advanced institution for the folk school. Latin schools would cease serving the function of a foundation institution.

Nissen resigned his post with the Department of Church and Education in December, 1854, and returned to his private school, but he tirelessly continued his fight for the improvement of the folk school. Of course, there had been bits and pieces of change, but he recognized it was necessary for the schools to undergo a comprehensive reform. In 1856 Nissen drafted just such a proposal for the changes which must come, both in the city and the countryside, and presented it to the Department of Church and Education.

The proposal was comprehensive in that it included provisions for teacher qualifications and salary, school days per year, curriculum, etc.[14] Of course, the plan included provisions that went to the heart of the social reform issues of the day. Some of these were rather bland and stirred little controversy. For example, Nissen had recognized in his investigations of other countries that many were giving greater attention to the education of girls than was the case in Norway. He even saw the potential of using women as teachers.[15] The explosive aspect of the plan, however, had to do with his proposal that each county have its own school administration, that would oversee the education budget and the distribution of funds throughout the county.[16] In other words, he anticipated that the administration of schooling would shift from ecclesiastical to civil authority.

In the past the school had been essentially a religious institution, with Christian studies being the most important aspect of instruction. Teacher appointments were made under the direction of diocese authority, and the focus of the visits of the bishop to the schools was mainly on the quality of religious instruction. The parish priest was the unquestioned director of the local school commission, and the priest was expected to oversee the yearly examinations, which themselves focused on religious matters. All of these traditions had been retained not only in the 1827 school law for the countryside but in the 1848 folk school law for the towns.

Of course, the church was intent on retaining its hold on the school. The minister of the Department of Church and Education was Hans Riddervold, who had served as bishop at Trondheim prior to his appointment in 1848. He remained as the Department head until 1872 trying to prevent erosion of the link between church and school.

Upon receiving Nissen's proposal for folk school reform, the Department of Church and Education distributed the proposal to church, civic, and school leaders requesting responses. It inspired a rash of reactions, including a number of alternative proposals.[17]

As a consequence of this activity, a royal commission was set up in 1857 to assess the matter. That commission consisted of a chief county administrative officer, three parish priests, and a theology student, who was teaching at a teachers seminary.[18] Needless to say, the Department of Church and Education, headed by the somber and dignified Hans Riddervold, had stacked the deck against Nissen's proposal, and its recommendations, published in 1859, clearly deviated from the proposal of Nissen.

The two particular recommendations that caused the most tension had to do with administrative structure and finances. The administrative structure would remain as it had been, except that the school board would have a teacher representative.[19] Financial matters would also be carried by the community, as in the past. A centralized budget would be set up, but only to deal with higher common schools and teacher seminars.

The upper chamber of the *Storting* took the matter into consideration, forming its own commission to come up with recommendations. It deliberated for over half a year without coming to a resolution. Finally,

Nissen laid before them a revised plan that paved the way for a positive resolution. A pervasive element of Norwegian political mythology is that Nissen's proposal to the *Storting* was quickly accepted and sanctioned by the King, and the program of the Department of Church and Education and its commission never really got off the ground. The law, which the *Storting* passed has since been identified as Hartvig Nissen's law and he, with full mythical justification, stands as the father of the Norwegian primary school in its modern democratic sense.

Recent more thorough documentation of events has demonstrated that Nissen's plan came after a full half year of deliberation of the Department plan, and is, in reality, a compromise plan that got the *Storting* off dead center. Johannes Helgheim, for example, found that Nissen's plan was essentially drawn from the Department plan, with the chapters following a very similar pattern. Of the 102 paragraphs, Nissen included 50 with no change, 16 with some changes, and 36 with his own form.[20] Tønnes Sirevåg concurs with Helgheim in suggesting that at least 60% of his proposal is drawn from the commission recommendations.[21] Even at the critical points of controversy this compromise is most apparent, as we shall point out.

In principle, the school would represent a Christian-civic institution, but possess a degree of social independence, providing the youth with knowledge and the ability to judge while becoming productive citizens of a free, democratic society. This is a decided victory for Nissen. However, Riddervold and the Department appears to have gained the edge over Nissen in that he allowed the regional administrator, who would oversee the schools in the diocese, which served as the county administrative unit until 1912, to be a representative of the bishop. Because this representative had the responsibility to undertake inspection visits, keep the accounts and supply appropriate information to the Department, set the budget for the schools in the district, and insure that adequate teachers were in the schools, his role would be vital. On the other hand, each municipality or parish district would actually run its schools through an elected school board. The chair of the board would be the priest, but the board would consist largely of civil leaders, thus insuring a balance between church and state. Nissen was successful in obtaining a separate school budget at the county level to finance folk schooling.

We see in this outcome a process of compromise and negotiation, a process of give and take on both sides. The notion that Riddervold was an uncompromising defender of tradition, pitted against the visionary and modern oriented Nissen is somewhat overdrawn. In fact, Riddervold had extensive involvement with modern schooling trends. As a young man he had served for twelve years as head master of the burgher school at Frederikstad and had been instrumental in seeing the school bloom into a respected institution. One incident in 1822 suggests that he was not a blind defender of church control. A priest was visiting Frederikstad to inspect the schools and Riddervold challenged the priest's right to visit his school, claiming that a *realskole* is not the concern of the clergy.[22]

If he had been as conservative as some make him out to be, he probably would not have enrolled his four sons in Nissen's school at Christiania. One of these sons even went through the *real* track in preparation for the Military academy.

Most of the provisions of Nissen's proposal were acceptable to all parties. Teachers would be required to meet certain qualifications. The conventional route would be through a county teacher seminar, but some could qualify by going to a so-called lower seminar that consisted of an higher common school experience, by apprenticing as a teacher, or by taking an examination approved by the king.[23] The law also recognized the possibility that women could serve as assistant teachers in the folk schools.[24]

No school was allowed to have more than thirty pupils; if it exceeded that figure, the school would be divided. In those "undivided" schools, the school year would last a minimum of twelve weeks, while in the "divided" schools the school year would last a minimum of nine weeks. As would be expected, there was enormous variation in the number of school days required in the various school districts. Some maintained a program of 250 days a year, while others maintained as few as 30. In the far north, conditions were such that even the minimum attendance requirements were not met.[25]

The required subjects in the law were reading, Christian studies, nature studies, history, singing, writing, calculating, and some optional subjects such as gymnasitics and military exercises.[26] Probably the surest sign of secularization was the development of a new reading book. Reading books had existed in the past,[27] but the major reading material had always been the *Bible* and a teaching book on *Bible* history.[28] In 1859, the *Storting* appropriated 4000 *national dollars* for the purpose of developing a new series. P. A. Jensen, a diocese priest was contracted to develop the series and in 1863 a three volume text appeared having five major sections: The Home, The Fatherland, The World, The Church, and a Miscellaneous selection.[29] It gave the children of Norway their first introduction to their own heritage, their social existence, their aesthetic potential. It also raised a few eyebrows with its romantic display of the old Norwegian tales, folk songs, and poems.

A graphic picture of what happened as a consequence of the law of 1860 can be seen in the Ullensvang region. A school board was elected in December, 1860 and consisted of the parish priest, the mayor, the church song leader, and ten board members from the community. It was a large board but had a difficult responsibility in setting forth the various school districts. The board finally settled on having a total of thirty-four school units, seventeen of which would be travelling schools, and seventeen of which would be permanent schools. The permanent schools ranged in size from twenty-one of fifty-nine pupils, while the traveling schools ranged from six to thirty-five pupils. Some of the school units possessed so many children that it was necessary to divide those schools.[30]

The parish of Bø experienced great difficulty deciding on the school boundaries, and several shifts were experienced in the first five years. In 1865 there were approximately 345 children being divided up into sixteen different school units. The district possessed four teachers, and each teacher was responsible for four schools. Each school lasted nine weeks, for a total of thirty-six weeks. In this district, there was already a permanent school in the town of Bostrand, built in 1853, which served the needs of two of the schools. Rented halls were used for the other fourteen schools.[31]

It was typical at the time the law was passed to rent school facilities. More than two out of every three permanent schools were in a rented facility at the time the law was instituted, and it was 1880 before the number of owned school houses equaled the number of rented school houses.[32]

In some parts of Norway, it was impossible for some parishes to initiate the 1860 law with any permanent schools. At Namdal in South Trøndelag, for example, there was really no central town and only an occasional industrial operation, such as the glass works at Åsnes. The elected school board divided the parish into six school units, but it was 1868 before the first building could be constructed. Three appeared that year, with the other three being build five years later. In 1891, a seventh school was constructed in the northern part of the parish.[33]

The development of the common school represented a decided step in Norwegian education, but it had little to do with the major social divisions symbolized in the school structure, which remained dualistic with the common people rarely being represented in the array of schooling alternatives for the official class and the new class of businessmen. The children of these classes attended the higher schools, which manifested great stresses and tensions in their own right. The role and relationship of modern languages, science and mathematics, and the classics in these schools was not yet resolved, although the outcome was inevitable, because the law would ultimately only confirm what was already a fact.

THE HIGHER COMMON SCHOOL

Of the 196,000 school age students in 1853/54, approximately 7,000 were being educated outside the common school and poor schools. No less than 4,000 were now being educated by home teachers and another 3,000 were attending higher public and private schools of one kind or another. Most of these were attending burgher schools, but approximately 700 students were enrolled in combined schools having a modern foundation with a Latin and *real* (modern) branch beyond that foundation.[34] Then there remained the three prestigious Latin schools in Christiania, Trondheim, and Bergen. The size of these schools had not appreciably changed over the years. For example, the number of students at Trondheim never exceeded eighty students and in 1852/53 there were only sixty-six students.[35]

In other words, of the 7,000 students who could be regarded as receiving education beyond that offered in the folk school, only about one in thirty-five was in a purely classical school. Of course, the influence of these schools was disproportionately large, but it was not enough to stem the tide of fundamental change, particularly when we recognize that the common classes would join with those stressing modern languages or science and mathematics.

During the 1850s a major issue that occupied the elite educators was the nature of the *examen artium*. The mainstay of that exam had traditionally been the difficult *latin stil* (Latin composition), which required translation from Norwegian into Latin. The defenders of traditional values, having witnessed the erosion of their sphere in the 1848 higher school ordinance, spoke out vigorously against the advocates of change. From the university, professor of philosophy, M. J. Monrad, a genuine Hegelian idealist with a conservative bent, would argue against the whole tenor of national romanticism, social reform, and more open religious thinking in trying to defend classical studies.[36] And when the proposal emerged from the *Storting* in 1857, Monrad joined with J. S. Welhaven, P. A. Munch, O. J. Broch, Tønder Nissen, and C. R. Unger to protest.

The major resistance, of course, came from the Latin schools themselves, including Carl Müller, rector of the Trondheim Latin School, Jacob Løkke, from Lillehammer, and Johan Edvard Thaasen, teacher at Christiania Latin School. Even the colorful and bombastic owner of the "student factory," Henrik Heltberg would join the chorus of defenders.[37]

Protest would not come only from the academic world, but from broader circles, the most vocal group calling itself "The Learned Holland," which gathered for informal discussions of literature.[38] Of course, many in the group were educators, including professor of history, Ludvig L. Daae, who defended the worst of classicism as well as a revival of the Dano-Norwegian union. He was joined by medical doctor, Jens Andreas Holmboe, who waged an active campaign in the public media against the proposal.

Many of these defenders of tradition were able to speak from direct experience about the encroachment of modern subjects, because they had taught in a school that included *real* courses. We recall that Ole Broch had helped Nissen establish his first *latin- og realskole*, and Carl Müller had also taught there. Thue had been a head teacher at *Arendals middel- og realskole*, while Løkke was still teaching at *Lillehammers lærde- og realskole*.

Actually, those educators in the combined schools did not speak with one voice, as there was bitter fighting among them about what should be done. Fr. M. Olsen, rector at Drammen, took advantage of the debate to point out that the process of translation in the upper levels of the Latin school was a scandal.[39]

In spite of the voices of protest, the issue had long been settled within the value system of Norway, even though it represented a radical move in international terms, because no other country in Europe had gone so far as to eliminate Latin composition. And so, on 12 Oct. 1857 a supplementary law was passed withdrawing Latin composition from the examination and introducing English as an optional subject in the Latin school.[40] However, the examination would remain lodged in the university until 1882, so the university continued to exercise enormous influence over its content and form.

One consequence of the 1857 law was the emergence of a series of private Latin schools similar to Heltberg's "student factory," which focused on older students that wished to obtain quickly the minimum competence to pass the *examen artium* and qualify for university study.[41]

While Latin was in a state of some decline, the development of a rigorous and consistent tradition in the *real* subjects had not yet been realized. The combined schools especially continued to pay great deference to the traditional subjects and the students were actually neither well prepared in the classics nor the modern subjects. Granted, there were programs of high stature and good repute, but *real* programs were generally relatively shorter and possessed very few students. In fact, the average size of the *real* class was only seven in 1853. The dropout rate was also relatively high. For example, at Skien, thirty-five students were enrolled in the *real* classes between 1852-1858 and only two finished the full four year course of studies.[42]

It was becoming more and more apparent that something had to be done, and it fell ultimately on Hartvig Nissen's shoulders to come up with a viable solution. In 1865 he formulated a plan for the higher schools that would lead to a school law in 1869. Major elements of his plan were not revolutionary in that they had been a part of the discussion on upper school reform since Nissen had been appointed to the three man committee in 1845 and they had been anticipated in the 1848 ordinance. His 1853 report of Scotland had included a suggestion that a folk school be established, which included all classes of people. Thus, his proposal would be no surprise to the schooling world when it appeared in a series of articles in the *Morgenbladet* in January, 1865.[43]

It was not a full blown proposal and would change in subsequent years, but the basic ideas remained firm: (1) A common higher school curriculum would form the foundation program, (2) The mother tongue, rather than Latin, would constitute the first language to be studied, and (3) *real* instruction would have an equal standing with the classical studies.

In his *Morgenbladet* proposal he saw a common school (*fellesskole*), a year later called the middle school, which all would attend for six years (ages 10-16). During these middle school years, the focus of the program would be on the all-round and harmonious development of the young person. The students would not engage in studying segmented and separate subjects so much as gain a grounding in those things that best define life itself. They would be learning in the spirit of the humanities, though the subject matter would be quite different.[44] Pupils would concentrate initially on the mother tongue, then take up German as the first foreign language followed by French or English. In addition, they would study religion, history, geography, natural history, nature studies, arithmetic, geometry, drawing, writing, and gymnastics.[45]

At the conclusion of the middle school students would be separated into one of two three year tracks: *latin gymnasium* and *real gymnasium*. The *latin gymnasium* would devote twenty-three of the thirty weekly hours to classics instruction, one to math, three to Norwegian, and three to history and religion. The *real gymnasium* would provide eighteen of the thirty-six weekly hours to mathematics and science with three to Norwegian, six to modern languages and two to northern history. No Greek or Latin instruction would be given.[46]

Nissen's proposal had an immediate impact on the Department of Church and Education, where Hans Riddervold was still the minister. Riddervold invited Nissen to become a section chief in his department which gave him much more leverage than he had been able to exercise as a consultant. At the same time Nissen was invited to form a royal commission, with himself as the chair, having the task of drawing up a plan for a higher school ordinance. Named to that commission three months later were rectors Hans Julius Hammer, Carl A. Müller, Johannes Steen, and principal Jacob Aall Bonnevie.[47]

The committee was in no way beholden to Nissen, and several members differed sharply with him. In 1867 they submitted a large three volume report. The entire second volume provided an overview of schools in Great Britain, France, Belgium, Zürich Canton in Switzerland, Prussia, Austria, Baden, Bavaria, Russia, Sweden, and Denmark.[48] Nissen had suggested that the school actually begin when the young people were ten years old. The name of the first stage was also changed to middle school, which implied that the beginning stages of education for the upper school take place elsewhere. The preparatory options available to the young were as follows: the folk school, home teaching, and a preliminary stage of higher schools. Nissen visualized the folk school serving the broader purpose of schooling for everyone, but this idea was too radical, and it was not seriously considered to be an appropriate option. The commission visualized the development of private preparatory classes in its proposal, which would be run without state support and which would last three years.[49]

At the conclusion of these preparatory experiences, pupils would enter the middle school. There was apparent consensus in the commission that it was, indeed, possible to maintain the lower stage of the school as a common middle school for higher schooling students. However, Steen,

Müller, and Hammer were especially dedicated to the value of Latin instruction during that common schooling period. Steen was also concerned that a six year common school was much to long and he drew up an alternative plan with only four years. A compromise was quickly reached in that the six year middle school was retained but it was divided into a lower stage and an upper stage. The first three years would, indeed, remain free of Latin, and would maintain a common curriculum. In the fourth grade, pupils would choose either Latin or English as a first language. Those choosing Latin would begin preparation for the *latin gymnasium*, and those choosing English would begin preparation for the *real gymnasium*. In other words, a two track system would already be in place after three years of common middle schooling. In spite of this, the middle school retained the encyclopedic character so cherished by Nissen. Pupils were expected to receive a liberal, general education in the best sense of *humanitas*, rather than a specialized education.[50]

At the end of the middle school, pupils would take a general examination to determine if they qualified to move to further schooling. Those qualifying would move either into the *latin gymnasium* or the *real gymnasium*, where they would remain in specialized training for another three years. In the Latin branch pupils would study religion one or two hours a week, Norwegian and Old Norse four hours a week in each of the three years (4-4-4), Latin ten or eleven hours a week (11-10-10), Greek seven hours a week (7-7-7), and two or three hours of history (2-3-3), mathematics (3-3-2), and French (2-2-2), two hours of English or Hebrew in the last two classes (0-2-2). German, which was begun the last two years of middle school, would continue with three hours a week (3-3-3).[51]

The *real gymnasium* would have a program of comparable length as the *latin gymnasium*. This decision had not received unanimous support. Steen, for example, believed that it should have been two years shorter than the Latin program, but it was retained as a three year upper school. Just as in the Latin program, students would study religion (2-1-1), Norwegian and Old Norse each year (4-4-5), and they could choose between Latin and English as a foreign language (3-3-3), but they would also study German (1-1-0) and French (3-3-3), history (3-3-3), geography (1-2-2), natural science (5-5-5), mathematics (6-6-6), and drawing (2-2-2).[52]

At the conclusion of the *gymnasium*, the *examen artium* would be administered, which would admit students to the university. This was one of the more difficult issues facing the commission. The *examen artium* had focused on a classical education although students had been admitted to the university in great numbers without having passed that hurdle. The examination was the responsibility of the university and not the Department of Church and Education, and so a request was made for the university to express itself on the issue.

Each of the faculties expressed its judgment. For example, the historical-philosophical faculty fell back on the old argument that a "classical educational preparation is an important and necessary foundation for academic study," and those who received a *real* program were simply not a party to this foundation. At the very best they could become but partially "academic citizens."[53] A similar position was taken by the theological and the medical faculties. The science and mathematics faculty took issue with the idea that the study of these spheres would result in a partially academic citizen, and supported the notion of "individual differences" and its positive possibilities at the university.[54]

These responses were forwarded to the commission and three university people, Monrad from history-philosophy, Tønder Nissen from Theology, and Bjerknes from math-science, were added to the commission as it deliberated this part of the plan. Monrad was the only member who believed that it was out of the question to consider *real* students for university study. In a major breakthrough, the commission recommended that the *real* students would, indeed, be eligible for study in the science and mining branches of the university.[55]

A final element that the commission deliberated on had to do with teacher preparation.[56] Teachers of higher schools received their education at the university, and it would be necessary to insure that adequate provisions were available to provide teachers for the subjects in the new school structure. In 1851 the storting had determined that an *embetseksamen* would be available for *real* school teachers, but it was necessary to make provisions for exams in the mother tongue, newer languages, etc., that were not tied to classical studies.

Hans Riddervold relied on the work of the commission to submit five separate proposals to the *Storting* pertaining to the school structure, examinations and the university role in the process. As could be anticipated, it was met with mixed reaction, including two competing proposals from the private sector, the one from a teacher and the rector at Arendal, and the other from J. Aars and P. Voss of Christiania. The Arendal proposal, very similar to Nissen's, was that Latin be excluded from the middle school altogether and had no chance of receiving a serious hearing. The Aars and Voss proposal was to separate students into the Latin and *real* branches much earlier than the fifteen-sixteen age period agreed on by the commission. They recommended that it come at age eleven, or at age twelve at the latest. They also recommended dividing the *real* branch into three tracks: mathematics and natural science, modern foreign languages, as well as Norwegian and Old Norse languages.[57] The Norwegian and Old Norse recommendation reflected a continuing pull toward national romanticism that had been so strong at mid-century.

In 1868, the Church Committee of the *Storting* was given the charge to draft the actual propositions of the law. Johannes Steen was the foreman of the work. By and large, the Committee supported the recommendations of the Nissen commission feeling that it would, among other things, help bind the people, strengthen the citizenry, raise the level of education, extend higher schooling, and give education a national element.[58]

The actual debate in the storting reflected a variety of views. Jaabæk and Ueland, for example, thought too much deference was being paid to classical studies. As the farmer spokesmen, they felt the classics were both unnecessary and even harmful to the national purposes. Johan Sverdrup, the nephew of the classics professor, Georg Sverdrup, and one of the first men in the Storting to be identified with the labor movement, agreed with these men and spoke out for emphasis on a school based on modern subjects.[59]

The major concern expressed on the other side of the issue was the difficulties the *real* studies presented for university study. In general, however, the debate did not lead to dramatic tensions, and on June 17, 1869, the law was passed which provided a science stream to be established having equivalent standing as the classical stream. Two years later the university followed up with its own reform to accommodate to the law. In that reform modern languages and mathematics/natural sciences were given complete parity with the classical languages in the examination system.[60]

The steps toward a fully integrated schooling structure, which Norway had taken in previous decades were not yet complete. It remained to unite the folk school with the higher school in a formal sense. The first step in accomplishing this task would be when the folk schools would replace the private preparatory classes for children preparing for the middle school. This would be accomplished in the School Law of 1889. However, it was clear even as the 1869 law was being passed, that a folk school was inevitable. Models were already being considered, and North America provided some of these models. In fact, Nissen published a full report on the schools of Massachusetts in 1868, which provided a genuine folk school.[61]

Actually, prototypes of the kind of schools necessary to satisfy this need were already in rich abundance in Norway immediately after the 1869 higher common school law, particularly in the small and middle-sized towns where there were insufficient numbers of children to justify privately financed preparatory classes. The young were given either home teachers or they were placed in regular folk school classes for these years. In the latter cases, pressure was placed on the schools to upgrade their programs so that these children would not be overly disadvantaged when they entered the middle school.

Hartvig Nissen had been appointed to chair a commission in 1871 which was given the charge to develop an "instructional plan for folk schools" (folkeskoler).[62] The commission did not realize its plan, but its work signifies the level of awareness of such a possibility. New political developments during the 1870s and 1880s would be necessary before such a decisive step could be taken.

Section III

Second Reform Cycle —
A Norwegian Folk School

---

8 A Common Foundation School

As Norway moved deliberately and forcefully toward a common folk school structure, certain questions surfaced. Should children of the official class receive the same education as those from the more common classes? Should girls receive the same education as boys? Should normal children receive the same education as the physically or psychologically abnormal children? Should those in the countryside receive the same education as those in the towns?

Ultimately, Norway would opt for policies that would answer these questions as vigorously in the affirmative as any country in the world. Even in the nineteenth century the country would move far beyond any other European country with regard to specific aspects of its program. The first major integrative accomplishment had to do with the integration of social classes into a common foundation school for all classes of people.

Significantly, Scandinavia was the only major European area where successful legislation was passed during that century. In Sweden, for example, a three year foundation school was adopted in 1894, while Norway came to such a decision as early as 1889.

Norway's legislative accomplishment was a direct consequence of the political upheaval that took place in the 1870s and 1880s, which witnessed the development of a modern political structure with an integrated parliamentary system and formally organized political parties. Of course, political factionalism had existed since 1814, but the country was initially run by the upper strata of the country. The differences of opinion among the upper strata were at times intense, particularly with regard to issues surrounding relationships that should be maintained between Denmark and Sweden. However, they were never serious enough to break into political factions.

The first major political split came with the growing agrarian political movement, which was led, not only by farm leaders such as Ole Gabriel Ueland, but by members of the official class itself, such as Henrik Wergeland. At mid-century there had even been signs of an incipient labor movement, but this did not result in a formally organized political party. The labor societies perceived their role as pressure groups working to influence the formal governmental process. The first genuine political party to emerge was an amalgam of several elements, including the new middle class from the towns, the growing labor class, the farmers, the lower levels of the bureaucracy, and dissatisfied students from the university. In fact, it was a protest party, a party that stood in opposition to the official class, the mainstream thinking of the old guard, the conservative sentiments of the older generation.

Political leadership for this opposition party was Johan Sverdrup, who had served in the *Storting* since 1850 when he was the single representative to come in on the wave of the young labor movement. He was joined by the farm representatives such as Ueland and Jaabæk to form the nucleus of the new organization. However, the Liberal Party was not just an organization of politicians. It gained sustenance from intellectuals and literary geniuses. For example, Bjørnstjerne Bjørnson viewed himself as Wergeland's successor in professing the claims of the common folk. He did not hesitate to use his talented pen to expound the cause of justice, of democracy, of devotion to a glorious and independent Norway. His pen was as committed to propaganda as it was to literature. He was beyond comparison the greatest orator of the country, an actor, a dramatist, both writing and acting in plays. He produced the most beautiful lyrics since Wergeland. He was the spiritual leader of the country for almost half a century.[1]

From the intellectual ranks came men such as Johan Ernst Sars, the foremost historian of the day, who conceptualized a Norwegian history that was democratic to the core. Whereas the work of earlier historians had concentrated on the early period of Norway, Sars stressed that the country had evolved even during the time of dependence on Denmark. In fact, he claimed that it had been a necessary period in the development of Norway as a full blown democratic people. His history was deeply nationalistic, it proclaimed the high stature of the Norwegian people.[2]

The Liberals identified themselves as the Left Party (*Venstre*), and they actually met little organized opposition during the first decade of their existence. It was repugnant to the old leaders of state that they should identify themselves with a faction of the people. They perceived themselves as "servants of the whole people" rather than as a segment.[3] Eventually, the official class was forced to organize itself and in 1884 the Right Party (*Høyre*) came into existence.

The major issue that initially separated the two groups was constitutional in nature. The Liberals coalesced around the desire that the *Storting* be recognized as the final source of authority. The Conservatives maintained that the king and his ministers stood outside the *Storting*, and that they provided a sound separation of powers that would insure balance and proportion in decisions. After bitter controversy and struggle, including three vetoes by the Swedish king to a constitutional amendment voted by the *Storting*, the resignation of the distinguished statesman, Frederik Stang, who had led the government from 1861 to 1880, and the impeachment of the members of the subsequent ministry in 1883, the Liberals were able to force the acceptance of parliamentarianism on the king.

At the time the Liberals controlled more than two-thirds of the *Storting*. However, the Liberals were held together by their opposition to the Right, and when they came into power they quickly fell into warring factions so that by 1888 there were the "Pures" and the "Moderates," at least in terms of the relationship that should be maintained toward Sweden. There was greater consensus in terms of certain reform measures that pointed toward greater democratization, including increased suffrage and folk schooling measures.

SUFFRAGE

Norway was the first country in Scandinavia to institute broad manhood suffrage when it became independent in 1814. However, the number of persons entitled to vote in the country had remained constant or even fell from the time of independence until 1888. Until 1884, suffrage was limited to government officials, landholders, and businessmen, and the decline in suffrage was occasioned because voting rules favored the farm population, which decreased during the century. Even before the Liberals actually gained control of the *Storting* they helped extend the voting rights of some by encouraging people to obtain title to worthless land, such as marshy or isolated, unproductive plots, thus, giving them the right to vote. After they gained control, qualifying criteria were extended so that by 1897 Norway became the first European country to grant universal male suffrage.[4]

The women's issue had remained somewhat dormant after Camilla Collett's novel, *The Governor's Daughters*,[5] had appeared in 1855 until the 1870s when people such as Aasta Hansteen began to push their cause. Their plight gained worldwide recognition, when Henrik Ibsen published *A Doll's House* in 1879,[6] which contributed to rapid changes in national policy. In 1884 the Norwegian Society for Women's Rights (*Norsk kvindesagsforening*) was organized to give women the rights and place in society they were entitled to and by the end of that decade most positions were made legally open to women. In 1907, women were given limited suffrage and in 1913 universal suffrage.[7]

From Table 8.1[8] we see that the number of persons entitled to vote increased dramatically during that time frame.

Table 8.1

Persons Entitled to Vote per 1,000 Population in Norway

Year	Number
1815	65
1870	47
1882	52
1888	65
1897	91
1906	193
1909	321
1918	460

THE 1889 SCHOOL LAW

The Liberals took formal control of the government on 26 June 1884, under the direction of Johan Sverdrup. On 25 September, Sverdrup sent his minister a letter and two weeks later, that letter was made public in the *Dagbladet*, a Christiania newspaper.[9] The letter represents the basis for what would ultimately become the school law of 1889, the teacher seminar law of 1890, and aspects of the higher common school law of 1896.

He begins the letter by reviewing what the *Storting* had initiated since 1848. He observes that an increasing interest in expanded educational experiences is being felt both in the towns and the countryside, to which the government must respond. However, the serious deficiency is in the countryside cannot be compared with those in the towns. This must be corrected. Both town and countryside citizens have the same rights "to a helping hand from the state." All sections of the country have the resources to participate in extended education to insure a "firm and inner connection between individuals, communities, and districts, which will bring the people to an integrated, harmonious, developed nation."[10]

Two things must be accomplished if this is to occur. The schools in the countryside must be made comparable to the town schools, and the national element must be strengthened in all schools, particularly regarding the New Norwegian language.

Sverdrup then proceeds to outline eight major points about how the folk schools must be revised.

First, schools must become regularized in terms of the years of study and the length of the school year.

Second, the subjects of study must be expanded and regularized. Until that point, Christian studies had been the only aspect of the curriculum that had been adequately regulated. The children must receive regular instruction in civic oriented studies, particularly the mother language, including New Norwegian, and history, including social studies. They must learn to read and write both forms of the official language.

Third, the language issue must be resolved so that "it can be considered to be the mother tongue." In other words, the nation must decide what role New Norwegian will play in the school. Children and teachers must be allowed the choice to use that language as the language of instruction, and where it is used, books must be available in that language.

Fourth, consideration must be given to the role of gymnnastics and handicrafts in the school.

Fifth, teacher training must be strengthened and redesigned toward national interests, including New Norwegian and an understanding of the role of the *folkeskole* as a national school.

Sixth, teacher salaries and pensions must be reconsidered. A reasonable funding relationship must be reached between the state, the county, and the community.

Seventh, the whole school administration, from top to bottom, must be overhauled. Diocese control must be curbed and be replaced by a county school inspector, and the school committees must be community based.

Eighth, the boundaries between central and local administration must be clarified, as well as the relationship between teacher independence and parental rights to exercise some influence on the school.

Sverdrup then proceeds to outline the most revolutionary aspect of his proposal. The folk school cannot be considered in isolation, but it must be articulated in a direct and meaningful way with the middle school. The children must be able to move from the one school to the other without interruption of time or having to engage in additional studies. The link must be direct, the way straight and clear.

Thus, the vision of reformers such as Nissen was finally on the agenda as a political priority of the ruling party of the government. In fact, a genuine folk school had been the "first and last" priority of the Liberal Party since its inception. "An assault on general education is an assault on the nerve center of society," exclaimed the party, "therefore, without an independent teaching profession and a strong folk school it is impossible to maintain democratic social development."[11]

A royal commission had been set up in 1871 to deal with the folk schools in the towns in order that greater coordination be achieved between them and the higher common schools. The commission contained some of the main spokesmen of the infant Liberal Party and it came to perceive its main task as one of articulation between the folk schools and the middle schools with the folk schools serving as preparatory institutions. The transition from the one to the other must be "smooth and natural." Both the higher and the lower schools were to be viewed as institutions appropriate to all social classes.

The Liberal Party, with all its fragmented interest groups, was absolutely united in regard to the role of the school. The first level of the folk school must be so structured that it provides a foundation for the higher schools. When the recommendations of the 1871 commission finally reached the floor of the *Storting* in 1880, all of the Liberal supporters fell in line in support of its provisions for the first level, which had been set at five years (ages 7-12). The only disagreements from the Liberals came in that some leaders pushed for even stronger conditions than the commission had recommended.[12]

For example, Jacob Sverdrup, nephew of Johan, was not satisfied to deal only with the first level and proclaimed that all schools, in town and countryside, must be so aligned that all young people can progress to the point "that they are sitting on the benches of the university lecture halls."[13] Johannes Steen insisted that any consideration of a genuine folk school must include more explicit time requirements for reading and writing. Even Johan Sverdrup, a firm believer in local control of schools, supported Steen and suggested that the state is the only element of government "that has the power and authority to put the folk school in organic relationship with the land's broader education system."[14]

In 1880, the Liberals were still the minority party and were unable to sustain the thrust for a genuine common school. It would be necessary to wait another four years before Sverdrup became the head of government and began the final step toward the realization of the Liberal Party goal. Even so, it would take another five years to become law, and some understanding of the political process in Norway clarifies the necessity for that kind of time span.

The Conservatives remained a powerful voice in public affairs. When Sverdrup announced his plan in the *Dagbladet*, opposing voices rose and sustained their argument through the long period when the proposal was taking legal form. The Church and Education minister of the recently deposed government, Nils C. Hertzberg, took the lead in challenging the Sverdrup proposals. Within two weeks from the time the letter was published, Hertzberg would write a series of articles in *Morgenbladet*, where he replied to Sverdrup, point for point and where he made his now famous statement: "There are some things of it that are good, and some that are new, but that which is good is not new and that which is new is not good."[15] From 1884 to 1889 he would write no less than four brochures against the plan, he worked actively in the public media, and he participated as a member of the *Storting* to get it defeated.[16]

The immediate political consequence of Sverdrup's letter was a proposal by the Department that the *Storting* establish still another school commission to come up with a plan for the revision of all folk schools. The *Storting* took up the matter, but found it necessary to hear many arguments before a commission could even be named. For example, Johannes Steen proposed that the town school law of 1880 be revived and action taken on it before consideration of a new law be initiated.[17]

Steen was a powerful figure in school politics. He had entered the *Storting* in 1859 and had been an active supporter of the 1860 school law. He had been a member of the 1865 and 1871 school commissions. He had long been a member of the so-called Church Committee (*Kirkekomiteen*) in the *Storting* and was its chairman from 1877-82. His voice must be listened to. The major issue at stake in this move was whether there would be a combined law governing both town and countryside schools or whether there would be two separate laws. It was decided that two separate laws would be written, but that they differ only in specific issues, particularly related to administration.

Other issues that came up were external to the folk school itself, such as adjustments that would be necessary in the middle schools, and the New Norwegian language issue. Worker organizations in the country had formulated many proposals about how middle schools would be joined with the folk schools. (For example, the Christiania workers organization had debated the issue in 1880 and had made specific recommendations about middle school reorganization.) It was necessary patiently to review these position papers before moving forward.

Further, New Norwegian was, for all intents and purposes, an artificial language, and there was intense allegiance to the Norwegian spoken not only in Christiania but in the isolated valleys throughout the country. Even if New Norwegian were instituted, special measures would be required to help teachers work comfortably and competently with it.

Even though a commission was recommended in January, 1885, it was November before things were far enough along to name the commission members and have them set to work. The commission members represented every shade of political bias in the country, and as would be expected, it worked deliberately and carefully in drawing up its proposals. In fact, it is remarkable that it was able to issue its recommendations to the Church Committee of the *Storting* as early as November, 1887.[18]

The greatest obstacle facing the proposal was the fact that the Liberal Party had already broken into factions. The "Pures" and the "Moderates" were warring with one another with the "Moderates" flexing their political muscle by pressing for a delay in action during that session of the *Storting*. Such tactics were meant to embarrass and compromise Steen and his "Pure" colleagues. Indeed, the "Moderates" were successful in postponing action.

The following year, a new *Storting* had been elected and it was not only necessary that consideration begin anew but the Liberals were not as strongly represented as in the previous year. Steen was gone and the chair of the Church Committee was now held by the Conservative, Bonnevie, who believed that you can't use the law to bring about a sudden change in the existing and evolving order of things.[19]

The *Odelsting* began discussion of the law on 15 May and held no less than 14 meetings on the issue.[20] The school law that was ultimately passed conformed, in its major outlines, with the recommendations

Sverdrup had made five years earlier, although it contained provisions not mentioned by Sverdrup and various degrees of compromise are noted in some of the measures.[21]

The 1889 school law actually signifies more than a simple victory of the Liberals in the political sphere. That law symbolizes a much broader social, economic and educational transformation that had taken place in the country. It would be a mistake to suggest that those who identified themselves as Liberals were completely responsible for that transformation. The changes that took place in education during the last half of the century indicate that even while the official class was running the government, it had fostered a cumulative, additive evolution in schooling. Certain policies may have required the emergence of the new political alignments to see their ultimate conclusions, but the progress made was impressive even prior to that time. We shall attempt to draw attention to some of these developments in discussing provisions of the law in the context of that evolution.

A COMMON FOLK SCHOOL

The name of the common school was changed from *allmueskole* to *folkeskole*, signifying that the school was now intended to be a school of the entire people, not one class, one strand of the population. It would also be a school run by representatives of the people rather than run by a segment of the official class, the clergy. Finally, the school would be free and open to all.

Sverdrup had intended that the differences between countryside and town common schools be erased. That was found to be impossible, not so much because of political divisions, but because of the radical differences in conditions between the towns and the countryside. In a technical sense, the result was actually two laws, one for the countryside and one for the towns, although most of the provisions of the two laws were comparable.

A major problem the legislators faced was, once again, the dispersed population in the countryside.

PERMANENT SCHOOL ISSUES

Hartvig Nissen had proposed in his 1860 school law that the travelling schools, which prevailed in the countryside, be systematically eliminated and that permanent schools represent the norm as a common school form. In the next decades, as noted in Table 8.2,[22] the travelling school would almost disappear as steady progress was made in satisfying the law.

Table 8.2

The Number and Percentage of Permanent and Travelling Common Schools between 1840 and 1890

Number	1840/41	1853/54	1861/62	1867/68	1875/76	1885/86	1890/91
Travelling	7133	6996	3620	2241	1806	968	732
Permanent	311	519	2569	4212	4714	5450	5600
Total	7444	7515	6189	6453	6520	6418	6332
Percentage							
Travelling	95.8	93.1	58.5	34.7	27.7	15.1	11.5
Permanent	4.2	6.9	41.5	65.3	72.3	84.9	88.4

We are able to observe a dramatic shift in the ratio of travelling to permanent schools at the time of the 1860 law. In 1853/54 over 93% of all common schools were travelling and in 1861/62 this had been reduced to 58.5%. Six years later the percentage of travelling schools had dropped to 34.7%. From that date a more gradual decline is noted until, in 1890/91, only 11.5% of all schools were travelling.

By the time of the 1889 school law, the schools in both town and countryside could be dealt with as permanent schools. However, by that time, still another school form had rendered the focus on a single permanent primary school obsolete. The new school form would have internal divisions and even grade levels.

School Size and Age Grading

From Table 8.2 we see that even though the number of pupils almost doubled during the 50 year period covered in the table, the number of schools actually declined from 7,444 to 6,332. Even though schools were consolidated, they remained somewhat small. In 1875, for example, the permanent schools in the countryside only averaged 39 students, while the travelling schools averaged 17 students. A significant consequence of this consolidation effort was the notion that children could be grouped more homogeneously according to age levels.

The practice of grouping students is almost as old as schooling itself, although modern practices have uniquenesses.[23] The initial grouping notions for the lower or common schools seems to have come from the Germans, who, from the time of the Reformation, prescribed three divisions in their schools, at least in terms of reading instruction. Even so, the greater part of the school day was communal in nature. When the eight year *Volksschule* was set up by the Prussians, they continued to divide the pupils into three groups. Even the one roomed schools were directed to maintain such a division for instructional purposes.

In Norway the norm was to divide the school into two levels, rather than the more typical three levels, although that latter arrangement was becoming the norm in the countryside by 1890. It was a more difficult matter to arrange for physically separate classrooms in the countryside. Very few schools existed with multiple classrooms prior to the 1870s, but in the next five years the number of separate classes increased by more than a factor of 10, and as we see in Table 8.3,[24] after 1875 the number increased steadily into the 1890s.

Table 8.3

Classes in Countryside Schools

Permanent Schools	1875	1880	1885	1890
Those divided into Classes	2527	2840	3140	3319
Schools with Separate Classes	55%	56%	59%	61%
Total Number of Classes	5800	6698	7540	8139
Ave. Classes in Divided Schools	2.3	2.4	2.4	2.5

By the time of the 1889 school law, certain conditions for classes were set. For example, no class could have more than 35 pupils in it. The normal division was set at two classes. The *smaaskolen* (small schools) were for children from 7-10 years of age, and the *storskolen* (large schools) were for children from 10-14 years of age.[25] Following the European pattern, it was expected that if enough pupils were available the *storskolen* could be further divided into two groups (10-12 and 12-14 years of age).

Quite a different situation was found in the towns. As new school buildings came into existence after the school law of 1848, enormous institutions were often the norm. A school built on Møller Street in Christiania in 1861 had no less the 1,957 students, and it was not uncommon for schools to have more than 1,000 students. Initially, large schools were not subdivided in any special way. That is, the conventional three level groupings were retained even in the large schools, but multiple sections of each level were arranged rather than dividing the students into more discrete levels. Consequently, it would be more accurate to describe the Møller Street School as a school group, because of this subdivision arrangement.[26]

With the expansion of school size a different organizational plan began to permeate the system so that by 1871 Christiania mandated that schools should rearrange themselves into age-graded institutions. By the mid-1870s the larger cities had moved to a system of from five to seven age grades, while the smaller towns usually remained constrained to operate two level schools. In spite of these developments, the 1889 school law defines the norm as being three levels, corresponding to that in the larger countryside schools (7-10, 10-12, 12-14).

Extension of the School Year

One of the crucial elements of modern schooling is its encompassing nature. During the first years after independence, even those young people who attended the common school were in the institution so few weeks that it did not occupy their lives. In fact, a 12 week attendance experience would have been extreme in the early days. The school law of 1860 had set minimal requirements at 9 weeks a year in divided classes and 12 weeks a year in those which were not. This remained the norm even to the time of the 1889 school law.

A major weakness of the 1889 school law in relationship to the recommendations of Sverdrup, had to do with the failure to extend the school year.[27] In contrast to many countries at the time, the school year was extremely limited. The United States, for example, averaged 27 school weeks.[28]

There was some consideration about extending the school year beyond 12 weeks, and the school commission came up with the notion that the compulsory attendance period remain the same, but that three weeks be added for enrichment purposes, although attendance would not be mandatory.[29]

One of the critical differences between the town and countryside had to do with the school week. Whereas in the town children were expected to attend five days, in the countryside the time of attendance was usually half that, and even as little as two days a week. Actually, the law mandated hours rather than days; the children would attend 24 hours a week although this could be reduced to 18 hours under certain conditions.[30] According to the 1889 school law, countryside children would only receive 2,800 hours of instruction over a seven year period, while those in the towns would receive 5,200 hours of instruction.[31]

Subjects of Study

Nowhere was the national form of the school to become more visible than in the subjects of study that were mandated. Social studies became an integral part of the curriculum, and history, geography, and nature studies would no longer be general in nature but would concentrate on the people, the land, and nature in Norway itself. The school had indeed taken on the nature of all modern common schools. It was a civic school devoted to national purposes and national development.

This was occurring throughout Europe, but quite a different tone in Norway than was found in most European countries. Prussia, for example, had defined patriotism in conjunction with devotion, loyalty, and obedience to the Prussian state.[32]

In Norway, patriotism did not imply a heavy sense of deference to the leaders of state. It did not suggest obedience to leaders and the military, but a sense of national identity, a sense of membership to a democratic tradition worthy of taking pride in. Citizens were not to be simply obedient servants but were to be productive citizens in a free, self-directed nation-state.

Language of Instruction

In 1878 the government had ruled that "instruction is to be given as far as possible in the children's own vernacular. Gradually they can then be taught to understand and write the Danish-Norwegian book language."[33] Curiously, the sentiments of the ruling class were that New Norwegian was the vernacular.

In 1885 Countryside Norwegian was legalized in the *Storting* by a 78-31 margin as a standard official language equal to Danish-Norwegian. The motion directed the Department of Church and Education "to make arrangements that the Norwegian vernacular is placed on an equal footing with our regular literary language as an official and school language."[34]

Thus, even before the school law of 1889 came into being the language policy of the country had been established, although it has to this day never really been settled. It was certainly unclear what it meant to be on an "equal footing." Obviously, it meant that adequate instructional materials needed to be developed and competent teachers needed to be trained. However, the teacher training seminary had at the time no mandate and it would be 1901 before the language was introduced in the teacher seminary on an equal footing with Danish-Norwegian.

Administrative Arrangements

Probably the most hotly discussed issue relating to the school was its administrative structure. Basic to this issue was (1) the relationship between the school and the state church, and (2) the relationship between local, district and central administrative authority. One of the major political distinctions between the Right and Left during the early years of party politics was the clear division of sentiment about centralized and local control. The Right during those early years was clearly sympathetic toward centralization and the control of the official class, while the Left was clearly partial to local control, the independence of the communities, the rights of the people to run their own political lives.

Such sentiments on the part of the Left derived in large part from the historical suspicion of the farmers toward the official class dominated central authority, and it was also within the mind set of men representing the workers groups. Such an orientation had been tempered with experience. We recall Jaabæk and Ueland had resisted extending the 1848 common school law to the countryside because the central government was not willing to participate in paying for the common school. Farmer support for the 1860 school law required assurance that the central government would help pay for the schools. In 1880 Sverdrup had also recognized that a genuine common school required the heavy arm of centralized authority if it were to be realized.

Such experiences did not alter their basic commitment to local control, and in the 1889 school law, the Liberals determined that the major authority over the folk schools would be local, and it would be lodged with representatives of the community. In the past the local countryside school committees had been dominated by the church, with the chair being the local priest, with committee members including other church underlings. That would change. The priest would henceforth remain a member of the school committee, but everyone else would be seated through local school elections, and anyone of those on the committee would be eligible to be elected as chair.[35] Thus, the school was separated formally from the church, making it a truly state institution.

In addition, diocese supervision of the school was eliminated altogether, although the bishop and priests would continue to oversee religious studies.[36] Diocese oversight was replaced by a new county organ: the county school board. Its authority would be secondary to that given to the local school committee, which would have the right to determine the school program and to select the teachers.

There is substantial evidence that the common school was essentially serving as a folk school even before the law formally confirmed it. That law was the first step taken by the Liberals in their quest to reform the educational system. Other laws would soon follow that would address issues such as teacher training, and reorganization of the common higher school.

SUMMARY

In the latter part of the nineteenth century in Europe, the concept of a common school, which would form the foundation of all subsequent schooling, finally began to become a reality. Certain nations had progressed sufficiently in terms of political and social mobilization to begin legislation of such schooling, and among the various nations of Europe, Norway was the first to pass legislation, which would provide for a school intended to be free and open to all children, regardless of social background. Of course, a broad spectrum of alternatives remained for the better classes, including private preparatory schools and home teachers, but the State declared itself unwilling to support any other form of primary school except the compulsory folk school. Thus, the stage was set for the integration of further schooling with the folk school.

9 Education Beyond the Folk School

While the folk school was now universally required, there was yet no comprehensive national system of schooling beyond it. The 1889 school law had made some oblique references to the possibility that young people might attend some form of schooling beyond the compulsory school age. That law suggested that some provision be made for those in the countryside who did not enter conventional advanced schools. It was assumed that in the towns any further schooling would begin with the middle schools, and in 1896 a separate school law would be passed relating to those who would enter the middle school and the *gymnasium*. It is our aim in this chapter to look at this broad spectrum of what we would today call secondary schooling, as it existed just prior to the turn of the century.

NONFORMAL HIGHER SCHOOLING

A number of possibilities existed for young people to continue education beyond the folk school that was outside the conventional college preparatory program and the *gymnasium*. Nonformal educational activities were becoming widespread during the last part of the nineteenth century. By nonformal education, we mean those educational programs that were systematic and organized but which took place outside the formal framework of schooling and did not lead to some formal certificate or diploma. At that time a multitude of rural organizations had sprung up, focusing not only on economic development through cooperative ventures, but focusing on educational programs as well. The Inner Mission was strongly educational in its orientation. Sport clubs, choral groups, music clubs, and literature societies became commonplace and developed their own educational programs. One of the earliest groups was the Norwegian Union of Total Abstainers, which was founded in 1859 and conducted an active adult education enterprise, focused mainly on the evils of alcohol.

In 1868 the first rural liberal youth association was established, while in the towns "workers" academies came into being, the first established in 1885. Their expressed aim was to organize lectures to provide "healthy, interesting and stimulating entertainment devised to develop and educate their hearers."[1] Over time they became somewhat more formalized, receiving, from the mid 1890s, state subsidies and taking on the name "folk academies." In 1905 a national organization of Norwegian Folk Academies was organized. The most visible nonformal institution, however, was the folk high school.

Folk High Schools

The major nonformal innovation in the country during the nineteenth century was the folk high school. We recall that the Danish Grundtvig was hostile toward much of what went into classical education, particularly Latin schools, claiming they were undemocratic and foreign. As early as 1837 he had proposed the establishment of "schools without books" and in 1864 the first such school in Norway was opened at Sagatun, near Hamar, by Ole Arvesen and Herman Anker, for the purpose of giving the sons of farmers an education beyond the folk school experience.[2]

The program would not be structured around formal knowledge but would awaken the youth to their nation and religion. It would have as its ultimate aim, the spiritual life of the youth. The means to this awakening would be to introduce the youth to the folk tradition as exemplified in the old folk tales, adventures, folk songs, poems, and myths of Norway. Young people, such as Viggo Ullmann and Christopher Bruun, gave themselves to the cause, doing so out of an intense sense of commitment and idealism as symbolized in Grundvigian Christianity and even liberal political beliefs.

That first folk high school began through private subscription and in the first year eighty people enrolled, some coming from distant districts to learn. It was a boarding school charging relatively low fees and conducting a six month program of studies. The teaching method was the "free lecture," stressing "the living word." No homework, examinations, or diplomas were given. Some of the greatest literary artists and educators took part in lectures during the first year forming a special bond between aesthetics and education in the schools.[3]

In 1867 Christopher Bruun opened his folk high school at Romundgaard in Gudbrandsdalen. He is known generally as the real father of the Norwegian folk high school movement, having set much of the model for schools to come.[4] Bruun down-played conventional modes of learning and stressed awakening the emotional side of human beings through word of mouth.[5] The high point of the movement is found in a series of lectures Bruun gave to the Norwegian Student Association in 1866, which were published in 1878, having the title *Folkelige grundtanker* (Foundation Thoughts of the People).[6] In the book the term "fatherland" takes on special meaning, with its focus on home, poetry, and history of the folk.[7]

In quick succession, many other institutions came into being so that within three years, twenty schools were operating, although many were so small that they could hardly be called schools. For example, Viggo Ullmann and an assistant teacher began their school by conducting sessions for three subscribed students.[8] Other schools were forced to adopt a moving school format to attract enough students.

The enterprise was not without its detractors. The folk high school at Lofthus, for example, opened its doors in November, 1969, beginning with only eight students but quickly expanding to twenty students by the end of the year. It even opened a summer course in 1870 for females, but by the next fall the school was enmeshed in a terrible controversy that quickly spilled over into the Christiania and Bergen public media. At the heart of the matter were challenges and counter-challenges between a young theology student, Vilhelm Poulsen, who had been sent from Christiania to take over the school, and an assistant teacher, Johannes Helleland, who was a local school instructor and who had taken time actually to visit folk high schools in Denmark. Claiming the enrollments were too low, Poulson attempted to dismiss Helleland.

It eventually became clear that there was a fundamental disagreement between the two men. Helleland claimed Poulson feared the real purpose of the folk high schools, as conceptualized by Grundtvig, feeling that they were little better than "Satan's Synagogue." Poulson wanted to institute a religious oriented school, with morning and evening services, Christian history, and military discipline, while Helleland wished to stress general enlightenment.[9]

In fact, Poulson's position was much like that of those Pietist clerics, who saw genuine danger in Grundtvigian thinking. They believed much like the conservative, Nils Hertzberg, who exercised a great negative influence on the movement in his position as Division Chief and Minister in the Department of Church and Education between 1873 and 1884. The number of folk high schools had reached thirty-five by 1876/77, and in an attempt to counteract the movement, Hertzberg began establishing a series of *amtskoler* (county schools) after 1877 for youth wishing for further common schooling. Of course, he intended their orientation to be toward orthodox Christian studies although certain counties chose their own course of action.

He was able to convince the *Storting* to support his plan, with the arrangement that the state pay 2/3 while the counties pay 1/3 of the costs. Of course, the folk high schools were eligible to be transformed into a county school, but this would mean that they would loose their autonomy. The Lofthus school, mentioned above, actually tried to receive funds from time to time, but was denied by the local governing board.[10] The winter term was typically devoted to study by males, while the summer term was for females. In addition, a teacher course of studies was often conducted in the summer time.[11]

There were some differences between the county schools and the folk high schools, beyond the religious-secular issue. The county school that was in competition with the Lofthus Folk High School, for example, focused on young people from 15-17 years of age, while the folk high school usually took in students from 20-25 years of age. However, in many respects the county schools attempted to replicate the folk high school format. There were permanent and traveling schools, male and female programs, and practical as well as theoretical studies.

While all this was going on, a few private orthodox Christian schools also came into being, these also being coeducational and residential in nature. Their focus was originally based on the desire to provide a more Christian learning environment alongside the national emphasis of the Grundtvigians. The first such school was established by Asbjørn Knutsen in 1893 at Heddal.[12]

The consequence of these counter-activities was that folk high schools were markedly curbed, and by 1898 there were only six genuinely private folk high schools in existence. They had, however, accomplished a more important aim as continuing education became an established part of the educational experience. By 1885 the number of public and private schools was fifty-seven, with 2,091 students enrolled. These enrollments would hold steady for the next two decades then climb rapidly so that by 1920/21 5,033 students would be enrolled.[13]

In spite of the historical importance of these institutions, particularly in terms of adult education during the twentieth century, the type of nonformal school providing education beyond the folk school that would ultimately be fully incorporated into the system of higher schooling was the continuation school (*framhaldsskole*).

The Continuation School

Continuation schools constitute a special type of schooling intended for young people who had recently completed the folk school. These were public schools, set up strictly through local initiative. That is, local authorities in various parts of the countryside began to recognize the need to provide their youth with some form of general and/or practical education beyond the seven year folk school.

Because it was from local initiative, the forms the continuation schools took were quite unique. In some localities the school addressed vocational crafts needs, in others vocational farming needs, in others religious needs, in others national needs, and still others a combination of needs. In Aurland, for example, the school board decided, in 1891, that a five week continuation school ought to be initiated having a program both general and theoretical in nature.[14]

Two years later, the board organized a different kind of continuation school, this one focusing on crafts for the boys and domestic studies for the girls. Funds to conduct the ten week school were sought from various sources, including private donations. The main problem, however, was not so much money as enrollments. In fact, the school interrupted its program between 1898 and 1900 because of low enrollments.[15]

In the Odda, Ullensvang and Kinsarvik area a number of continuation schools came into existence around the turn of the century. The fjord area communities had maintained a folk high school and a county school for some time. The teachers of the folk schools in Odda, Vikebygd, and Hauso had, for some time, been conducting six week continuation classes at their schools, and the notion took hold that it might be possible to establish more expanded continuation schools. In 1895 a crafts school for boys was set up at Lofthus, using the local folk school facilities, and in 1900 the school board adopted a plan to set up a full six month general education program at Ullensvang, using public subsidies. Two years later a domestic studies school for girls was also set up at Lofthus, which relied on local public funds.[16]

In the Stord region, a special crafts course had been conducted for youth after 1890, as a consequence of the 1889 school law, but in 1896, the local board decided to set up a special school for that purpose. In 1916 a private middle school was set up at As, but the region decided to annex the school and turn it into a folk school and a general continuation school.[17]

What we find during this time is an active recognition on the part of public and private groups that an extended education was becoming more and more necessary. The type of schools that resulted were not dictated by any centralized controlling body. The local groups and authorities were "entirely free to build them up on lines best suited to the people living in their particular part of the country."[18] It is with the continuation schools that we see the nearest European equivalent to the nineteenth century American high school. Edgar Wesley could well have been speaking of them as he described the American high schools:

> Democratic, untrammeled by tradition, rooted in local situa-
> tions, sensitive to popular demands, relatively free to evolve
> as conditions warranted, they began their spectacular rise.[19]

The state had established a uniform minimum schooling standard, but it was the local districts that chose to provide further schooling, and it was the local districts that chose whether to make such school compulsory or not. In other words, a growing number of communities were establishing a compulsory attendance law that exceeded the state requirement of seven to fourteen years.

The local communities decided how long such courses would be. Some set up short courses of a few months duration, while others set up a full six month term. Other courses were designed so that students could attend part-time and complete the course over two or even three years.

The local community also decided what the content would be. Generally, however, the content fell into two major categories: general (mathematics, Norwegian, hygiene, history and citizenship) and practical (craft courses for boys and domestic studies for girls).

The continuation schools were somewhat formalized in the 1889 school laws; however, the law simply defined a course as something running from one to six months and adhering to a developed plan.[20] This brings us to formal schooling beyond the folk school level.

FORMAL SECONDARY EDUCATION

A major political triumph of the Liberals just prior to the turn of the century lay in the changes they would render in the higher common school. That would be clarified in the 1896 common higher school law, but it would have enormous consequences for all of common schooling.

The 1896 School Law

The traditional higher school was not a popular institution among the Liberal Party leaders. It had represented the exclusive domain of the official class legitimizing its claim to national leadership. While the form and content of the higher school was very similar to that throughout Europe, it had taken on the aura of illegitimacy because it was so foreign and contrary to genuine feelings of nationalism. Even the classical schoolmasters were seen as being so remote and somehow alien, that an account such as that described by Thomas Krog in his short story "Jørgen Dom, Philologist," about the loves and dreams of such a person, takes on a peculiar, unreal charm.[21] Any institution that was based on the Latin language, would certainly symbolize an artificial and capricious key to positions of authority in democratic Norway.

The Liberal Party was interested in doing away with these symbols and wished to replace them with a mechanism that would more nearly represent the political leadership structure that existed in the country. A school commission was named in 1890 to consider questions surrounding the higher schools. As is the case with commissions at the time, its composition was structured to represent the various facets of schooling.[22]

It was a hard working commission and gathered a good deal of information. Its major defect, if it could be so identified, was that it was made up of professionals, while the real battle to be fought was ultimately political in nature. Of course, these men represented political leanings. O. E. Holck was a Conservative, P. Voss a Moderate, and H. S. Horst a Liberal. In fact, Horst was a member of the *Storting* and had taken an active role in getting the 1889 school law passed.[23]

George Klem has identified three major areas of interest in the 1896 higher common school law: (1) administrative issues, (2) organizational issues, and (3) curricular issues.[24]

Administrative Issues. The general policy regarding local control over central control had been set in the debate concerning the folk school. That held firm regarding the higher common school debate, but another aspect of school administration emerged that was not a part of the earlier considerations: public vs. private schooling.

While the folk school had been recognized as a public institution, it was not at all clear in the minds of many of the Liberals if the higher schools should be accorded such a connection. Certain members of the *Storting* had long attacked the notion of state support for higher schooling.[25] Jaabæk, for example, declared to the Church Committee in 1871, that the state should not be in the business of higher schooling. He had consistently taken the position that higher schools were simply institutions dedicated to particular vocations. They should be treated in the same way as commercial enterprises and crafts enterprises were treated. Groups sponsoring these vocations enter into competition with each other, without state intervention.[26]

As a young man, Johan Sverdrup had also been against higher state schools, though his position was a bit more tempered than was Jaabæk's. He had declared that he simply did not want the state to gain a monopoly over the higher schools, because that would have "unfortunate consequences." The private schools, except for the traditional Latin grammar schools, are bound by law, and that is enough. According to the young Sverdrup, they require the ability to "possess great elasticity, so they can bend themselves to the forces of life and reality."[27] It was his belief in 1871 that the state had become too involved in the sponsorship of the higher schools. At that time he had felt that the state must put all of its resources and strength behind the general enlightenment.

The attitudes of Jaabæk and Sverdrup were expressed at a time when the Liberals were with little political power, and the attitudes would change as these leaders moved into positions of genuine power and recognized the potential of gaining control over the higher schools and molding them to their own designs. At the time the budget for the common higher school was being debated in 1889, certain issues were raised concerning the role of the state in higher schooling. Moursand, the representative of Tromsø, reminded his colleagues that they were deliberating the budget issue on the assumption that the common higher school was a state issue and that it was a state school. He requested that the government actually consider to what degree the higher common school has become the responsibility of the state or should be given over to private or community care.[28]

This recommendation set off a whole parliamentary and public reaction, which revealed a change in the position of the Liberals.[29] The folk school was assured and now it was time to deal with the higher common school, turning it into a national and democratic based institution, the likes of which was not yet known in Europe. It would be a state school, but a state school under parliamentary rather than official class leadership.

Maintaining a continued commitment to local control, the education commission that was established in 1890, the Church Committee of the *Storting*, the *Odelsting*, and the *Lagting* all held firm that the higher common school be a public institution, that it be administered through a cooperative arrangement between state and community, that the public middle school be a community school, that the state be responsible for the public *gymnasium*,[30] and that the private school come under the same regulations as public schools.[31] These regulations pertain specifically to the organizational and curricular issues of the law.

Organizational Issues. The major organizational issue surrounding the higher common school had to do with the structural levels and divisions that would exist as a student progressed through the school. The issue was not new. In fact, it had occupied the attention of those who had considered school reform from the time of independence.

Any consideration of structural levels must begin with the relationship between the folk school and the middle school. We recall that the 1869 school law operated on the assumption that the folk school could serve as a foundation school for three years, and the state would not participate in the operation of any other foundation school. One of the specific intentions of the 1889 school law was to strengthen the folk school so that it would be as adequate as any school in preparing the youth to enter the middle school.

The political discussion of the 1890s had nothing to do with whether the folk school was the proper foundation school. That issue had been settled and the focus of attention was now on which level of the folk school the student would conclude common schooling and enter the middle school. We recall that the fully developed folk school had three main levels, the first lasting three years, the second lasting two years, and the third lasting two additional years.

The commission discussion centered on adopting the first two levels of the folk school as the foundation program. There was near unanimous opinion that the foundation program should be five years and consist of the first two levels of the folk school.[32] Holck, being the Conservative member, was reluctant to go with the others, arguing that many students would not receive a proper foundation for middle school. He proposed that the middle school set up its own one year preparation class, which would essentially reduce the foundation program to four years. His suggestion was not taken seriously and the *Storting* received the recommendation that the foundation school be five years, taken at the folk school.

Within the *Storting*, the points of view were much more divergent than in the commission. The least radical position taken in debates was that the foundation school remain the first level lasting but three years, although there was almost no support for this position among the Liberals. The leaders of the party, Steen and Sverdrup, had recommended a five year foundation school since 1880.[33] Some of the representatives even advocated that the full seven year folk school should serve as the foundation school. Viggo Ullmann, for example, maintained that so long as there was any separation or division between the middle school and the upper levels of the folk school, the folk school would remain a second class institution.[34]

Certain supporters of the full seven year foundation school recognized, however, that such a step was too great to take at one time. Horst, for example, was sympathetic to the full seven year school, but having participated as a member of the 1890 school commission, he was sensitive to the pedagogical discussion that had been conducted about when a foreign language ought to begin. Agreement had been reached in that forum that it should not be postponed beyond the sixth year, and being sensitive to the temper of those who supported this point of view he pushed his colleagues for a compromise position: the foundation school would comprise the first two levels (3–2) of the folk school. At that point, the students would separate, some going on to a four year middle school, while others would go on to the final level of the folk school.[35] Such a position gained quick and extensive support, even from the Conservatives. Actually, the leading Conservatives, such as Bonnevie, were not hostile to the idea of an integrated foundation school. Their major concern was that it provide a sufficiently strong foundation program to prepare the young people to cope with the rigors of higher schooling.[36]

Subjects of Study. The aspect of the 1896 school law, that was more radical than anything else, pertained to the subjects of study. In fact, the very first issue that the 1890 school commission took up was the role of the classics in the higher common school. It was the issue that came under extensive public discussion.

The outcome of this consideration was that the classics were, for all intents and purposes, declared obsolete and irrelevant to the purposes of Norwegian education. This declaration against Latin had its theoretical foundations, including its nonscientific, reactionary tone, but Klem stresses that the fight against Latin was particularly political in nature.[37] It had both an internal and an external dimension. Internally, if there had been anything that had symbolized to the farmer, the laborer, the crofter, that he was not an equal to those of the official class, it was the classical schooling that seemed to be such an arbitrary and irrelevant barrier.

Externally, Norway was still in a state of symbolic dependence on Sweden, although that condition was coming to a rapid conclusion. Norway would ultimately win its total independence in 1905.[38] Latin, being inextricably linked with that which is foreign, with the negatives of the dependent past, would also have to go.

As the 1890 school commission set to work, a number of proposals came before it. The most radical was that of Rector H. J. Horst, who proposed a single track throughout the middle and higher school. Greater sympathy in the commission was toward a middle school with Latin and English constituting optional languages. The *gymnasium* would consist of the two tracks that had existed since 1869, the one stressing math/science and the other classics. However, different forces were at work to counteract the commission's sentiments. The Department, for example, pushed the notion of a Latin free middle school with a three pronged *gymnasium*, including the two old branches just mentioned, but adding a new history/ modern languages branch.

The majority of the members of the Church Committee of the *Storting* were opposed to a classics branch, so that when the issue reached the *Odelsting* and *Lagting*, it was clear that Latin was in jeopardy altogether. In a last ditch attempt to salvage something, the Conservatives recommended postponing action, hoping that sentiments might somehow change over time.[39] Indeed, if the Liberals could be persuaded to look more closely at the rest of Europe, their attitudes might change. No other country had come even remotely as far as Norway in its policy toward the classics in school. Germany would not even recognize the modern languages and math/science branches of study as equivalent to the classics in terms of the *Abitur*, or secondary school leaving examination, until the turn of the twentieth century.

Even in England, where Herbert Spencer had proclaimed that science was the study of greatest worth,[40] and where secondary students could concentrate on sciences, the tendency to remain with the classics was pervasive. A survey in 1875 of 40 of the best schools in the country showed 438 requesting examinations in Latin, 433 in Greek, 21 in mechanics (physics), 28 in chemistry, and 6 in botany.[41]

Of course, this tendency coincides with the tendency of secondary students at the time in Norway, where only one of the 158 *artium* students between 1871-1875 had passed the examination in the science branch. All the rest had passed in the Latin branch. This was shifting quickly, however, as is seen in Table 9.1,[42] so that by the turn of this century more science examination passes were being recorded than were classics passes.

Table 9.1

Graduates from Secondary Schools in the Latin, Science, and English Branches between 1871 and 1910

| | Branch of Study | | |
	Latin	Science	English
1871-1875	157	1	
1876-1880	104	27	
1881-1885	212	97	
1886-1890	232	84	
1891-1895	146	101	
1896-1900	130	192	
1901-1905	126	247	
1906-1910	151	208	63

And so the Liberals held firm in their resolve to consider the issue in that session of the *Storting*. The arguments for retaining Latin would be predictable and not very strong. It would not be possible for the defenders of the classics to argue the role of the classics in Western civilization, nor the bond of a common European heritage. Norway had only suffered humiliation through unions, integration, and broader connections. Nor would it be possible for them to argue for an intellectual aristocracy. The official class had used its educational advantage to perpetuate its political power and social influence against the growing democratic spirit. Now the power of the official class was in a state of real decline.

The tenor of the times was to sweep away any symbols of elitist and foreign domination and replace them with symbols of the growing democratic, national spirit. Bonnevie weakly argued for the retention of Latin on the grounds that it represented the best preparation for "scientific studies" at the university.[43] The priest, Christian Knudsen, argued the specific case of religious studies, claiming that it constituted an essential background for those who were preparing to study religion and dedicate themselves to the church.[44]

Johannes Steen, recognizing the futility of any arguments, expressed high regard for classical studies, but he explained that a proper preparation in the classics would consume most of the curriculum and result in a subject bound preparatory school. Such a course would be counter productive of the reform intention, which was to institute a unified higher school appropriate to the entire population.[45]

On the initial vote of the two houses of the *Storting*, it was concluded that Latin and Greek should be eliminated altogether from the higher common school. However, Jacob Sverdrup, the Minister of the Department of Church and Education, intervened with a proposal for an addendum,[46] before the final vote was taken. That addendum stipulated that the king, with the approval of the *Storting*, may designate specific higher schools, "until further notice," that could retain the right to instruct in Latin. Such a move won immediate praise. The representative from Arendal, Klem, suggested for example, that it was just too dangerous for a tiny people to be the first to eliminate the classics from the schools.[47] The role of Latin was salvaged momentarily, although the Liberals were convinced that this was a temporary situation, believing that Latin would eventually be totally done away with. In fact, such a step would never be necessary. The war against elitism in Norwegian secondary education had already been won, and Latin would quickly disappear as a political issue.

SUMMARY

A British report on Scandinavia shortly after the turn of the century indicates that the school law of 1896 provided certain major innovations among the countries of Europe. First, it provided an organic relationship between the primary school and the lower division of the secondary school (middle school). Second, it made coeducation compulsory in all schools receiving aid. Third, it eliminated Greek from the list of school subjects and placed enormous restrictions on the use of Latin as a special subject.[48] Other innovations were included, but those mentioned in the report were obviously some of the most important, and they set Norway apart as having such a peculiar school structure, that it seemed it would exercise no influence on other countries. It is important to note, however, that Norway was to serve as an important model for reform. Within seven years after the Norwegian law was passed, Denmark also passed a school law, which paid Norway the compliment of being a "fairly close imitation" of that passed in the country to the north.[49] Norwegian education had come of age, it had completed its second major cycle of educational reform, but soon after the turn of the century, the third cycle would already be under way.

10 Extension of Participation in Education

A major indicator of the degree to which the school had been democratized by the time the Liberal Party passed its school laws in the 1880s and 1890s, is the degree of participation of various groups in the educational process. We shall begin with a general assessment of attendance patterns at the various levels of education, after which we shall give special consideration to two populations of people: females and special needs children. In the next chapter we shall discuss opportunities for vocational training through the nineteenth century.

ATTENDANCE PATTERNS

A type of compulsory education law had been in Norway since the 1739 ordinance in that parents were legally obliged to instruct or cause the child to be instructed in reading and religion. In other words, parents were not obliged to send their children to school if they are able to provide home teachers or otherwise instruct their children. By 1860 only 3.3% of the young people of compulsory school age were not receiving instruction of some kind.

Even those who did not attend school usually learned to read, because it was the parent's responsibility to teach reading to the children. Bjørnson's *Arne* typifies the type of person who would not have gone to school. He was so isolated from the rest, that he never attended school, and so, in the tradition of Norway, "the mother taught the boy to read." He then gained a companion, Kristian, for a time, who "discovered Arne's fondness for reading, and now carried up to him those books he had read himself. After Arne had finished these, Kristian brought him new ones."[1]

As we see in Table 10.1[2] almost all of the children who were in school were in one of four school types: folk, middle, *gymnasium*, or special education. That is, by 1875, 97.6% of all school aged students were in one of these four school types, and this rose to 97.9% in 1880, to 98.0% in 1885 and 1890, and 99.3% in 1895. Because home teaching was such a common mode of instruction, it could be taken for granted that almost all of the children engaged in alternate instruction were engaged in that type of instruction.

Between 5% and 6% of the students were attending the middle school during those years, while less than 0.2%, were at the *gymnasium*, and an even smaller percentage were attending special education schools.

Table 10.1

The Number of Students in the Folk School, the Middle School, the *Gymnasium*, and Special Schools between 1860 and 1900

		School Type		
Year	Folk	Middle	Gymnasium	Special	Others
1875/76	244,998	14,274	370	245	6,124
1880/81	247,303	15,289	686	298	5,678
1885/86	261,378	17,086	958	452	4,508
1890/91	287,400	17,980	676	443	5,152
1895/96	331,133	18,485	855	303	2,594

A crucial issue here is the degree to which the folk school was being used as a foundation school for the middle school prior to the 1889 school law, when it became the norm. Two quite different conditions are found in the towns and the countryside. In the countryside, the number of youth relying on the folk school was very high relative to those in other forms of instruction, although the percentage of youth actually decreased between 1860 and 1890. At the time the 1860 school law came into effect only 1,564 youth out of 200,273 school attenders were receiving instruction outside the folk school. In other words, 99.2% of the youth attending school were in the folk school.

By 1890 5,757 of the 238,184 school attenders in the countryside were engaged in some other type of formal schooling. Thus, 98% of all school attenders were in the folk school.[3] Dokka laments such a trend as a sign that the folk school was not serving as a foundation school for an increasing number of school youth.[4] To some extent this observation may be accurate, but it needs qualification. First, the foundation school represented the first three years of schooling, and the figures cited above are for all school aged youth, including those in the middle school and those in the upper levels of the folk school. We must assume that a major portion of these youth in the middle school actually did use the folk school as a foundation program before moving on to a middle school. Second, the increased number reflects a democratization process of another sort in that increasing numbers of children from relatively poor families were entering higher schooling and sitting alongside those of the more privileged classes.[5]

Table 10.2

The Percentage of Youth not Receiving Education, Receiving Home Teaching, or Attending Some Form of Formal Schooling in 1870, 1875, 1880, 1885, and 1890, in the Towns of Norway

	1870	1875	1880	1885	1890
Receiving no education	1*	1*	1*	1*	1*
Home teaching	1*	1*	1*	1*	1*
Public Folk Schools	67.9	66.5	69.6	71.8	74.8
Private Folk Schools	6.9				3.5
Middle and Higher Schools	22.1	25.3		20.0	

*approximate percentages

In the towns, quite a different pattern of school attenders is found. This pattern takes on increasing importance because Norway was becoming a more modern, urbanized country. Whereas 10.8% of the population was in densely populated areas in 1837, that figure had risen to 19.6% in 1865, to 24.4% in 1875, and 31.3% in 1890.[6] From Table 10.2

folk schools, although another 6.9% were in private schools giving a similar type of schooling. During the next two decades the number of private pupils in these types of institutions declined while the folk schools took on greater and greater percentages of the youth. In spite of this, by 1990, approximately one quarter of all pupils were in other schools, particularly the higher schools.

We have seen that over the years, more and more people began attending middle school and the *gymnasium*. Over time a broader spectrum of people gained access to the institutions and even went on to the university. Unfortunately, we have very little data about the social class origins of students during the nineteenth century, at least concerning the middle school. We do have information on those completing the *examen artium*, or those who finished the *gymnasium* in the last quarter of the nineteenth century.

From Table 10.3,[7] we find that over one third of those graduates between 1870-79 had fathers whose occupation was as an academic. Another 22% were sons of businessmen, and 17.6% were sons of white collar workers, or a heterogeneous group made up of civil servants, executives, sea captains, etc. About one in four, however, came from that group of people who previously had rarely participated in higher education, including farmers, folk school teachers, craftsmen, and laborers.

Table 10.3

Male Artium Graduates in 1870-79 and 1910-1914, by Father's Occupation in Percentages

	1870-79	*1910-14*
Academic	34.6	28.1
Businessman	22.0	22.9
White Collar Worker	17.6	20.5
Farmer	9.0	11.8
Teacher	5.4	7.3
Artisan	8.2	5.5
Worker	2.0	1.8
Other	1.2	2.1
Total	100.0	100.0

While contemporary social scientists tend to use such data to show the inequality of opportunity that existed, it represents a remarkable historical shift in participation in higher education on the part of these groups.

Many students had made their way through the system and even to the university in ways that are not reflected in the formal statistics. The student factories continued to operate, and foreign experience remained a vital source of enlightenment. Even so, the lot of those from the lower ranks, who made it to the university remained difficult. Arne Garborg has provided the world with a description of one farm boy's experience in a world quite foreign to that of his own, in his novel about one Daniel Braut, supposedly taking place during the 1860s.[8]

During the next three decades, this ratio did not change dramatically. More than half of all *gymnasium* finishers continued to be children of academics or merchants, and the number of finishers whose children were from the lower social classes rose so slowly that the shift in percentage points was minimal, amounting to a rise of approximately 3%.

A number of factors come to play to explain the different patterns of enrollment. It is clear that a critical mass of people is usually necessary for an extensive schooling tradition to develop in the first place, and the towns had long served as advanced education centers, not only for the youth of the towns but the youth from the countryside. Dokka stresses that economic impulses had contributed largely to the shifts in school attendance rates in the towns. The country was taking on the trappings of a modern nation state. He also notes that religious impulses were mainly behind the existence of private folk schools at the time.[9]

WOMEN IN SCHOOLS

Females had long attended folk schools. The value system of the early part of the nineteenth century dictated that males and females be schooled separately, and this was instituted as far as possible. In practice, however, countryside schools had usually been coeducational simply because the school population was so sparse. Over time this value system began to change, and as the Liberals came into power, they took the position that coeducational institutions were appropriate for a democratic society. The political agenda of the schools was to prepare all people, including females, to participate in society. Consequently, women were seen to possess the same social rights and obligations as the men.[10]

As the 1889 school law was being debated in the *Storting*, the Liberals made clear that they were oriented toward coeducation; the schools must be built having a coeducational program. The Conservatives could not be described as being fully against coeducation, but the active role taken by the Liberals against separation led them to point out its virtues and resist unquestioned adoption of coeducation.[11]

Because the Liberals dominated politics in the last decade of the century, they were able to take specific measures to rectify injustices. Girls schools had never received state support, but on 27 July 1896, that policy was changed by the *Storting*. Just one year later, as the budget for higher schools was being debated, the issue was raised about the support of coeducational schools. A decision was made that state funds, whether they be for public or for private schools, would only be given to schools that did not discriminate between the sexes in terms of their admission policies.[12]

It would, however, require a number of years to gain any sense of parity with males, particularly regarding higher schooling.

Women in Higher Schooling

Certain girls had long been well educated at home or at a few womens schools, but females had systematically been denied access to almost all formal schooling at the higher levels during the first three quarters of nineteenth century Norway. In 1875, Rasmus Tønder Nissen, the brother of Hartvig Nissen, was appointed Minister of the Department of Church and Education. He had been a diligent advocate of a higher quality of girls schooling and through his leadership, the Department suddenly issued a circular announcing that the way was open for girls to attend middle school and take the middle school leaving examination.

This announcement was not quite as radical as it appears on the surface. Throughout the early 1870s, girls had prepared themselves through tutors and in private schools, and had then taken the examination, even though this practice had not been clarified in previous legislation. In June, 1878, a law was finally passed allowing this to happen.[13] The *Odelsting* debate over the issue gives some insight into the attitudes of the time, particularly of the Liberal politicians.

There was positive sentiment among law makers to extend schooling opportunities for girls, but there was an underlying current of thought that girls were not as intellectually capable as the boys. Some consideration was given to creating a simplified examination, particularly in mathematics, though the leaders of the Liberals quickly dismissed this possibility. Johan Sverdrup mentioned that he knew a school where the girls exceeded the boys in mathematics. "There is so little difference between the true intellectual education of man and woman," he claimed, "that it is not possible to speak of a heart side and a leader side, where one side should belong to the one sex and the other side to the other." He maintained that a proper education consists of instruction of both the head and the heart.[14]

Johannes Steen joined Sverdrup in maintaining that "our girls schools are common schools," implying that they provided a general education expected of everyone. He even cautioned against a policy of establishing special schools for girls, because "in that moment they become such, they have done the greatest damage in the female development, which society could perpetrate."[15] P. Quam, the head of an important private middle school for girls in Christiania, explained that his experience had demonstrated they are equal to the boys, even in mathematics.[16]

The decision was made to retain the same requirements for girls as for boys. By 1880 sixty-three female graduates of the middle schools had been recorded, although the common assumption remained that middle schools remained, by and large, boys schools, because their purpose was ultimately for university entrance purposes and girls were not deemed suited to engage in the most advanced higher studies. In fact, girls schools were not even allowed to administer the middle school examination. Girls wishing to take it were required to go to a boys school at the time of the examination. In spite of this, between 1880 and 1890 twenty-one percent of the 1994 middle school graduates would be female.[17]

A significant step for women's education would come in 1882, when Cecilie Thoresen registered a direct request to the *Storting* to be allowed to take the *examen artium*. Representative Hagbard Berner, a well-known supporter of women's issues,[18] drew up a proposal that women be allowed to take not only the *examen artium*, but the alternative examination at the university. The *Storting* responded positively to the proposal and, in paternalistic fashion, some discussion was even conducted about the possibility of excusing women from the mathematics section of the examination, substituting German in its place, because women were thought to be unable to master higher mathematics. Fortunately, no decision was made to excuse women, and Cecilie passed her mathematics program with distinction, becoming the first woman to pass the *examen artium*.[19]

From 1885-1890 twelve more women accomplished this task, from 1891-95 sixteen more, and from 1896-1900 thirty-one more. The ratio of women to men was, of course, still highly disproportionate. In the

1890s only eight percent of all those passing the examination were women, and it would be another seventy-five years before the number of women passing the examination outnumbered the number of men.

Having technically qualified for university studies in 1884, the way was open for Cecilie Thoresen to enter the university. All degrees and professional examinations were made available to her although there was strong protest from some Conservatives. The faculty of the School of Medicine, for example, published the following declaration:

> The study of medicine will take women outside their natural field. Their intelligence will be developed at the expense of their emotional life; they will lose their womanliness.[20]

Cecilie Thoresen came to the university but failed to complete her studies, having married in 1887. However, by then others were taking advantage of the opportunity. In 1889 two women finished their studies, the one in sciences and the other in law. In the 1890s, women had also been admitted to medicine, philology, and even theology. By 1903, sixteen percent of all young people qualifying for university study were women. This figure had climbed to over 31 percent by 1913. In that brief ten year period, 1,378 of the 5,673 young people qualifying for university study were women.[21] Of course, the number of women actually going through university studies was much more limited. Less than three percent of all *embetseksamen* in that ten year period were given to women.[22]

Emergence of Formally Trained Women Teachers

The school law of 1860 anticipated limited participation of women in teaching, although it did not provide for the education of women teachers, who were excluded from the teacher seminars at the time.[23] However, training became available to women through The Association for the Advancement of Women's Handicraft Enterprises, which was organized in 1862 and fostered the development of handicrafts, shops, and offices for women.[24] The group established a private school for girls which quickly grew to about 100 students. Because handicrafts for girls was one of the subjects women were allowed to teach, many of these school leavers were hired as teachers at the folk schools, even though that private school for women provided no preparation for teaching. In 1865 the Department of Church and Education proposed to the *Storting* that a teacher seminar for females be set up in Christiania. At the same time, a sister association of women in Bergen was campaigning locally to the diocese officials for a similar kind of seminar.

There was positive response, but the *Storting* was not inclined to enter into a change of laws, which would have been necessary to accomplish the task. The Department was able to provide, on an experimental basis, some funds, but lawmakers were opposed even to that. The Associations in both Christiania and Bergen finally took matters into their own hands and applied for permission to run two-year institutions for girls from private sources. In 1867 the two schools were opened.

In the next four years the debate continued in the Department and the *Storting* as to the place of women teachers in the folk schools. At the time, there were relatively few women working full time. For example, in 1867/68 only 72 (0.2%) of the 3,533 full time folk school teachers were women, but pressure was on to raise that number. In 1869, a proposal was submitted that would allow women to work as teachers of the lower levels of the folk school and in those classes that contained only girls. Such a proposal was passed in the *Storting* in November, 1869, providing for an examination structure that would qualify women for these positions.[25]

In the next two decades the debate over teacher seminars would continue, but little concrete was accomplished to further the cause of women as teachers, although we see in Table 10.4[26] that the number of women teachers grew considerably during that time.

Table 10.4

The Number of Common School Teachers between 1875 and 1890

	Total	Females	% Females
1867/68	3533	72	2.0
1875/76	3911	312	8.0
1880/81	4358	578	13.3
1885/86	4726	858	18.2
1890/91	5128	1187	23.1

There was a great difference in participation rates of women between the countryside and the towns. By 1890 62% of all folk school teachers in the towns were women, while in the countryside only 13.3%

(429) of the 3,478 teachers were women, in part, because there were so few girls schools.[27] Significantly, the social class background of women teachers was strikingly different from the men. Whereas almost all of the men teachers came from farmer and lower class backgrounds, the women came almost exclusively from families which had the resources to provide private higher schooling and home teaching for their daughters.[28]

As a part of the Liberal Party reform activities, the first independent law concerning teaching seminars was passed in 1890. Sverdrup had recommended that teacher training be strengthened in his open letter of 1884,[29] and teacher education was a part of the broader discussions of the school commission and *Storting* considerations that led up to the 1889 school law. The major point of discussion had to do with the length of time one should attend a teachers seminar. The Church Committee of the *Storting* had already gone on record in 1881, in favor of a three year course of studies, and Sverdrup had this notion in mind with his recommendations of 1884.[30]

Enormous debates ensued over the value of such a course of studies, the value of theoretical studies, the differences in training for teachers of lower levels and upper levels.[31] The outcome was that a two year course in teacher preparation was instituted, and that course was open both to men and women. At the conclusion of the course, teachers would be examined, mainly on the practical side of their preparation, to qualify to teach both in the lower and the higher levels of the folk school. In fact, many of the seminars extended their programs beyond the minimum time requirements and provided a three year course of studies.[32]

An additional recommendation of Sverdrup had been that the teacher training be redesigned toward national interests, including exposure to New Norwegian. The 1890 law mandated that all students learn New Norwegian or Countryside Norwegian grammar and be able to write in an appropriate New Norwegian style. Old Norse would be made available as an optional course of studies. In addition, history, geography, and natural science would be strengthened and included in the leaving examination, while handicrafts would also be made mandatory.

The law came under strong criticism and only twelve years later a new law was passed mandating a full three year course of studies, and the Dano-Norwegian language was given a status equal to New Norwegian in terms of its availability to students.

A major consequence of the 1890 law was that women quickly almost gained parity with men in terms of numbers undertaking training.

Five years after the law was passed, 45.1% of all seminar students were women. This figure dropped to 38.4% five years later, but by 1905/06 it had risen again to 44.8%.[33]

With the decision on the part of the *Storting* in 1897 that coeducational schools were the desired form, a genuine concern was that women teachers would systematically be denied access to mixed classes and mixed schools. The sense of the law was, of course, contrary to this concern, but in 1902 an adjustment was made in the law insuring that women had the same rights to civil service appointments, which included directors, headmistresses, and teachers in the higher schools.[34]

SPECIAL EDUCATION

At the time of the 1889 school law, it was simply taken for granted that a certain portion of society did not possess the same legal rights and obligations that were being imposed on society in general. Even while the major political purpose of the common school was being formulated, it was taken for granted that some segments of society would not participate in that common experience.

The 1889 school law allows for the exclusion of the feebleminded, the crippled, children with contagious diseases, and even misbehaving children.[35] Today, such an orientation is usually defined in negative terms, suggesting that such children were "segregated" or allowed to remain in a "neglected" condition by the common school provisions.[36]

From a historical vantage point, this is only partially so. Even before the 1889 school law, a number of steps had been taken to provide for special needs children, or to enhance the environments which contributed to certain problems, including the homes where certain children were living. The school laws of 1848 and 1860 had specifically stated that parents who were "so indifferent, disorderly or dissolute" that their children were neglected or corrupted could have their children taken away from the family and placed with another until they were sixteen years old if they lived in the countryside or nineteen if they lived in the towns.[37]

These legal provisions stemmed from a longstanding point of view that youth could be placed in a corrective facility if that was the only way to get them through the basic elements of religious studies and confirmation. Such measures attempted to regulate social problems, but it was more difficult to manage problems that were physiological in nature, such as blindness, deafness, or mental retardation.

The handicapped in nineteenth century Norway were treated in a rather similar way as were other such children throughout Europe. They often received specialized training of one kind or another, mainly in some private enterprise. Initially, this type of training usually came in the form of individualized help, exemplified by those well known cases of Victor, the wild boy of Aveyron in France, being tutored by Itard in the early 1800s. Or the reading experiments of Valentin Hauy in Picardy, France on the blind youth, Le Sueur, before bringing him to Paris in 1784 to exhibit him as an example of what might be done.

However, those tutors, who were successful, usually established their own school or became associated with an asylum that housed the mentally retarded, the blind, or deaf. Hauy's demonstrations in Paris proved so popular that he received funds from the Philosophical Society of Paris to establish the National Institute for the Young Blind in 1785, the first educational institution for the blind founded in Europe. Soon similar institutes sprang up in various centers of Europe. Norway was a party to the Royal Institute for the Blind, which was established in Copenhagen in 1811.[38]

It was 1861 before independent Norway was able to provide its own institution for the blind, with the opening of a private home where two students were instructed at the *Arbeidskole for blinde* (Crafts School for the Blind). It won almost immediate support by the Department of Church and Education for a yearly stipend. The program consisted of the folk school subjects as well as general living skills. The girls learned useful skills in hand crafts and needle work, while the boys learned wicker work, stool seat weaving, lathe operations, broom construction, and piano tuning. A second institute for the blind was under way in Trondheim in 1884, and by the time of the 1889 school law the two institutions existed serving approximately 130 pupils.[39]

Schools for the deaf in Europe can be traced back as far as the efforts of the priest Charles Michel de l'Epee, born in 1712, who had taught two sisters not only how to read and write but to speak and eventually established a school to grew to international fame. L'Epee has the distinction of opening the first state school for the deaf, which occurred in Vienna in 1779.[40] Subsequent to that, a number of schools for the deaf had come into operation. Norway was a party to the Royal Institute for the Deaf (*Det kongelige døvstumme-institut*) in Copenhagen, which was established in 1807. In fact, one of the early teachers of the institute was the Norwegian, Andreas Møller, who taught there from

1817-22.[41] In 1824, Møller initiated the first institute for the dumb (*Døvstumme institut*) in Norway, which was set up in Trondheim. By 1875 no less than four schools for the deaf were in operation in Norway, serving 245 pupils, and by the time of the 1889 school law seven such schools existed, serving over 450 pupils.[42]

It was with the deaf and blind that the policy makers took the first steps. In 1881, the first law was passed concerning instruction for the "abnormal," and it pertained specifically to these groups.[43] Norway was well into the next century before provisions were passed for educating other types of "abnormal" children. Of course, assistance of other types of handicapped children was not uncommon. The Frenchman, Edouard Seguin, who is usually identified as the father of special education, began a private school for mentally retarded youngsters in 1837, but eventually moved to the new world, leaving the task in Europe to others.

The first residential program in Europe for the mentally retarded was initiated in 1848 by Carl Saegert in Berlin, and these quickly proliferated throughout Europe. By 1887 there were at least fifty-five residential schools. The first such program in Norway came into being in 1877. The treatment in these programs was typically "substantially less than adequate and often brutal."[44]

Still another type of schooling for the mentally retarded came through so-called *hjelpeundervisningen* (auxiliary instruction). This notion had come out of Germany, where in 1859, a school headmaster in Halle set up a special class for children showing marginal mental ability to receive two hours of special instruction each day. By 1867 a special school had been set up in Dresden and the notion quickly spread to other cities in Germany as well as throughout Europe.[45]

In Christiania, the Work School for Crippled opened in 1892, later named Sophies Minde.[46] Unlike the typical residential programs, this consisted of a genuine educational endeavor. Participants spent six hours a day in extensive practical studies giving students occupational skills such as weaving, leather work, lathe work, shoe making, and basket making. Of course, students were also exposed to a heavy dose of *Bible* studies with psalm reading.[47]

By the turn of the century, programs similar to Sophies Minde had been set up in Bergen, Tromsø, Trondheim, and other towns. These came largely from private initiative, although the state quickly became a partner to the activities. Sophies Minde was receiving funds as early as 1902.[48]

We are able to make certain generalizations about the early activities for special needs children. These took place largely in the private sector, but the state was beginning to assume some responsibility for them. Whereas, in the earliest days of Western civilization, children showing signs of some acute disability were simply done away with, they were now accorded the right to live and even learn some productive skills. This was a period of humanitarian protection in which special institutions were set up to provide for the disabled.[49] Those critical of the period might claim that the children were institutionalized so that they would be "hidden away" from society, but that is only a partial explanation of the situation. It would be accurate to say that Norway, and all of Europe, had not yet reached the point that these youth would systematically be given the assistance necessary to become integrated into society. Certainly, they were not accorded the privilege of joining together with the rest of the youth as an integral part of the people's school.

While the folk school claimed to include most people, those young people moving beyond that school into the more practical spheres of work world were forced to rely on educational channels that were not yet recognized as a part of the educational system. We look more closely at those channels in the next chapter.

11 Workers and Their Education

The emergence of Norway as an advanced industrial-commercial state had altered the very nature of its social structure. Two traditional social groups which we described in Chapter One were fundamentally altered in the process. The rising burgher class of the eighteenth century had actually become absorbed into the official class, the bureaucrats, or civil servants. The group that actually transformed the Norwegian economy, the new burgher class, the entrepreneurs, the risk takers, the industrialists, were typically sons of that small middle class consisting of sea captains, ship owners, and small business people, or they were immigrants coming out of Denmark or northern Germany, who came attempting to make good in this underdeveloped land.[1]

The technical skills which the early entrepreneurs possessed were relatively superficial. The machinery they used was imported and the technical personnel needed to repair and adjust the machines were initially imported as well. By the turn of the century, however, Norway had come to possess its own corps of highly skilled technicians and engineers. By and large, these had actually been trained in the technical schools outside Norway, particularly in Germany. By 1910, Norway would finally have its own Institute of Technology at Trondheim, where its own engineers and technical experts could be trained.[2]

The second major social group, described in Chapter One, undergoing dramatic change, was the cotter class, that underprivileged group of tenant farmers, who had stood on the fringes of society, without a legal voice in politics and with little means to raise themselves out of their status beyond their own sense of personal worth. During the last half of the nineteenth century, the cotter class simply disappeared as an identifiable group. Surely, many of them became small farmers, but most of them moved into the towns where they formed the nucleus of a new class of people, a so-called working class.[3] It is questionable if that transition represented a true improvement in the lot of the old cotter class, but the one thing it did provide, was a concentration of people sufficient to organize themselves and demand redress for injustices. Whereas those of the cotter class, even in the days of Markus Thrane, were too dispersed to organize themselves effectively, the industrial workers were concentrated so that they could organize, and organize they did.

These changes brought about radical realignments in the political sphere. The Labor Party was formed in 1887, although it was for some years almost nonexistent in terms of successful participation in the electoral process. In 1903, it made its first successful bid for *Storting* representation, gaining four seats. Prior to this the party tended to support Liberal candidates, at least on the national level, rather than run its own candidates.[4] The Labor Party was the most radical of the many parties coming into existence at the time, being socialist and advocating nationalizing the means of production.

Other alignments were also taking place. The Conservatives, for example, had been dominated in the past by the civil servants, but they were becoming the party of the urban middle class, the industrialists and the commercial leaders.

During this period of time the political process was focused on the Swedish union, and the country finally became an independent state in 1905, which contributed mightily to a state of optimism. Just prior to World War I Norway was in a state of euphoria, having entered a period of good will, self assurance, prosperity and freedom.

Central to the feeling of independence was the expression that Norway was an open society where every member had worth and the right to participate in the decisions that guided the country. The notion of direct elections to the *Storting*, of proportional representation, of universal suffrage were all realized in the first two decades of the twentieth century. Male suffrage was introduced in 1898, allowing workers and tenant farmers the opportunity to vote. Female suffrage was also introduced by the reforms of 1902, 1907, and 1913, which contributed further to the already altered political picture.

It was fortuitous that in the decade following independence from Sweden the economy of Norway exploded. The country had witnessed "an astonishing growth in the number of small farms" immediately after 1905.[5] These averaged less than 10 acres but they also gave access to outlying pastures and woods, hunting and fishing that increased the value of farming. The fishing industry was becoming modernized with motorization and the use of the steam engine. This added both to the value of large fishing enterprises, but also to the possibility of smaller vessels and inexpensive equipment. Weather monitoring also diminished the dangers of the sea.

Railroading had entered a new era after 1908, when many lines were authorized throughout the Southern part of the country. At the same time the shipping industry also experienced great growth, especially with steamers and tankers becoming the dominant mode of shipping.

Industrial expansion also took an upswing as the number of laborers increased by sixty-six percent between 1905 and 1914. A major reason for this growth was the development of electrical power stations throughout the land. Water power was quickly turned into electrical power, which led to paper mills and wood pulp factories, chemical plants, and mining mills.

As more and more young people were entering into the modern work world, the industrial labor force spoke with a sense of competence but a sense of need for new programs to be taken on by the schools. Actually, vocational schooling had a long tradition in Norway. As we noted in Chapter Three, it was already firmly established in Norway at the time of independence in 1814. Of course, it continued to grow and become regularized during the nineteenth century, although it remained, in most spheres, mainly a private enterprise.

VOCATIONAL AND TECHNICAL SCHOOLING

Schools and training opportunities became more and more plentiful during the nineteenth century, helping young workers gain skills necessary to work in factories, in shipping, in the commercial world and even on the farms, but those enterprises were initially not thought of as the responsibility of the state, nor were they considered to be part of the "educational system." One reads in vain for any reference to vocational schooling in the standard historical accounts of education during the century. It is almost as if vocational schools did not exist. However, a rich tradition had come into being. That tradition merits some description, and in the next pages we shall outline the evolution of vocational programs in shipping, crafts and technical skills, commerce, and farming.

Seaman's Schools

At the time of independence in 1814, at least six seaman's schools were in operation in Norway. By the 1850s and 60s, the shipping industry had expanded to the point that it had reached what some describe as its "golden age."[6] At that time public seaman's schools could be found in Fredrikstad, Fredrikshald, Kristiania, Drammen, Arendal, Grimstad, Kristiansand, Mandal, Stavanger, Bergen, Kristiansund, and Tromsø. In 1868 alone at least 1,076 students were attending school at these seventeen institutions, and 450 passed the qualifying examination.[7]

At the same time, a far greater number of young sailors were taking private instruction. In Chistiania alone, over a five year period between 1864 and 1868, only 81 (14%) of the 580 candidates being examined at the school had actually attended the school, while another 499 (86%) had prepared for the examination through private instruction. This does not mean the young men were privately tutored; rather, private teachers were running their own narrow courses preparing groups of boys for nothing but the examination. One private teacher, Hans Anderson, boasted of having no less than 97 students in a single year. O. Mikkelson was restricted to teaching only 60 students a year because the hall he rented held no more. As would be expected, the private students had a much higher examination failure rate (40%) than did the public seaman's schools (21%).[8]

We might look more closely at the Christiania school to gain a greater perspective of such schools. It was begun relatively late compared with many other schools, mainly because that town had never been a major center of the shipping industry. Finally, in 1845 the school was begun on the initiative of a businessman and a sea captain, because they were attracted to the advantages of the local public auction fund (*auktionsfond*), that was made available to supplement tuition and small sums of money from the town treasury.

Such was the case until 1863, when the school began receiving support from the state on condition that it conform to special conditions. To qualify for funds, the school was directed to provide instruction at three levels: navigator, mate, and seaman proper. The administration was also defined in such a manner as to make it a fully public institution.[9]

In 1867 a fourth level of instruction was added: the skipper class. This provided the highest type of instruction available at the time with a program that included the study of Norwegian language, accounting, English, seamanship, meteorology, and writing.[10]

Toward the end of the century, still other types of schools came into existence, training personnel having to do with the sea. For example, a sea stewards (cooking) school was established in Sandefjord in 1893 sponsored by the Norwegian Shippers Association. This was in response to a movement begun in Great Britain some twenty years earlier. With this successful endeavor, an appeal was made to the *Storting* to support such activities. Having received the assurance that state support was available, other schools came into existence in nine other towns, although they were quickly brought under stricter control so that by 1915 only the schools at Bergen, Fredrikshald, Drammen, and Stavanger continued to operate.[11]

Craft and Technical Schools

At the time of independence in 1814 most craft and technical skills were being learned under a master tutor arrangement for journeymen and apprentices. However, even at that time the value of general skills and theoretical training was recognized. This training was being given to budding craftsmen in part-time courses conducted in the evenings and on Sundays, where workers learned writing, calculating, drawing, geometry and other subjects. Over the years the number of schools increased throughout the country so that by 1840, seventeen such institutions could be found in Norway.[12]

In the early period after independence the rules governing the qualifications of journeymen and masters remained essentially in effect in Norway. Consequently, the evening and Sunday schools addressed themselves to these specific demands. It was, of course, recognized that more general learnings would enhance the quality of craftsmen, and as new institutions, such as the Crafts and Art Industry School in Christiania (1818), the Graphics School run by *Det nyttige selskab* in Bergen (1824), and the Skien graphics school (1832), attempted to provide basic skills learnings as well as crafts learnings.

In a significant move, the *Storting* resolved to provide financial support for these three schools as early as the 1830s, which established a tradition of state support for workers education. But the most important action taken by the *Storting* in that decade was an 1839 law which shifted regulations regarding standards for craftsmen. For example, a master must now be able to "calculate with accuracy, write plainly and use the language tolerably correctly." The law also stipulated that in twenty-one named crafts the master must be able to do graphics with competence.[13] This ruling placed unusual stress on the value of drawing, graphics, and even architecture in the craft spheres. This was reinforced by an 1848 *Storting* decision to support graphics schools for some years, including the Drammen school begun in 1845. In fact, the Norwegian Art Academy, run by the Art Association, was actually converted into a graphics school for handworkers in 1869, because the school had, for all practical purposes, been doing that kind of training for several years.[14]

The 1840s and 50s were important decades in the development of the Norwegian economy and vocational education. Probably the most important public figure acting as a driving force for both these spheres of activity was Frederik Stang, who was appointed to head the Department of Interior in 1845. Stang would ultimately be identified as one of the important conservative politicians of the century. In the 1830s he had been a supporter of Welhaven in his conflict with Wergeland, but he recognized the necessity of technical competence if Norway were to realize its economic potential.

In 1847 Stang named a special commission which was charged with the responsibility of developing plans for a polytechnical institute. Its report came out in 1850 and in it the commission had conceptualized three classes of industrial workers; those requiring (1) scientifically trained engineers, (2) workers who could apply the results of scientific activity, and (3) handworkers needing crafts or graphics training.[15]

The major concrete consequence of this thinking was the establishment of Norway's first technical school, *Hortens tekniske skole*, which was so named because it existed as a part of the industrial works at Horten, just south of Christiania along the Oslo fjord. The school began operations in 1855 with an 18 month training program in mechanics, both theoretical and practical.[16]

The three major categories set by the 1847 commission held somewhat firmly in a later plan drawn up by physics professor H. Christie, who was asked in 1867 to develop a national technical training system. Based on a trip to Sweden and Denmark, were he saw a number of institutions, Christie drew up a fairly lengthy description which was ultimately submitted to the *Storting* in 1868.[17] In the plan he recommended three levels of schools:

1. Sunday and evening schools that were already in existence.
2. Elementary technical schools lasting three years, having no divisions and providing a general introduction to elementary knowledge and technical competence. It would include a practical component.

3. A polytechnical institute with one year of common instruction and two years of specialized instruction.

Christie's plan took almost immediate effect as representative Motzfeldt proposed to the *Storting* in 1868 that funds be appropriated for an institute similar to the polytechnic institute conceptualized by Christie and for an elementary technical school in Christiania. Funds for the higher institute were allocated a year later and a program was initiated in Trondheim.[18]

At first, the school, called the Trondheim Technical Training Institution (*Tekniske læreanstalt*), was housed at the Latin school and enrolled only fourteen students. It expanded quickly and by 1890 it was nearing the quality of an institution of higher learning. Its four major divisions were architecture, engineering, mechanics, and chemistry. In addition to the Trondheim school, funds had been appropriated for a school in Christiania. It opened its doors in 1873, was of the elementary technical school type, and provided common instruction for the three years rather than specialized instruction.

The city of Bergen, through the initiative of the local craft association, proposed in 1870 that an additional school be set up in that location, using local funds. Fortunately for the association, before the school got under way, the *Storting* approved funding for it. It began instruction in 1875, with courses in mathematics, mechanics, graphics, physics, chemistry, and statistics.[19]

We must keep in mind that all of this activity was outside the realm of the Department of Church and Education. It was 1878 before technical education was formally moved from the Department of Interior to Church and Education.[20] When that was accomplished, a commission was set up to consider how to organize technical education throughout the country. Its report, issued in 1880, was that three main classes of schools should exist, essentially replicating the 1847 and the Christie conceptualizations:

1. A four year institute of higher learning.
2. Two year technical schools, divided by specialization.
3. Technical evening schools.

The commission recognized that the evening schools ought to be allowed to exercise complete local control. They had become enormously successful in providing general training to those in the work world and apprentices. In fact, 1878 is the year these schools reached their peak in terms of popularity, with over 2,213 schools providing instruction to

20,790 boys and 7,438 girls, mainly in Norwegian and calculating with a little composition, geography, history, singing and other subjects thrown in.[21]

Actually, the involvement of the Department of Church and Education does not appear to have done much at the time in terms of enhancing technical education. Even the evening schools quickly died out, although some of this can be explained in terms of the emergence of continuation schools as a part of general education. It was also during this time that more specialized vocational schools began to appear. Thus, we find Skien's *Fjordens mekaniske fagskole* (1885), Bergen's *Fagskole for træ- og metalindustri* (1887), and Christiania's *Elementærtekniske dagskole* (1893), providing expanded versions of the evening schools in day-programs. These educational options were not just available to boys. In fact, *Den kvinnelige industriskole*, a school for women came into existence in 1875. Gude-Smith was at the time chair of a commission leading the Association for the Advancement of Women's Handwork services and had traveled to Germany and France only to return with a plan for a Norwegian school like those she had seen abroad. The Association carried the major share of finances, along with student tuition, until 1888 when the Department of Church and Education assumed major responsibility.

These funds were given in recognition of the importance workers education had come to play in the country. As yet, all of these schools were not linked in any conceptual way with the rest of the system. In fact, they were administratively not yet under the Department of Church and Education. This would begin to change in 1898, when the Department was finally given jurisdiction over the schools. The Department quickly recognized that certain adjustments must be made in the structure of things if technical schools were to become rationalized with the rest of the system. The first important decision to come down was that a technical institute of higher education must be set up to satisfy the pressing needs of advanced technology. The *Storting* concluded, in 1900, that the institute would be established at Trondheim, and a decade later it opened its doors to the first students.[22]

The Department also recognized that most vocational schooling was taking place in evening schools, where apprentices and other workers were engaged in part-time education. Between 1878 and 1913 a number of very large evening schools came into existence throughout the country. One of these enrolled no less than 809 pupils in one year alone (1913), another 361, and another 263; several others enrolled more than 100 pupils, while the majority had less than 100 students. Even so, this constituted several thousand students.[23]

While the existing technical schools would satisfy the vocational education requirements of those young people just finishing the folk school, it was decided that another "middle-level" school must come into existence for those young people who had passed through the middle school but did not plan to qualify for higher education studies.

Consequently, in 1911 a new school, a middle technical school, was defined. Admission requirements would be the middle school leaving examination or its equivalent, and the school would provide a two year program in technical chemistry, building technology, machine technology, electronics, and ship building. The schools were allowed to provide preparation courses lasting for six months for folk school leavers, who wished to prepare for this skill level. A passing examination score would be required for all candidates.[24]

Thus, we find that the schools for those in the craft and technical fields had finally begun to become a part of the total system of education. A similar pattern of activity is found with the training of commercial skills.

Commercial Schools

Commercial schools in Norway came on the scene somewhat later than the seaman and technical schools. One reason for this is because the *real* schools, which were specifically designed for the burgher classes, often included some commercial component in them. Even when the common higher school reforms of 1869 had created a middle school as the institution beyond the common school, private *real* schools continued to exist in sufficient numbers to allow for some commercial learnings to take place. In addition, it was possible for private tutoring and apprenticeship arrangements to be made. Still another option was for commercial study to occur in foreign countries, particularly Germany.

Within the business community a continual thrust could be found for commercial schooling to be initiated, but it was 1875 before the first such institution, the Christiania *Handelsgymnasium*, came into existence. That was originally a two year school with a dual purpose of giving a foundation in commercial understanding as well as a general education. The school was founded by the Christiania Commercial Community Association, which had been reorganized in 1872 and had laid down as one of its three major goals "to realize the extension of commercial, scientific, and general education."[25]

The committee responsible for developing the plan for the school considered but rejected those purely vocational models so often found in Germany, and they opted for a less popular German model found in cities such as Dresden, Leipzig, and Chemnitz, which provided a full general education in connection with the vocational training. Because of financial and practical constraints, the Christiania Association opted for an abbreviated two year program.

The Association realized that it could not survive without partial community support, so it petitioned to have community representation on the board, then requested that Christiania supplement the funds donated by generous members of the commercial world. By taking on the name "*gymnasium*," the Association also committed itself to a certain admission standard, i.e. middle-school examination, although it did make provision for exceptions.

Because the *Handelsgymnasium* had chosen to be a more general institution, a need remained for training possibilities of a strictly vocational nature. Otto Treider, a bookkeeper in Christiania, saw the possibilities of a private venture and in 1882 he opened a private school and gave it his name. The school offered one year, six month, and three month courses. With such competition, the *Handelsgymnasium* was forced to begin offering its own short courses and it also quickly opened its doors to women students.[26]

Over the years, other communities opened their own *Handelsgymnasier*, using the Christiania model.[27] Private commercial ventures became even more popular, so that almost every town of any size came to possess at least one private commercial school.

The Farm and Forest Schools

Farming has traditionally been the most resistant to change and innovation. The farm was traditionally passed from father to son, and the skills needed to conduct farming were similarly inherited.

As with most other practical spheres, the first agricultural school was private, set up in 1825 by Jacob Sverdrup on the estate of Count Wedel-Jarlsberg, where he served as manager. The school introduced the upper classes to the latest farming practices, but it also included four farm boys each of the first two years and eight boys in each of the next years as "private students."[28]

In succeeding years two other private schools were set up. Peter Sverdrup, the oldest son of Jacob, started a second farm school on Jarlsberg's farm at Rise in 1827. Just as his father had done, Peter maintained a practice orientation, rather than concentrating on theory and general studies.[29] A third private school came into existence in 1843 at Linnes in Baskerud Amt, set up by a former student of Jacob.

The government had passed a law in 1837 that encouraged the support of farm schools, but it quickly found such a move to be rather expensive and it took a compromise move in 1842 by making 2,400 national dollars. (600 maximum per school) available to communities or private groups interested in starting their own schools. Another 4,000 national dollars was made available in 1845, this time coupled with the condition that a district must commit itself with matching funds, and also that at least one school be in each county.[30]

In the next years, a remarkable array of county farm schools came into existence. By 1848, schools were found in twelve of the eighteen counties, and five years later only Oslo, Tromsø, and Finnmark were lacking such schools. In 1857 the high water mark was reached with eighteen schools, then in the next decade the number of schools declined again until only six schools were in operation during most of the 1870s.

There are a number of reasons why the schools declined so rapidly after such a glowing start. Hasund and Nesheim suggest the following: 1) The number of qualified teachers could not keep up with the number of schools coming into existence, and the educational quality dropped after a time. 2) The schools came into existence in relatively good times and the state began to cut back on its share of the costs in the 1860s, leaving the counties to carry a larger burden. 3) The farm movement, led by Søren Jaabæk, had a clear socio-political character. In the early period the official class not only supported farm school developments, but usually supplied its leaders and teachers. However, as farmers participated actively in the labor movement of the early 1850s they began to challenge that leadership in their schools, which resulted in a decline of support on the part of the official class. 4) The schools had no firm base. It was not possible to buy a separate farm, in many instances, and over the years the schools shifted from place to place, bringing further instability. 5) Most of the students had received only a common school education in the countryside, which meant they could often not even adequately compose a written document. The level of instruction was rather primitive in many instances.[31]

As a consequence, the schools began to disappear and farming education went through a period of real stagnation. In the mid-1890s a second cycle of farming education came into being and by 1900, no less than twenty farm schools were running. This number held steady for a decade then rose to thirty-eight schools in 1920 and forty-one schools by 1925. In the new cycle the schools were much more developed and each typically enrolled two to three times as many students as did the schools in the earlier cycles.

There are a number of reasons why the second cycle came into being. Farming, as we have noted, had grown rapidly and because the farms were small farmers needed the best techniques to be successful. In addition, modern standards were being applied, requiring a sense of competence and occupational pride. It was becoming more and more important to diversify the types of crops and to expand into untapped spheres, such as fur farming. Finally, and probably most importantly, in 1893 the *Storting* declared itself prepared to assume 3/4 of the costs of each farm school, although it also placed tight control over schools.[32]

One of the interesting developments in farming instruction after the turn of the century was so-called small farm-holder schools (*småbruksskoler*). In 1907 the Ministry of Agriculture Farm Committee began working on the possibility of improving the quality of small farm holdings. After many years, the *Storting* proposed an instructional program based on the work of the committee. The school would run during the winter months with the prospect that the students could engage in an apprenticeship during the summer months, although they could do practice on their own farm if necessary.[33] A law was passed in 1915, and the first school went into immediate operation in Asker. Most of the instruction actually took place during the first years in several folk high schools, although a number of schools sprang up after World War I.

GENERAL VOCATIONAL EDUCATION DEVELOPMENTS

Vocational education was taken for granted to be a private enterprise in the early nineteenth century. In fact, so deeply was vocational education embedded in the private sector that Jaabæk used it as a major argument against state support for higher common schooling. "The same fundamental thinking, which has held for commerce, for crafts and work," he argued, "must also hold for the position which people take regarding the learned school."[34] That meant that the state should do very little for the learned school, that it ought to be seen as a "privilege" to engage in it and not as something connected with "public" education. Vocational education was typically conducted by associations connected with a particular type of work. These went by names such as the Christiania Seamans Association (*Christiania Sjømandsforening*), the Bergen Craft Association (*Bergen Håndverkerforening*), the Christiania Commercial Community Association (*Christiania Handelstands Forening*). These associations usually appealed to the local communities to help them run a particular school. In most cases where schools were set up, the town or community took on some responsibility for assisting vocational training, even though it was mainly a private affair. And so we see communities participating by providing space in common schools, by proving officials to oversee programs, by supervising examinations, or by providing outright grants of money.

Farming deviates in some respects from this pattern in that the initiative for schools came from the public sector with substantial public funds either from the state or the counties. Even here, however, a small number of private schools maintained a successful program throughout the century.

The state typically became initially involved in vocational schooling by defining by law the kinds of qualifications necessary to perform specific tasks. For example, the first law on navigation was passed in Norway in 1839, which defined the means by which an individual could qualify to be a navigator or a skipper, and also included specific spheres of knowledge that the candidate must demonstrate.[35]

Eventually, the state would begin to participate in the support of quasi-public schools. In the process, the state would begin to define the nature of the programs of study. Some of these institutions even became state or county enterprises.

In spite of this, a substantial private dimension continued. Some of this was in the form of strictly private schools somewhat reminiscent of Heltberg's student factory, which drilled aspiring candidates for specific examinations, for a fee. Others were institutions that had taken on a quasi-public nature, receiving heavy contributions from the community and the state.

It is impossible to determine the relative significance of vocational schooling in comparison with other forms of higher common schooling, but we shall see that it had come to play a dominant role in the total educational enterprise by the turn of the twentieth century, in spite of the fact that vocational education had not yet been recognized as a part of the educational system of Norway. Whole sectors even remained outside the jurisdiction of the Department of Church and Education. For example, farming education remained clearly a part of the Ministry of Agriculture. Nevertheless, by the turn of this century the educational establishment had at least come to notice the existence of vocational education, and some small inroads had been made in the system through continuation schools.

SCHOOLS FOR A PROGRESSIVE, INDUSTRIAL STATE

Even before the turn of the century, a growing sense of the importance of an understanding of the practical side of life had led to framers of the 1889 school law to require that boys be exposed to a crafts and the girls to a domestic studies program as a part of their general schooling at the folk school. In addition, a growing number of continuation schools were coming into being through local initiative, which maintained a craft, farming, or domestic studies orientation. These activities must be viewed as propaedeutic in nature and were simply too telescoped to provide more than a general understanding of the world of work. They could best be described as something akin to industrial arts, a liberal education about the work world, or work literacy more than occupational training comparable to that given in the vocational schools or through apprenticeship.

The activities were spurred as the New Education Movement began to permeate every culture of Europe, although it took on special characteristics in each culture. In Germany, for example the New Education Movement came in a four major spheres, including Country Home schools, Art Education, the Self-Directed Activity Movement, and the Activity School Movement.[36] In Norway, the major outlet for these values lay in the Activity School Movement, which had two major dimensions. First, it was connected with the notion of learning in a concrete, real environment. Second, it was connected with the notion that manual work has value.[37]

A major incentive toward the Activity School Movement came through the work of a folk school teacher, Anne Holsen, who received a stipend to travel to Germany, Austria, and Switzerland in 1897 to study continuation schools. Indeed, she found a number of good models. She was particularly impressed with the programs in Bavaria, where Georg Kerschensteiner, superintendent of schools at Munich had revolutionized the schools in his district.[38] Kerschensteiner recognized that all schooling in his country was plagued with a distant, abstract, and alienating form of learning. The children were not engaged in vital, real experiences, but in meaningless exercises, which were not connected with the demands of real life. It was his conviction that general education must become connected and integrated with vocational education. Character education must become attached to a sense of service and productivity in the community. The best instrument to achieve these ends was the vocationally oriented activity school.

After having observed schools practicing these ideals, Holsen returned to Christiania with the objective of changing the situation in her country. She was joined by a colleague at her folk school, Anna Rogstad, and together they lectured to those who would listen that most young people leaving the folk school at the age of 14 years have no other alternative than to enter the work world for their "daily bread." The only schooling alternative open to them were academic institutions or special vocational schools. There was no institution that brought the two together. Their solution was to develop: a general education school, that does not lead away from productive work, but which enhances it and respects it, while simultaneously develops and supports the ethical and religious impulses in people.[39]

There were schools in Europe, which had realized that aim, particularly in Munich and Leipzig, but also in other places. They were there, in place, and the Norwegians needed only to emulate them.

Indeed, within a year Christiania introduced some small continuation classes, which they chose to call *fortsettelsesklasser*, rather than the more conventional *framhaldsklasser*. The two women were even able to get a small stipend to begin continuation classes at their own folk school, which enrolled its first girls in 1900. Of course, this was not the first such program. We recall that Article 1 of the 1889 school law had made provisions for a countryside community to establish brief continuation classes, but the movement had not yet realized its potential. In 1900, there were only 191 continuation schools in the entire country,[40] and the figure had actually declined to 182 schools by 1910,[41] although it rose to 223 schools by 1920.[42] Approximately 70% of all young people leaving the folk school were not going on to any further schooling, and a major reason was that they were expected to pay heavily toward their own schooling.[43]

For dedicated teachers such as Holsen and Rogstad, it was an insult that the girls must pay tuition, so a campaign was launched, first with the Norwegian Women Teachers Association, but their ultimate goal was the Department of Church and Education, which eventually passed a law in 1908 providing for continuation schools in the towns giving courses lasting from four to ten hours a week. With this provision, the women focused directly on Christiania and were finally able to realize a full continuation school in 1909, at least as an evening school. Finally, seven years later the school was able to initiate a full day school program for girls.[44] Because the two above mentioned laws had used the term *fortsettelsesskoler* rather than *framhaldsskoler*, which had become the conventional term in the countryside, the countryside continuation schools and the city continuation schools took on two different names. The city continuation schools quickly became identified for their vocational orientation, while the lack of middle schools in the countryside forced a large percentage of them to continue with a more theoretical, academic program, as a substitute for the middle schools.

The ultimate aim of those early advocates was some general policy on the part of the Department of Church and Education. That did not occur until 1919, when the Department finally mandated a general review of continuation schooling. A nine person committee was named, including Anna Rogstad, which submitted a full report two years later. That report was sympathetic with a full development of the schools serving a dual role: providing an introduction into the world of work as well as furthering the intellectual development of participants.[45]

Thus, the public sector became a partner with the private sector in ensuring that the growing labor force of Norway would be adequately prepared. We shall see that deliberations about the role of vocational education were taken up by the commission that would ultimately define schooling in the mid-1930s. However, it would be 1940 before the first modern law regulating vocational schools would be passed.

Of course, the Activity School Movement did not remain restricted to continuation schools. Primarily through the efforts of enterprising women such as Anna Sethne in Oslo and Frida Lund in Bergen, progressive education ideas became a part of a whole inner school movement in the country, helping to transform the school into a social institution as much as an instructional institution.[46]

Section IV

Third Reform Cycle — Toward a Unified School

12 Education in a Free Norway: 1905 and Beyond

In 1905 the formal union between Norway and Sweden came to an abrupt end. It had been a union lasting for over ninety years, based almost entirely on political rather than cultural or spiritual bonds. Because the union with Sweden had been limited to political relations, primarily connected with foreign affairs, education policy was rarely bound in any significant way with Sweden. The break with Sweden in 1905 did provide the Norwegians with a new sense of freedom, a strengthened sense of courage and self-assurance. In addition, the first decade after independence represented a period of economic prosperity that allowed policy makers to set their sights on an expanded role of rural education and a broader view of secondary education.

The 1889 and 1896 school laws had represent watershed marks in Norwegian schooling. The conventional dualistic European school, that had been imported to the country was now broken, having been replaced by a Norwegian oriented school system possessing a five year foundation school. The Liberal Party, which had carried the reform sentiments of the last century to a successful conclusion, was able to retain its power in the *Storting* between 1905 and 1918, with the exception of the 1909 elections. And so, the first years following these laws represented a time of incremental change, of solidifying and adding to the school form that was in place.

The first decade of the new century draws the previous reform movement to a conclusion, and it also represents the beginning of a new reform cycle that is not completed until the 1950s. The initial issues of this cycle focused on (1) the fate of the middle school, (2) the emergence of the countryside *gymnas*, (3) the brief revival of classical studies, and (4) the prospects of comprehensive education through the first seven years of schooling.

THE DILEMMA OF THE MIDDLE SCHOOL

During the *Storting* debate on the budget for the higher common school in 1909, a full discussion ensued regarding the relationship between the folk school and the middle school.[1] Some Liberals and the budding Labor Party members were pushing for an extension of the folk school so that the full seven years would constitute the foundation program of the middle school, which would consequently be required to reduce its program from three years to two years of schooling.

The Conservatives expressed grave reservations about the ability of the full seven year folk school serving as a foundation school for the middle school, there was some empirical data to support that position. The town of Gjøvik, across the lake from Hamar, had tried a seven year folk school plan leading to a two year middle school, but the operation had been abandoned because too many of the children had failed the middle school leaving examination.[2]

In addition, the Conservative position was given leverage by the existence of an extensive private school operation in the towns. In fact, 17.1% of all compulsory school children in Norway were gaining education outside the public sector in 1900/01. This had dropped to 13.9% a decade later, but still represented the absence of a large part of the children of the better classes in the public folk schools, at least in the towns.[3]

The situation was even more challenging to school authorities when they looked at the middle schools and *gymnasier*. In 1900 there were only twenty-three middle schools in the entire country holding the right to give the middle school leaving examination, fourteen of which were in Kristiania, four in Bergen, two in Drammen and one each in Trondheim, Stavanger, and Fredrikstad.[4] These included those distinguished private institutions such as Quams School and Gjerstens School, which provided so many of the examination passes. The number of middle schools had increased to forty-six by 1911-12; but 28.5% of the students remained in private schools.[5] If government policy pushed too far, there would likely be a shift back toward the private sector, which would be untenable to the Liberals and Laborites.

The major solution to the relatively poor performance of middle school students who had completed the seven year folk school was not a happy one. In 1900, Kristiania had decided to try and overcome such deficiencies by establishing some three year middle schools that would take in the brighter youngsters from the working classes who had completed the full folk school, because they had not previously considered going beyond that point.[6] It had proved to be successful, but it had also added a full year to the student's program. In 1908, the *Storting* tried to ensure that the town folk schools would provide adequate instruction by mandating a minimum of thirty hours a week in the so-called small schools and thirty-six hours a week in the others.[7]

In the countryside, the stress points pushed the issue of the middle school in a different direction. Higher schooling was, for all intents and purposes, still an urban enterprise, which placed an enormous hardship on families in the countryside wishing to have their children engage in higher studies but also wishing to keep their children at home. In addition, the old distinction between town and country was no longer nearly so marked. The urban dwellers, many of whom had come to the towns in the last part of the previous century, felt an affinity for the country through family ties and a growing appreciation for their folk heritage. An expanded communications network also allowed them the possibility to participate in outdoor sports activities, to build cottages in remote places, to take vacations in isolated areas. The mountains, the woods, the lakes, the farms constituted a cherished part of what it meant to be a Norwegian.

The rural dweller was also able to participate in the advantages of urban life in a way that had never before been possible. Energy sources provided electrical lighting and heating. Store bought articles were becoming plentiful. Fashion, books, manufactured furniture, and finer foods were becoming a part of rural life. The disparity between countryside and town was disappearing. This melding of society translated itself into important social policies. For example, in 1910 and again in 1917 the *Storting* adopted an extensive language reform, which brought *bokmaal* much closer to *landsmaal* in its written form and also much closer to the daily speech of the people.[8] In conjunction with these changes, it became clearer that some mechanism was necessary to allow the countryside children access to institutions of higher learning without engaging in costly home teaching or forcing them to leave home and reside in the towns.

In 1911, the Department of Church and Education organized two special school committees to explore possible solutions to the issues being raised both in the towns and the countryside. Each committee came up with important recommendations that would be adopted within the decade.

THE LANDSGYMNAS

One committee was given the charge of exploring the situation related to those middle schools having the right to offer the school leaving examination. Since 1869 the middle school leaving examination had served as a prerequisite to admission to the *gymnasium* and the right to take the *examen artium*. This placed a real hardship on the young people from the countryside, because the middle schools were, for all intents and purposes, town schools. The 1911 committee issued its report in 1913,[9] and policy deriving from the work of the countryside committee was adopted prior to the beginning of the war.[10] It did not have much impact in terms of actual practice, but it did contribute to the creative use of certain institutions and legitimize their activities. Folk schools in the countryside were engaging in continuation programs, which gave instruction to young people who had graduated from the seven year folk school. These were similar to the folk high school programs in that they did not lead to formal certificates or to further schooling.

In contrast to continuation schools in the towns, which had become more and more practical and vocational, the countryside continuation schools had remained rather theoretical and general, but they had not served as stepping stones for young people wishing to go into higher studies, because it was necessary for a student to have passed the middle school leaving examination in order to qualify for the *examen artium*. If a young person in the countryside wished to go on to higher studies, it was necessary for him/her to leave home at the end of the fifth year of the folk school and journey to where a middle school was found. Even then, the young student would be disadvantaged because of language differences between town and countryside.

The Department committee recommended that the middle school be bypassed in the countryside, and that young people could participate in an expanded continuation school program, then enroll in a *gymnasium* program that would be extended one full year. In other words, the two year middle school would be replaced by one year, actually six months of study, at the continuation school or an *amt* school and one extra year at a so-called *landsgymnasium*.

The *Storting* approved a plan for such *gymnasier* in 1914, and the first school actually opened its doors in 1916 at Voss. A private *landsgym-*

nasium came into being at Horten in 1918 and became a public school four years later. The Eidsvoll *landsgymnasium* admitted its first students in 1922.[11] The term *landsgymnasium* was shortened in many cases to the term *landsgymnas*. The term *gymnas* eventually gained currency in the Norwegian language, and the term *gymnasium* slowly disappeared.

A number of private endeavors with the *landsgymnas* were successful. In fact, the first private school, which was at Volda, had been set up as early as 1910. In the 1920s other schools were set up at Firda, Orkdal, Rogaland and Steinkjer, but it was after World War II before they were recognized as public schools.[12]

Built on the assumption that the schooling background of the students would be deficient, a typical program demanded no less than seven hours of instruction a day and added certain other requirements. The *landsgymnasium* notion was not only a mechanism to provide countryside youth with a more equal opportunity for access to higher education. It also represented an institution that could be based on the old Norwegian culture and the medium of instruction would be *landsmaal* rather than *bokmaal*. That was not the original intention of the framers of the institution, but in 1922 Voss took the initiative to obtain a special line of study called a *norrøn* (Norse) line.[13]

Such an idea was not new. It had been suggested as early as 1868, and Knud Knudsen had written a book entitled *Latin School without Latin*, in 1884, whereby Norwegian literature, history, and Old Norwegian language would become the new classical study.[14] These were an explicit part of the folk high school movement, but Old Norwegian had never received serious consideration as a major part of a special line leading to the *examen artium*. The board of directors at Voss petitioned the Department of Church and Education to allow them such a privilege, but the matter became a part of the considerations of the Parliamentary School Commission, which met from 1922 to 1927, and would also have to be cleared by the historical-philosophical faculty of the university before the *Storting* would approve it in 1931.[15] The reason for that delay must be considered in a somewhat broader context, having to do with the temporary revival of the classics at the *Gymnasium*.

CLASSICS AT THE GYMNASIUM

The classical imprint of the schools had been declared obsolete by the 1896 directives, although the classics were allowed to continue in some schools. In fact, the number of students following the Latin stream remained extensive. As we see in Table 12.1[16], at the turn of the century twenty-eight percent of all graduates from the *gymnasium* were in classics, and that percentage held steady until the World War I years.

Table 12.1

Students Passing the Secondary School Leaving Examination between 1901 and 1940

	Latin	Science	English
1901-1905	126	247	63
1906-1910	151	208	137
1911-1915	201	350	181
1916-1920	297	508	211
1921-1925	517	685	357
1926-1930	654	702	359
1931-1935	654	762	427
1936-1940	603	762	427

We must keep in mind, however, that the *gymnasium* had been reduced to three years in 1869, and in 1896 the first of these three years maintained a common curriculum, which did not include Latin. In other words, Latin study was for only two years. Greek had long disappeared, so the "classics" now consisted of a little Latin grammar and the reading of a few selected texts.

The impact of these developments was best seen with the decline of Latin students at the university, where several graduating classes in the pre-World War I years did not have a single Latin major.[17] The battle against the classics had already been won, and "the classical heritage was no longer an enemy to be taken seriously, but just relatively unimportant, irrelevant to the vital problems of the time.[18]

After the war, classical studies experienced a brief revival. Greek was readmitted as an oral subject, and because the university began demanding Latin language preparation in several faculties, the secondary students once again flowed to the Latin stream of the *gymnas*. In fact, from Table 12.1 we see that almost 35% of all graduates in the 1920s were from that stream. In addition, the *gymnasium* ordinance of 1919 allowed differentiation to take place in the first year rather than allowing it only in the second and third year.[19]

A number of factors account for the Latin revival. Skard highlights three major elements.[20] First, Norwegians recognized that they had reacted more radically than necessary to the classics, which constituted a definite element of their own cultural roots and heritage. Scholars of history, art and literature had turning once again to antiquity as a source of research data and inspiration. Second, scholars interested in Norwegian antiquity were now able to shed the ethnocentrism that had earlier been brought on partly in defense of their own infant field of inquiry. They began to admit the importance of broader antiquity studies to their own work. Serious attempts were made by scholars such as archaeologist, Haakon Shetelig, the Old Norse student, Fr. Paasche, and the classical philologist, Eiliv Skard, to connect Norway's roots more firmly with broader Western classicism.[21] Third, in a more indirect way, other scholars recognized the links of a more contemporary Norway with the broader European currents. If Norway was connected with those currents, she was, at least indirectly, connected with the roots from which those currents sprang.

In spite of the rebirth of classical interests, there remained a real difference in the present and past role of the classics. In the past, to be educated was almost synonymous with having a common educational heritage. The claim had been that the classics represented the highest expression of mankind and anyone who would possess the qualities that set man apart from the animals, would possess a classical background. The Norwegians had challenged this claim, and had proclaimed that other courses of study were, if not more adequate, at least as adequate in helping to instill those traits that helped the young express the highest ideals of humanity.[22]

It is true that the decline of the classics was a general phenomenon throughout Europe, but the Norwegians had been much more resolute than others in transforming this thought into national policy. Not letting it die a natural death, they had consciously and deliberately rooted that tradition from their schools. Consequently, it is of little surprise that the revival of classical studies was short-lived. In the late 1920s the law and science faculties of the university abolished its Latin language requirements, and medicine reduced its requirements, with the consequence that the number of secondary students taking Latin fell dramatically. In the years 1935-1939 the percentage of students in the Latin stream had fallen to 16% and by 1949 it was 1.5%.[23] In the process, the way would be opened for other studies, including Old Norse, as the legitimate "Norwegian" classics. Much would happen, at least in terms of reform proposals by the time the Norse line was finally approved. The Unified School Committee, also named in 1911, would contribute greatly to the new reform cycle.

THE UNIFIED SCHOOL

The so-called Unified School Committee (*Enhetsskolekomiteen*)[24] was given the charge to come up with a proper plan for a two year middle school that would be built on the full seven year folk school.[25] The committee worked for two years and came up with a number of recommendations, including the recommended adoption of a folk school leaving examination, a reduction of the teacher-pupil ratio, an expanded number of hours in class, a greater uniformity in countryside schools, the introduction of a foreign language in the folk school, and a full proposal for a two year middle school program.[26]

These recommendations did not have unanimous support from the committee. Certain members strongly objected to the whole idea of a two year middle school, although even they recognized the value of working toward a full seven year common school. The committee did consider in its report the full range of options including a three year middle school beyond the seven year common school, a three year middle school beyond a six year common school, and the incorporation of variations in programs beyond the folk school, including the continuation programs.[27]

Neither the common school people nor the higher school people reacted positively to the recommendations.[28] The Department officials were also not taken with the proposals. They complained that the price to pay for this innovation, in terms of money, commitment, and program, would simply be too high, and their priorities were elsewhere.[29]

And within the leading political party, the Liberals, there was not yet the strong thrust for a seven year foundation school. In fact, it was 1915 before the Liberals established a party platform, that included the notion that the full folk school should serve as the common foundation school for all further schooling.[30] Even then, there was no consensus in the Party that the five year program that had been established in 1889 ought to be abandoned. The only party with a strong positive stand was the Labor Party, which had stepped forth with a full folk school proposal as early as 1900, but it possessed almost no power at the time.[31]

In spite of the fact that World War I broke out soon after the Unified School Committee issued its report, the review process continued. After considering all of the options that had been submitted, the Department of Church and Education chose to recommend one option that had been tried by Kristiania and a few other towns, and that had been recommended by Johan Gjøstein, one of the earliest important educational politicians from the Labor Party.[32] The normal school process would be the full folk school, followed by a three year middle school.[33] However, schooling arrangements included consideration of two, three, and four year middle schools, one and two year continuation schools, five, six, and seven year folk schools, four, five, and six year *gymnasier*, all working together to provide optional means to higher educational studies.

As long as the focus of attention was on the form or forms of the middle school, the entire issue remained muddied. As the time for a decision approached, the *Storting* shifted away from a focus on the middle school to the common folk school itself. That was the fundamental issue, and so the proposal came before the *Storting* to adopt the policy that the folk school serve as the only publicly supported foundation school.

Finally, the *Storting* acted on the recommendations on 20 March 1920, with a vote of 66-48 to the following proposal: "From the beginning of the school year 1921/22, state supported middle schools shall be built on full folk schools."[34] Missing in this proposal was any definition of a middle school. Remaining consistent with Liberal policy, the *Storting* recognized that the two, three, and four year middle schools would continue to exist, even though there was general agreement that the three year schools would be funded by the state. If a community wished to support any one of these types, they could, or if, through private initiative, they could be maintained, they were allowed to do so.

Thus, Norway had finally realized the full folk school as a preparatory institution for all other schooling programs. It had become the only institution which almost everyone was to attend during the first seven years of their schooling experience. The year 1920 marks one of the significant dates in Norway's educational history. More than that, Norway was the first country in Europe to realize that aim. The resolve of Sweden toward a similar end would not come until 1927, and that would allow transfer either in the fourth or the sixth year. Denmark, which had debated a similar possibility as Norway in 1920, would not even achieve a common school of four or five years until the end of the 1930s.[35] England, France, and Germany would not achieve such a goal until the 1930s and 1940s.

13 The Labor Party Takes Command

The years following World War I were sobering in many respects, as the country was thrown into economic turmoil that ended with the great depression. At the same time, political antagonisms led to further fragmentation and instability. The Labor Party even expressed a mounting distrust in parliamentary democracy, in part, because the representation process was not proportional. The party had won 32% of the vote in 1915, but had only been awarded 15 of the 123 seats in the *Storting*.[1] The representation process was changed in 1920, which added fuel to party fragmentation, because the proportional system allowed small parties to gain access to the *Storting*. In fact, the two party system that had dominated the scene since 1884 was replaced by a multiparty system. No political party was able to gain a political majority in the *Storting* between 1918 and 1945; Norway was not even able to coalesce its divisions enough to form a coalition cabinet prior to the period of exile during World War II.

Nevertheless, Karen Larsen reminds us: "In spite of sharp differences and bitter disputes between parties, classes, and schools of thought, there was a remarkable unanimity back of the efforts for social betterment" following World War I.[2] Even at this stage of Norway's development, the country was operating on what has been described as a consensual democracy.[3] Its social improvement agenda penetrated all facets of life. It became law that babies could not be burdened with a name that would cause it unhappiness. All children were to be given dental care, physical checkups, and instruction in hygiene. They were also relieved of unhealthy work requirements through a Labor Protection Act. Workers were provided with protection through the Unemployment Insurance Act. The retired were assisted through the Old Age Pension Act.

Schools were also the object of enormous attention. Even with the educational achievements of 1920, the decade of the 1920s is best known for engaging in a total assessment of Norway's educational system, which eventuated in important school laws that came, mainly after the mid-1930s. As early as 1919, the Church Committee of the *Storting* had once again taken up the issue of the unified school, but more particularly the issue that the common school, the continuation school, the middle school, and the *gymnasium* did not constitute an organic whole.

The Church Committee appealed to the government to establish a school commission to bring this about. It took a year for the Department of Church and Education to act, and finally in October, 1920, a "Great School Commission" was named, consisting of no less than 27 members, with Rector Anton Ræder as the foreman.[4]

At the time, the cabinet was dominated by the Liberals, who had been in power since 1914, and an immediate cry went up from the more radical parties, that the Commission had been balanced toward the conservative side. This agitation led to a crisis in the already unstable cabinet, leading to the resignation of the Minister of Church and Education, O. B. Halvorsen, who was replaced by J. L. Mowinckel. In spite of the fact that the Commission had been able to collect a good deal of information, including statistical data, the *Storting* quickly rendered the Great School Commission inoperable by withdrawing all its funds.[5]

THE PARLIAMENTARY SCHOOL COMMISSION

In place of the Great School Commission, the *Storting* named its own Parliamentary School Commission and invited Rector Ræder to act as its foreman.[6] Differing greatly from the previous commission, its members were largely politically more than professionally oriented, and its membership was tilted toward a more radical ideology.

That commission sat for five years, and by 1927 it had completed two major tasks. In 1924 it had issued a set of recommendations regarding teacher training institutions, and in 1927 its second major report had come forth having five divisions:

1. Commissions Appointment and the Unified Schools.
2. Law on Folk Schools in the Countryside.
3. Law on Folk Schools in the Free Towns

4. Law on Continuation Schools (*framhaldsskoler*) in the Country-side and Continuation Schools (*fortsettelsesskoler*) in the Free Towns.

5. Law on the Higher Common Schools.[7]

All reports had been written by Rector Ræder, who exercised a great influence on their form and content. Ræder had been for years one of the leading figures in school practice as well as school politics. He came from an established official class family and had been deeply trained in classical history and philology. His history texts had long been used in the middle school and *gymnasium*. He had been an active member of the Philological and Scientific Teachers Association, having served as its head. He had taught at the school run by Aars and Voss, and had established his own school, the Oslo *latin- og realskole*, and had served as head of the Kristiania Cathedral School. In addition, he had served as the Undersecretary of the Department of Church and Education, in charge of the primary and secondary schools.[8]

With such a background, it is easy to understand his desire to retain the best of the past in schooling. Most school people of his background would have preferred to function in their secondary schools undisturbed by the political winds blowing about them. Ræder recognized this was not possible and worked to bring about a sensible solution. Being a "charming and honorable" man, he was the ideal person to bring opponents to harmonious decisions.[9]

Curiously, the first commission report had to do with teacher training institutions. Rationally conceived, it would seem that teacher training should await decisions about the nature of the schools themselves, but a major issue necessitated a clarification of the status of the teacher training schools. A teacher surplus had come to plague the common school system, mainly because the rate of increase in the number of teachers had far exceeded the population increase. Between 1900 and 1920 the number of common school students had increased by 12.2%, while the number of teachers had increased by 34.3%, and the number of teachers completing teacher training institutions had increased by 59.5% during those years.[10]

Some of these new teachers had been absorbed into the system by lowering the pupil/teacher ratio, but there remained a surplus, and it would be necessary to harmonize teacher production with the growth in the student population by reducing the number of teacher candidates and training institutions. The Commission had received explicit instructions to work within the existing three year teacher training framework,[11] with an implied charge that it must deal only with the problem of oversupply of teachers and colleges.[12]

One of the most interesting issues surrounding the teacher education proposal, was a pamphlet, published by Professor Vilhelm Bjerknes in 1928, suggesting that teacher training institutions be moved in the direction of institutions of higher learning in that teacher candidates ought to have earned the *examen artium*.[13] At this point in time most of the candidates had simply completed the folk school, and Bjerknes' recommendation was quite radical, although it was not without precedent. Germany, for example, had resolved to begin requiring teacher candidates to pass the *Abitur* as a part of its liberal reform endeavors after World War I.[14]

Actually, the teacher training law of 1929 did not define any substantial changes in teacher training practice. It did not even reduce the number of institutions or the duration of training. However, the number of candidates at each school was reduced, which seemingly provided an opportunity for the schools to get something for nothing. That is, the teacher training schools had an opportunity to extend the period of training without raising the costs of the institutions. In fact, the *Storting* declared on 21 May 1930 that they could begin to offer a four year training course.[15]

The very idea of extending teacher preparation was repugnant to some people, and when the political picture shifted with elections that next fall, one such person, priest Nils Trædal, a member of the Farmers Center Party, became the Minister of Church and Education. He quickly directed the Department to draft a proposal to reverse the decision of the previous year. "Teachers are not just products of training time," he declared before the *Odelsting*, "but first and foremost they are dependent on the creator for the talents they possess."[16] If teaching talent was a gift of God, an inborn talent, and could not be taught, extending the training time of teacher candidates would simply be a waste of time. Fortunately, the *Odelsting* possessed a somewhat more enlightened view and soundly defeated the proposal by 64 to 37 votes.[17]

Having considered teacher training, the Parliamentary School Commission turned to the issue that had been central in school reform for almost a century: the unified school. Two quite different systems were functioning in the towns and the countryside, and a single, unified national school program was the Commission's ultimate aim.

There was some initial consideration in the Commission of the appropriateness of the undifferentiated seven year folk school. One outspoken Commission member was the Socialist instrument maker, O. G. Gjøstein, who wanted to extend the folk school from seven to eight years. His ultimate design was to move to a full ten year school that would serve as a compulsory institution for all children.[18]

Gjøstein had been a member of the Labor Party from its inception and had been enormously influential in Oslo school politics. He and his brother Johan, a school superintendent in Stavanger and later Agder, had helped formulate a socialist education platform, which included provision for attendance of all children, without cost, to an extended common school program that was freed from religious influence and which placed value on practical, work related learning.[19] The Gjøstein brothers proposal did not receive popular support. Even the socialist Edvard Bull saw little value in forcing youth, who had no interest, or history of success, into school for so many years.[20]

A second proposal envisioned a folk school that was reduced to six years with a two year continuation school built on it. That proposal was more attractive to people such as Bull, if attendance at the continuation school were made compulsory.[21] However, the committee in general favored the continuation of a seven year common school, and most of the deliberations focussed on what was necessary to improve that institution.

The countryside schools were the object of most of the deliberations, because this was where improvement was most needed. The recommendations for the countryside folk school included the following: that the school year in the countryside be extended, that school supplies be made available without cost to the student, and that schools develop school libraries.[22]

The major change recommended for town common schools was that the school introduce a foreign language during the regular school time.[23] This foreign language, typically English, would remain optional for students, as had been the case since the 1889 school law, but rather than being given in the program outside the regular school time, as were all other optional courses, it would be given during the regular school time.

The decision to provide foreign language instruction in the town folk schools was motivated by the anticipated reduction of higher school time from six to five years, as we shall discuss below. The Commission realized that it would be impossible to require a foreign language in the countryside schools, simply because the necessary teachers would not be available. Further, town folk schools would not have the resources to teach more than one language, so a decision would be necessary, at the school level, as to which language would be taught.[24] The decision to adopt a foreign language in town schools but not in countryside schools would lead to still another inevitable quality difference between town and countryside, in spite of all the rhetoric to the contrary.

With regard to higher common school issues, the task of combining different school types above the common school proved to be problematic. The Commission maintained that the middle school had ceased to have a functional value and must disappear. The simplest higher schooling mechanism would be to maintain a five year *gymnasium*, which students could enter right out of the seven year folk school. In addition, Commission members determined that a three year *realskole* should come into existence, which would provide some extension of general education as well as preparation for special occupations.

There was some mild challenge to this scheme by higher school teachers on the Commission, who claimed that *gymnasium* students would have a weakened background, because school time would be reduced by a full year. In the end, the general consensus was that the five year higher school should be the norm for those pursuing academic oriented studies.[25]

It was clear that time must be found within the five year program to make up for the lost year. A number of options were available. There was the possibility of providing two years of foreign language instruction at the folk school. Another option would be to drop certain subjects. Two subjects were considered: religion and French. Edvard Bull, Gitta Jønsson (a woman member from Tromsø), and M. Svebstad (a teacher from Støren), argued against religion on the grounds that higher students would already have had as much religious instruction as those who had left school and it would be discriminatory to exact even more religion from them. Besides, religion could be incorporated into history. Of course, this was not a popular view, and religion was ultimately retained as a subject of study. After some consideration of French, it was agreed that knowledge of the French culture was important, even though a student's grasp of the language would generally be very superficial.[26]

Unfortunately, the only time saving option that was agreed on, was to provide foreign language instruction in the town folk schools. This decision created a most difficult structural problem for the Commission. Because all common schools would not require a foreign language, it would be impossible to demand foreign language competence prior to entering the *gymnasium*. Of course, language would be available in town schools, but an admissions requirement not built on the countryside schools would discriminate against them, unless there were other attractive options available to them. The Commission decided to divide all *gymnasier* into two categories. An *A-gymnasium* would exist for students who had not taken English studies prior to entrance, while a *B-gymnasium* would exist for those who had taken two years of English. This was a simple political solution to the situation but it left unresolved the task of solving the pedagogical and status issues surrounding claims of equivalence in the two *gymnasium* types.[27]

A further Commission struggle centered around the need to address the growing demands of a modern industrial state. A certain proportion of the youth would have to be given some opportunity to participate in a more practical, even vocationally oriented, state sponsored educational experience. The Commission recommended that a three year *realskole* become part of the general system. This school would remain theoretical, and even replicate the program found in the *gymnasium* during the first two years, but the third year would deviate markedly in that it would concentrate on practical studies. Such an arrangement would allow students to attend the *realskole* for two years, then transfer to the *gymnasium*, if they wished to continue toward the *artium*. However, those who went on and took the *realskole* examination at the end of the third year would not be able to transfer into the *gymnasium* without loosing school time. The Commission recommended that the third year be divided into several lines, including a commercial-office work line and a domestic science line.[28]

In order to remain consistent with the *A-* and *B-gymnasium* structure, it was also decided that there would be *A-realskoler* for those without folk school foreign language training and *B-realskoler* for those with foreign language study.

Another major problem facing the Commission was the recommendations to include lines of study other than the existing three lines at the *gymnasium*: science, English and Latin. Three major proposals were considered. The first was for a line of study for girls (*pikelinje*). This special girl's line was recommended by the Association for Women's Education (*Forening for kvinnelig opdragelse*), but was strongly opposed by another women's organization, the Norwegian Women's Academic Association (*Norske kvinnelige akademikeres landsforbund*). The proposal was built on the assumption that certain subjects of study were particularly appropriate to women's needs and interests. These might include homemaking, needlework, child care, and mothering.[29] The proposal was looked upon by those in opposition as an attempt to give the girls an easier route to university studies. The Commission ultimately recommended against such a line, maintaining that females would have to compete on the same basis as the males.[30]

The second proposal was for a so-called *Norrøn* line based on Old Norse, Norwegian history and culture. This idea had been around for decades and was raised again with the petition of Voss *landsgymnas*.[31] The Commission invited the rector of the school to present his case, and recommended positively.[32]

The final proposal was for a nature studies line (*naturfaglinje*), suggested by the Norwegian Farmer Association (*Norges Bondelag*), and put forward by the Department of Agriculture. It would have a natural science base, particularly biology, and be intended for future agronomists, veterinarians, nutritionists, etc. Following a long presentation on the value of certain sciences and modern languages, the Commission tentatively supported the proposal, but stressed that the proposal had not shown a clear distinction between the new line and the existing science line.[33]

The end result of these proposals was that a fourth and fifth line of study leading to the *examen artium* were included in the Commission recommendations.

A final major issue facing the Commission was the problem of continuation schools in the towns and the countryside. There were isolated *landsgymnaser*, but the continuation school continued to serve most of those who stayed in the countryside. A Department committee of nine people, including Labor Party leader Johan Gjøstein, and school activists Anna Rogstad and Anna Sethne, had earlier been designated to develop a set of recommendations regarding the continuation schools. The committee had considered proposing mandatory attendance to some form of further education, but in its report of 1921, it had eventually opted for some form of choice in the matter.[34]

The Parliamentary School Commission also struggled with the issues, but decided that a separate law be negotiated which would clarify the role of continuation schools.[35]

The reports of the Parliamentary School Commission were forwarded to the Department of Church and Education in January, 1928. It would be more than eight years before the proposals would begin to be translated into comprehensive school law. However, certain specific items would be passed prior to that time. For example, on 19 June 1931 the *Storting* approved the Norrøn line of study at the *gymnasium*.[36]

A number of factors help explain the long delay in action. First, by the time action could be taken, Norway was in the middle of the Great Depression that reached to all corners of the globe. Reform costs money and the country was in no position to pay for the reforms. Second, the political picture was very volatile. No political party had been able to gain control of the government since the end of World War I, and there were constant shifts in power and leadership. Third, the consensus orientation of the Norwegians required a full airing of possibilities. Interest groups must be given the chance to react to the reports, which takes enormous time.

THE HIGHER COMMON SCHOOL LAW OF 1935

Three years after the major reports of the Commission appeared, the Department of Church and Education invited the four major teacher organizations to form a committee to review the issues anew. Curiously, the Department gave this committee the charge once again to consider the possibility of a six year as well as a seven year folk school program.[37] That charge came, in part, in reaction to the extensive negative reviews that the Commission was so politically inspired that it had not sufficiently considered the pedagogical implications of its recommendations. We must keep in mind the fact that countryside schools were as yet still in session only 12-15 weeks a year and were in no position to give the kind of preparation, which university and higher schooling people deemed necessary.

In addition, the conservative, Nils Traedal, was now heading the Department and he was most sympathetic to the idea of a six year folk school foundation program. However, a seven year folk school had already become a part of the common wisdom and commitment of most teachers and they took strong issue with the idea of a six year folk school, even though a minority pressed its cause. The notion of a six year school was actually given a fair hearing, but it was ultimately rejected because it was viewed as a political rather than a pedagogical alternative. To reverse Norway's commitment to a seven year common school would represent a retrogressive decision and the teachers claimed it would symbolize a "blow against the developments in our own land. . .and against the lead that other lands follow."[38]

In 1934, the Department issued its recommendations for the higher common school. After a thorough review of higher school developments since 1869, it concluded that it had no choice but to agree with the

Commission and the teachers that the higher common school would be built on the seven year folk school.[39]

Having made this decision, the rest of the story is predictable, even though the ultimate design represents a mishmash of options provided to students. The A (without folk school foreign language) and B (with folk school foreign language) *gymnasier* and *realskoler* could be 4, 5, or 6 years in length and 2, 3, and 4 years in length, respectively. The *gymnasium* could form five different lines of study: science, natural science, English, Latin and Norse, while the *realskole* could provide several lines of study in its third year.[40] In other words, Norway had adopted a higher schooling form that would address the diverse needs of a modern industrial state and declare obsolete any semblance of uniform traditional liberal studies that had characterized classical education.

In some respects, the Norwegian higher common school retained the traditional European concept that a "school" was an institution where everyone took a uniform course of studies, in contrast to the tradition in America, where a high school would offer a wide array of options to every student so that each student would build his/her own individualized program of studies. However, the Norwegians developed a wide array of school types so that students in each of these school types would engage in a program of studies quite different from the program in other school types.

Actually, the structure was not quite as wide open as these alternatives suggest. The major framework would be a five year *gymnasium* and a three year *realskole*. Those schools with an added year were intended to make up the English deficiency of students who had none at the folk school. Those schools with shorter programs would conduct regular transfer programs. In general, however, a common thrust in higher schooling was becoming evident throughout Europe. The emphasis was away from general liberal studies toward the utilitarian and even practical studies.

THE FOLK SCHOOL LAW OF 1936

The higher common school law of 1935 had essentially dictated what must happen to the folk schools. It would serve as a preparatory institution for the higher schools, which meant that it must extend the number of days in its school year and offer English if it was to provide adequate preparation. The Department of Church and Education established a planning committee in 1935 to prepare the law. Its major provisions were that the folk school be the fundamental institution of common instruction for seven years, that it adopt a standard leaving examination, that its countryside school offer 16-18 weeks of instruction a year, that its town schools provide a minimum of 176 instructional hours in age-graded classes (This was ultimately set at 168 hours), that English be offered in the last two years as a regular subject of study (as an optional subject but within the regular schedule). It was further decided that conditions in the countryside and the town schools would be differently defined in many paragraphs.

The law was passed with almost no debate, and the passage of the law also confirmed a value orientation that had gradually come into being with the emergence of the Labor Party. One of the working policies for over half a century and throughout the reform process had been to give the local community as much autonomy as possible. This policy had resulted in vastly different levels of performance and standards of excellence. The Parliamentary School Commission recommendations had signaled the establishment of policy that would set a centralization process in motion that would run almost unchecked for the next half century.

The major Commission recommendations toward centralization would be that a national folk school council (*folkeskoleråd*) be established to oversee the conduct of schools and to set policy within the framework of the law.[41] Ironically, this had inspired such controversy from other national bodies representing teachers, school directors, etc., that it had been dropped. Two other elements of the law would prove even more centralizing, these being (1) the standard leaving examination, and (2) educational finances.

The Parliamentary School Commission had debated the examination issue, and the Labor Party representative, Gjøstein pushed for its inclusion, maintaining that it should be a condition for admission to the middle school, although it was not included in the final draft law of the Commission.[42] The law would require that all children be tested in Norwegian and arithmetic through a uniform examination that would standardize performance measures throughout the country.

In terms of educational finance, we recall that the state, region, and local community had previously shared responsibility for funding. That design was altered in favor of a formula in which the state covered 50-80% of teacher salaries. It would also carry certain financial responsibilities previously carried by the county, including school buildings, inventory, the teacher's farm, and the teacher's home.[43]

THE CONTINUATION SCHOOL LAW

Since the 1889 school law, the continuation schools had been included in the legislation regarding folk schools, but the 1935 and 1936 school laws implied that continuation schools had become a part of further education and required a clearer definition as a part of that system. The Department of Church and Education designated a committee to assess the role of continuation schools in November, 1936, giving it a charge to design a theoretical, a practical, and a combination line of study requiring one or more years of study.[44] A year later the committee issued its recommendations, which mandated the existence of schools, but fell short of mandating attendance. Article five of the folk school law of 1936 actually allowed individual communities to require attendance, but it was not thought to be a wise move to extend compulsory education a further year at that point in time. Only about 22% of all folk school leavers were going on to the continuation school at the time,[45] while approximately 20% more were going into other forms of full-time education. More than half the young people terminated schooling at the end of folk school.

The proposal was still in process when World War II broke out, preventing any decision.[46] In 1946, the matter was finally able to be concluded and became law.[47] The law perpetuated the tradition of allowing great variation in the form the schools would take. The continuation school program could have theoretical and/or practical content; they could be evening or day schools, they could be one, two, or even three year programs; they could define a school year as 12 to 26 weeks to a full year; they could be optional or compulsory, depending on the wishes of the particular community involved.

The impact of the law was dramatic. The number of schools and students had progressed steadily, but slowly over the years. The number of schools had only increased 38% from 1900 to 1940 (191 to 262 schools), but in the 1940s they increased 309% (262 to 1130 schools), and were enrolling 17,395 students in 1950.[48]

THE VOCATIONAL EDUCATION LAW

Vocational education had been so tangential to the educational system, that the Parliamentary School Commission had not even considered it worthy of including in its comprehensive deliberations. With the emergence of the Labor Party as the dominant political force, it was inevitable that vocational schooling should take on importance in the educational system.

The formal incentive for the Department of Church and Education to begin considering how vocational education should mesh with the rest of the system came through a 1930 initiative from the community of Stavanger to operationalize a new dimension of the educational system: independent vocational schools (*fagskoler*) with short lower, middle level, and higher level courses.[49] In the next years, a great deal of deliberation was engaged in about the form these schools should take. In these deliberations reference was often made to the Department recommendations about continuation schools just after World War I.[50] Attention was given to levels of schooling, to the relationship between vocational schools and other parts of the educational system, but the major emphasis was placed on the necessity that the vocational students be in close contact with the actual work they would be engaged in.[51]

A committee set up by worker organizations in 1936, acted quickly in drawing up a set of recommendations for all youth who did not attend another form of schooling. Their program centered on two points: (1) a compulsory eighth year continuation school, and (2) a one year compulsory vocational school. The vocational school would be organized so that a young student could move from level to level until the highest level of technical training could be achieved.[52]

The Department finally took matters into hand, charging its council in charge of vocational education, the *Yrkesopplæringsrådet for håndverk og industri*, to come up with its own set of recommendations. Their recommendations were published in November, 1937,[53] and formed the basis for the vocational education law approved by the *Storting* on 1 March 1940.[54] Unfortunately, World War II interrupted the implementation of the law, so it was 1945 before it was fully put into effect.

The law mandated four major types of vocational schools. First, workshop schools (*verkstedskoler*) were intended to provide a 1/2 to 1 year foundation program for youth, who would later go into apprenticeship. Second, apprentice schools (*lærlingeskoler*) would give 10 hours of instruction each week during the time of apprenticeship, which usually lasted three years. Third, workers who had completed their apprenticeship could receive further practical and theoretical training in advanced vocational schools (*videregående skoler*), including those for foremen and craft masters. Finally, regular vocational schools, would provide one year courses in eight subjects.

Beyond vocational schools were technical schools offering a three year program with six specializations: electrotechnical, machine technical, chemical, house construction, road, bridge, and canal building, and ship building. The law regulating schools of technology would be subject to regulations dealing with higher education.

Enough cannot be said about the importance of this first major law related to vocational education as a part of the broader educational system. From the time of the Greeks, Western man had systematically relegated the practical side of life to a lesser place in his value system. This value system had penetrated the Norwegian culture in such a way that vocational education had not even been looked on as a part of the educational system. Vocational education had received its proper place, and in the next decades Norway would work as aggressively as any country in breaking down the distinction between the practical and the theoretical aspects of education.

The school laws that were passed in the 1930s were dealing mainly with structural issues related to different school types. At the same time, a general movement had been in motion throughout Europe, called the New Education Movement, which focused on the inner life of the school, on the relationships between teacher and student, on the way instruction was conducted. These issues found expression in a Department endeavor regarding curriculum policy, and it was given the label, the *Normalplan,* which we must consider next.

THE *NORMALPLAN* OF 1939

Norway has a history of curriculum planning, which laid down the instructional programs that were to be conducted in a school. The school laws defined the courses that were to be run, but the content and instructional process were undefined. To assist the teacher, instructional plans were occasionally drawn up, but they were quite free to modify them according to local requirements. The first major plan was drawn up in 1890, by the Department of Church and Education. The 1889 school law had mandated specific subjects of study, and it also mandated that the education committee should provide a plan to be made available to school leaders.[55] Matias Skard became the author of this plan, and he simply listed each course and outlined its main goals. Arithmetic pupils at the first level, for instance, were to understand the meaning of all numbers from 1-100, as well as use and write them.[56]

Over the years still other plans appeared. In 1902, the Rector Søyland in Tønsberg developed a plan for the seven year school,[57] and as the unified school became a reality, it became imperative that a general seven year plan become available. Consequently, in 1922 the Department of Church and Education came forth with a so-called *Normalplan* for folk schools in the countryside, developed by school directors and representatives of the teachers.[58] The goals outlined in the plan were as explicit about good conduct and proper behavior as they were about knowledge. Thus, the children were to keep their writing books clean and orderly. The writing books weren't to be handled by unclean fingers and certainly no ink splotches were to be found on them.[59] Traditional schooling was almost taken for granted in the plans, and it wasn't until the 1939 *Normalplan* appeared that evidence of progressive, new educational practices were becoming the norm.[60]

The 1939 *Normalplan* represented an enormous undertaking, the town folk school plan taking 265 pages and the countryside plan 276 pages. It was so expansive that the committee anticipated taking at least five years to be fully implemented. Indeed, one of the important innovations of this new plan was that it was to be implemented throughout Norway; it was to be binding on all schools. Norway was to become unified not only in its school types, but in the way instruction and curricular matters were to be carried out. This was declared, not with any sense of criticism or reserve, but with an optimistic sense that its "scientific foundation" would insure that it was the proper plan for all schools.[61] Of course, such reasoning would only reinforce the orientation of the Norwegians toward centralized control of the schools.

The plan not only outlined the minimal competencies that were expected in each subject, but how the students were to be evaluated, tested, and graded. It also outlined how instruction was to be given. Within this framework, the progressive education bias of the leaders in the committee, including B. Ribsskog and Anna Sethne, pervaded the plan. Schooling was to be conducted on the basis of the activity school. The children were to cease being mere passive learners where the teachers lectured and told information. Now the children were to become active and involved in the learning process. Not only were they to engage in silent reading, but to act out dramatizations of the readings. Not only was the teacher to explain things to the class, but the children were to tell of personal experiences. Not only were children to learn to follow directions, but they were to be encouraged to exercise personal choice in their learning experiences.

In a brief five year period, Norway had embarked on an ambitious plan of school reform, both structurally and internally. The next phase in this process was expected to be a period of time when these programs were to be implemented. Before this could become a reality, however, a new era in Norway's history took place. Some describe this as a brief interlude, a period when little happened in terms of modern Norwegian education, a period when Norway was once again occupied by a foreign power.

14 Education during World War II and Its Aftermath

April 9, 1940, is a date every Norwegian knows. Suddenly, without warning, German military forces moved into Denmark and Norway. While Denmark capitulated immediately, Norway resisted for two months before being overwhelmed. The country remained in a state of occupation until the war came to an end in 1945. That five year period represents a difficult episode in our story.[1]

The educational system during the war might be described as being molded by foreign influences and any changes might be described as amounting to something other than "Norwegian" education. However, it would be necessary for us to discount the role played by the members of the Norwegian National Unification (*Nasjonal Samling*) Movement and their collaborators. In fact, certain Norwegians acted with the conviction that the school system must be transformed to conform to a new societal model. Significant changes took place during the five years in question, which left a lasting mark on the schools, for good or ill.

An enormous literature exists on Norway during the war years, but most of the educational literature has glorified the resistance movement.[2] While this literature is inspiring and even helpful, it may be construed as myth making in that it highlights some incidents, but does not give a balanced, comprehensive picture of the schools and school people during the war years. While we wait for a complete account of the period, we must be content to give an abbreviated account of political events following April 9, 1940, and recount some of the changes in the schooling process that necessitated some response in the immediate postwar years.

By the time the German forces arrived in Oslo in the afternoon of April 9, the King and most of the members of the government had taken refuge in the small town of Hamar, near the Swedish border, creating an immediate vacuum of authority.[3] When it became evident that no body existed to speak for the Norwegians, in the early evening of that eventful day, Vidkun Quisling, the leader of the National Unification Movement, stepped into this vacuum declaring himself the Prime Minister, and he named a number of prominent individuals as ministers, including Professor Ragnar Skancke, Director of the Trondheim Technical University, as the Minister of Church and Education.

Although Quisling became immediately synonymous with the word traitor, the modern day Judas, he actually appears to have maintained some vestiges of independence during those first days. However, certain officials of the church, judiciary and local governments quickly gathered to form the so-called Administrative Council (*administrasjonsrådet*) that claimed to be in authority.

The Council operated in a patriotic though compromising posture. With regard to education, the Council, by way of the Department of Church and Education, advised the teachers, in a circular of 26 Aug. 1940, that (1) instruction should not deal with "the actual situation in our land," so that subjects such as history, social studies, mother language, etc., would be treated as they were in 1939; (2) school leaders and teachers should direct the students to act with discretion and caution; and (3) all should regard the provisional directives concerning schooling and instruction with a sense of goodwill and diligence.[4]

The first months represented a period of indecisiveness on the part of the German forces, but on Sept. 25, Josef Terboven, who had come to Norway to take over the reigns of power as the *Reichskommissar*, began to assert himself by replacing the Administrative Council with 13 state ministers, who headed the various departments of the government. Most of these ministers had been associated with Quisling's National Unification Movement, which allowed Quisling some voice even though he was not yet the Prime Minister. The most powerful minister was probably Viljam Albert Hagelin, who headed the Department of Interior. He was largely responsible for streamlining lines of authority, so that all political power was centralized and all civil servants and office holders at all levels became subject to dismissal if they failed to carry out their responsibilities related to the "new times thinking" in Norway.

The minister for the Department of Church and Education remained Ragnar Skancke, and on Dec. 16, Skancke issued an edict that all school leaders, headmasters, etc., were also subject to dismissal under the same conditions as had been laid down by Hagelin. At the same time he declared that all national councils for education were to be disbanded. Thus, all local and school powers had been consolidated by the end of the year.

The intention of the new government was much more than mere occupation. They intended to alter the very nature of Norwegian "cultural life." The school system and youth education, they claimed, "stand as a focus of these interests and will become one of the most important spheres of endeavor in creating this culture."[5]

If the schools were to become instruments of cultural transformation, it would be necessary for them to conform with the mandates of the new regime. On 20 Nov. 1940, the Department had already sent a forceful message to all teachers telling them that they were to serve as models to the youth, which meant they must conduct themselves properly and align themselves with the new educational program. Passive compliance would not be enough; it would require "enormous, diligent energy on the part of the teachers."[6]

However, the exact form of that new culture was not yet clear. Even Skancke wavered in what to do, and until that became clear, his clearest course of action was to quell any move on the part of teachers to propagandize against the Germans,[7] and to keep politics out of the schools altogether.[8] The teachers resisted cooptation, and the first major test of their resolve came in February, 1941, when the schools of the Oslo area were directed to participate in a Hitler Youth exhibition. The teachers banned together in one voice to send a protest to the Department. They were joined by their students, who refused to subject themselves to a propaganda exercise.[9]

Even more dangerous to the teachers' sense of autonomy was a move by the government, also in February, 1941, to established a national personnel office, which would approve all new appointments. Many work organizations, among them teacher groups, organized to protest such action and the occupation of Norwegian soil. The government responded by inviting 43 organizations to meet in the *Storting* on 18 June 1941, where Terboven announced that many of the organizations would be disbanded and the heads of others would be replaced by people appointed by the Commissar, including replacements for the teacher organizations. In fact, the teacher groups were already aware of plans to collapse them into a single association.[10]

The lawful leaders of the teacher organizations quickly regrouped, going underground and firming up a structure that would insure a place for teachers in the dramatic story of the resistance movement. The man to emerge as the leader of the secondary school teachers was Einar Høigård, a lecturer at the University of Oslo. In the fall of 1941, Høigård traveled the country holding meetings and delivering lectures of four "cardinal points." Teachers were to:

1) reject demands for membership of, or declarations of loyalty to the *Nasjonal Samling*;

2) reject every attempt at *Nasjonal Samling* propaganda in the school;

3) reject every order from unauthorized sources;

4) reject every demand for participation in the *Nasjonal Samling* youth organization.[11]

The groundwork for a major showdown had been set, and one of the first acts of Quisling, when he was finally appointed Prime Minister for the remainder of the occupation period, was to announce, on 7 February 1942, that all youth were to be inducted into a National Unification Youth Service (*Nasjonal Samlings Ungdomstjeneste*), and that the Norwegian Teachers Union (*Norges Lærersamband*)[12] would be organized into a single comprehensive organization led by Orvar Sæther, a simple and insecure man, who had functioned as the Commissar's appointee over the primary teacher association (*Lærerlaget*).[13] In actuality, the existing organizations were suddenly transformed into "illegal" groups working in a resistance capacity until the end of the war, when men such as Einar Høigård, would become immortalized for their covert dedication to the ideals of a free Norway.[14]

One of the stirring episodes of the entire resistance movement was the resolve of the teachers against induction into the new organization. In response to Quisling's mandate, action committees of the now illegal organizations hammered out a statement that each teacher would be invited to sign:

> I find myself unable to take part in the bringing up of Norwegian youth according to the line prescribed for youth service in the NS Youth Company, as this conflicts with my conscience. As membership of the Teachers Union, according

to the statement of the National Leader among other things, lays upon me the duty of such an upbringing, and furthermore other demands are raised which conflict with my terms of appointment, I am obliged to inform you that I cannot regard myself as a member of the Teachers Union.[15]

From 20 February 1942 onwards, thousands of signed statements came into the Department. By 4 March, between 6-7,000 signatures had been received, and Skancke felt compelled to send out a further notice that teachers were obliged to commit themselves to membership. When this did not happen, approximately 1,100, or one tenth of all teachers, were arrested. Over 500 were loaded into cattle trucks and sent to Trondheim, then placed in the hold of an old coastal steamer and delivered to Kirkenes in the far North, where they were subjected to hard labor for several months.[16] The example set by the teachers set a powerful precedent that helped the clergy and the lawyers resist membership in organizations set up for them.[17]

The war years represented a delicate period in the history of Norwegian education. A large number of educators took an active role in the resistance. Other educators remained on their jobs in the classrooms. Large numbers of those, who remained, had done so from a sense of responsibility to the youth of Norway. They "held out" in their own way, while others took more direct but covert action.[18]

Some teachers remained in the classroom out of fear, or because they lacked any sense of personal commitment and ideals. Still others were committed to the "new times thinking," and worked energetically to transform society. This was particularly the case with those who took leadership roles in the school system. In a survey taken in 1942, 58.5% of all school authorities (*skolestyrer*) in Akershus, the county where Oslo is located, were National Unification members. However, those figures dropped dramatically in other counties (Telemark, 33.3%; Buskerud, 28.6%; Vestfold 28.4%), and in the country as a whole the membership was only 18.8%.[19]

CHANGES IN SCHOOLING

Until recently few studies have been conducted on changes that took place in education, even though significant adjustments were made.[20] We have already noted the move to coalesce the teachers into one organization, and to abolish the national councils dealing with various facets of education. Sirevåg has discussed the changes that were made in the examination system.[21] In this chapter we shall look at three specific schooling issues under German occupation: (1) the implementation of the school laws of the 1930s, (2) the changes in the Normal Plan of 1939, and (3) the adoption of German as the first foreign language.

The School Laws of the 1930s

The passage of any school law in Norway had always been done with the assumption that it would take a number of years for the mandates to be implemented. The higher education law of 1935, the folk school law of 1936, the teacher training law of 1938, and the vocational school law of 1940, were just beginning to be implemented when the war broke out.

Many elements of these laws would be altered to suit the occupational forces. For illustrative purposes, we shall mention some alterations that took place with regard to the folk school. On 14 July 1941, the Department of Church and Education issued a statement regarding specific provisions related mainly to administration and finances.[22] First, the local authorities had been given the responsibility to set school boundaries. Now the Department and its authorities could determine them, if they wished. Second, if disputes arose between communities, or if a community decided not to operate a school, the Department could now step in and become responsible for the final decision. Third, if a community was responsible to pay another community, as laid down by the 1936 school law, the Department could now choose to make some contribution to the transaction.

Approximately three months later, on October 18, further changes were issued relating to teachers, their appointments, dismissal, and termination payments. These regulations were soon expanded to apply not only to teachers, but to school administrators and school inspectors. These new regulations also noted that community civil servants (*tjenestemenn*) in the schools had been eliminated.[23]

These changes were all part of the centralizing process. The Department of Church and Education was taking over schooling in a way that had never existed. Curiously, the new regulations also conformed to the long tradition of respect for the law in Norway in that they spelled out conditions as if they would apply to the occupying powers.

The directives just mentioned pertained mainly to people and lines of authority. The laws that had been passed in the 1930s continued to be implemented. The full seven year folk school was now universally in place and being attended by over 99% of the population that came under its jurisdiction. The *gymnasier* and *realskoler* were also almost entirely built into the system. The two and four year teacher preparation programs continued to develop.

One of the remarkable aspects of the implementation activities had to do with vocational education. We recall that the vocational education law was passed just prior to the occupation period in 1940, and by the end of the war an enormous complex of institutions could be identified which fell under the definition of vocational education. For example, in 1935 there were only 10 handwork schools in the country. This had expanded to 28 three years later, and continued to expand, so that 42 of these schools existed at the end of the war.[24] Telhaug lists 59 different school types that existed in Norway in 1945 and over half of them were vocational schools, dealing with general vocational training to specialized institutions for the training of seamen, craftsmen, fishermen, railroaders, artists, musicians, librarians, workers in various parts of business, forestry, hotel, health, and social welfare. In addition there were technical schools of various sorts.[25] Indeed, Norway had already begun to define education beyond the folk school as practical education as much as general education.

Some curricular adjustments were being made, particularly as they pertained to the adoption of German as the major foreign language, however, the timetable of the schools was also changed to reflect the new times thinking. For example, the number of hours for religious instruction was reduced from six hours to four hours a week,[26] which represented a change in the Normal Plan of 1939.

The Normal Plan *(Normalplan)*

In certain respects, that Normal Plan was ideally suited to the purposes of the new regime. The 1939 plan had represented a fundamental shift with regard to curriculum policy. In the past, normal plans had been drawn up to assist local communities and the folk school law of 1936 even stipulated that the timetable of the schools shall be set by local school authorities.[27] The Labor dominated government systematically moved to centralize the entire schooling enterprise, including the Normal Plan, which became mandatory throughout the country. When the National Unification advocates took over, they took advantage of that policy, because it represented a vital vehicle to dictate their own school programs throughout the country, and in a bulletin dated 3 March 1941, the Department informed local authorities that, while they could make "minor changes," they must conform to the requirements of the 1939 Normal Plan.[28]

While support for the 1939 Normal Plan was repeatedly expressed, in actuality, the inner purpose and general tone of the Plan deviated markedly from the purposes of the National Unification followers. The committee drawing up the Normal Plan had been dominated by some of the leading progressives in Norway, whose intent had been to turn the schools into activity based learning centers.

The ideals of National Unification were in direct conflict with humanistic, liberal impulses expressed in progressive education. While Orvar Sæther expressed appreciation for the value of the Normal Plan, he explained that it must undergo a shift in focus. For example, history must come to form a core study in the schools. Even with its positive focus on history, he maintained that the 1939 Normal Plan continued to give too much stress on such matters as the Greeks, commerce and dates, when it must deal more exclusively with the life of the people, it must teach the Norwegian the art of living, it must move away from broader themes and focus on the Norwegians' own national life.[29]

Other shifts in thinking would also be necessary. The contrast in the two modes of thinking are clearly spelled out in the thoughts of teacher, J. Eldal, in a series of articles about what changes were necessary in drafting a National Unification normal plan. Eldal begins by pointing out the obvious. Curriculum plans are under constant revision and as conditions change, so will the plans. Being a "product of its time" the 1939 Normal Plan was in conflict with the conditions.[30]

Eldal then chides the teachers, because most of them were continuing to implement the Plan without clearly seeing that it required criticism and assessment. The aims of National Unification was not those of "Jewish liberalism," which he saw imbedded in the Plan. National Unification was not in harmony with the "liberal-Marxist" poison that the Normal Plan wished to pour into the young mind. They were not consistent with the individualism and egoism that lurks behind the "smiling mask of the humanities."[31]

In a second article, Eldal concentrated on the section of the Normal Plan dealing with language instruction in order to show where the Plan fell short. To begin with, language as developed in the Plan was seen to be learned mechanically, and its whole style was materialistic, stressing grammar and rules, and minimal competencies, when the National Unification advocates recognized that language strikes at the heart of a people. "Together with the fatherland's history," wrote Eldal, "training in the mother tongue should create the foundation for the people development in a national sense."[32]

To Eldal, the Normal Plan was individualistic oriented to the extreme in that children would be encouraged to exercise freedom and personal choice in most of what they did in Norwegian language development. For example, third grade children were to write on topics of their own choice.[33] Fifth grade children were to read books that they had readily available and that they found interesting.[34] The composition exercises stressed "free style writing," on subjects of interest to the child.[35]

Eldal exclaimed that National Unification could not tolerate such self-serving education. The main goal of education was to restrict individualistic interests, subordinating them to the common interests. The common interest was to be a theme that pervaded all subjects, all spheres of education.[36]

Eldal criticized still another focus of the 1939 Normal Plan, which intended to make learning a game. Reading programs, for example, were filled with dramatizations of the materials being read.[37] The Plan turned exercises into games — poor games, because at any given time most of the children were passive observers while only a few were actively learning. Further, the Plan downplayed silent reading in the final year of the folk school, because, reasoned the originators of the Plan, the young people were mostly interested in their companions. Companionship had become the focus rather than isolating activities such as silent reading.[38] Eldal challenged such notions, because they failed to account for proper control in a large class of young people. Control must exist, the school must maintain silent reading.

There are other shortcomings, having to do with the distribution of time for Norwegian, and with other subjects. Ultimately, National Unification was dedicated to work for Norway, according to Eldal, within the Norwegian spirit. The Normal Plan could, with revisions, contribute to that end. The major curricular revision would be in the foreign languages, where German would dominate.

German Language

On 1 March 1941, the Department announced that in the fall, when school year begins, German would replace English as the major foreign language in the folk school. The 1939 Normal Plan had called for five hours of English in each of the sixth and seventh grades. These ten hours would systematically be replaced by German instruction, so that by the fall of 1942, German would be the only foreign language in the folk school.

Because it would be difficult to satisfy the demand for German teachers in the folk school, certain provisions were instituted including in-service courses and standards to be met. If a school did not have competent people, the students would have the right to transfer to a five year *gymnas*. The existing German language books were all found to be unsuitable and it was announced that new texts would become available.[39]

On 27 May 1941, the Department issued its plans for the *gymnas*. The five year *gymnas*, which would admit students having had German in the folk school, and would offer four hours of German instruction a week in the higher grades, while the four year *landsgymnas* would give five hours a week in the three higher grades. With regard to the *examin artium*, German would become the main foreign language within all lines of the *gymnas*.[40]

In January, 1942, the Department increased the hours devoted to German by another hour so that 13 hours were spent in all lines of the *gymnas* in the last three years.[41]

When compared with the 1935 and 1936 school laws, German had replaced the ten hours of English in the folk school, it had been increased by six hours in the science and Latin lines had replaced English in the English line, and had been increased one hour more than English had been given. German had also become the major language of the continuation school and the teacher training college.

The changes we have been discussing are at the national level. What actually went on at the individual schools was often quite a different matter.

EDUCATIONAL CHANGE AT THE LOCAL LEVEL

The author of this book conducted a number of interviews with people who were in the schools at the time of the occupation, hearing recurrent stories particularly of the "nice but incompetent" people who were suddenly placed as the head of a school, with the consequence that the staff was constrained to try and protect the integrity and quality of the school while attempting to work with the rector as best they could.

There are some anecdotal accounts giving us a small, incomplete picture of the situation at individual schools. In the town of Larvik the teachers simply made do as best they could. They actually operated at times in relative freedom, except when the Germans were paying attention to them or imposing their own people into leadership positions.[42] The children typically sang forbidden songs with no interruption and often enjoyed the simple pleasures of youth.

Major problems arose as the teachers tried to maintain the formal class schedule. Four of the eighteen male teachers from Larvik were deported with other teachers to Kirkenes in 1942, and three of them were subsequently interned in prison in or near Oslo. There were no substitute teachers to take over for them during their absence. The remaining teachers operated from a position of commitment to the ideals of Quisling's National Unification Movement, to one of peaceful cooperation, or of passive resistance. It was common knowledge which teachers and students were committed to the Movement. Apparently, the children who were in the Movement experienced few advantages. In fact, they often suffered from a sense of isolation.

In the isolated region of Hadeland, a sense of deprivation and hardship appears to have been minimal.[43] The new times thinking certainly permeated many groups, and there was open discussion about personal feelings. Those youth committed to the Movement seemed to keep more or less to themselves at the schools, which usually retained all the symbols of Norwegian independence and loyalty to the King.

However, at the primary school in Brandbu, one community of Hadeland, a large number of the teachers actually declared themselves committed to Quisling's National Unification Movement, although there was strong resistance on the part of the remaining teachers. In fact, all communities experienced genuine tension between teachers speaking out in favor of the Movement and those in opposition to it.

As a consequence of the teacher petitions that were sent in to the Department in February, 1942, one teacher in each school at Hadeland was singled out to be sent North. However, those others who remained in the school, were recognized and appreciated for their enormous contribution to the physical and emotional well being of the students.

THE POSTWAR ADJUSTMENTS

The first years after the war were, in the minds of many, as difficult as those during the occupation. The tensions had arisen between those who were in the resistance movement and those in support of National Unification were very high.[44] There was a natural tendency to cast all who had chosen, for whatever reason, to remain in the classroom, into a group as traitors to their country. Barely two days after the Germans had formally capitulated, the Department of Church and Education sent a notice to all primary and youth schools announcing that all unworthy teachers were to be suspended. The same notice to secondary schools went out on 30 July.[45] The notice stressed that membership alone in the Teachers Union did not constitute grounds for suspension, but it usually represented the major criterion.[46]

The government, which had been sequestered in London throughout the war, soon arrived back in Norway, where it assumed control. Norway has the distinction of being the first nation after the war to call a general election. On 8 October 1945 the Labor Party won a clear parliamentary majority, headed by Einar Gerhardsen, former mayor of Oslo, who had been held in a German concentration camp for much of the occupation period. Kåre Fostervoll, a rector of the higher school in Ålesund, was appointed the Minister of Church and Education.

The Right remained the major opposition party, but all parties joined together in a spirit of unity, none wanting to embark immediately on some new path, but all resolving to work together to fully implement an educational program within the structure that had been set prior to the occupation period. The foundation of that policy was that "the entire school system would constitute a unified whole so that the individual parts, from the foundation school to the highest instruction would follow naturally from each other, whether they lead to practical or academic school forms.[47]

Of course it was not possible simply to begin where the government had left off in 1940. Students had been preparing for examinations under unusual conditions, and they had been taking a different course of studies. Some accommodation was necessary, at least in the short run. It would be necessary, for example, for the university to accept students on the basis of the marks they had received during the occupation period.[48] The place of German in the curriculum must be preserved, at least so that students who were under way could complete the course of studies.[49] In fact, the whole course schedule must be accommodated before the Department could revert to the 1940 schedule.[50]

After a period of time, it became evident that some stock-taking was necessary to determine where the country stood. In 1947 a twenty-one member committee was constituted, called the Coordinating Committee for Schooling (*Samordningsnemnda for skoleverket*), with the chairman of Primary and Secondary Schooling in the Department, Einar

Boyesen, acting as its head. It received a charge to review the situation with regard to the (1) the different school types, (2) teacher education, (3) school administration, and (4) revisions that might be necessary in the law to achieve coordination.[51]

In the next five years nineteen different reports were submitted dealing with every facet of the school system. In its summary report issued on 28 April 1952, the committee went far beyond its charge and looked forward a decade, declaring that by the 1960s a new school form would be necessary, if Norway was to build a school consistent with the changing times. It would be a common school for all Norwegian youth, having a comprehensive program and competent teachers who had been so trained that every community would be obliged to require its adoption.[52] This declaration helped precipitate a new reform cycle in education that has been under way until the present day.

Section V

Fourth Reform Cycle — Structural Reform Completed

15 Experimenting with New School Forms

Although the wounds of the occupation period would heal slowly, the country quickly resolved to operate on the basis of political unity, even though the Labor Party continued to dominate the government, garnering 41% of the *Storting* seats in 1945, 46% in 1949, 47% in 1953, 48% in 1957, and 47% in 1961.[1]

The Party had long since shed its connections with Marxist ideology and was now appealing to members of all social groups. At the same time the Conservatives were also moving toward the center. Even the smaller splinter parties worked with a spirit of cooperation and progressive intention, so that the country operated on the basis of tranquil development for over a decade.

In spite of the political resolve to work on a basis of political unity, from a long range perspective, life in Norway was anything but tranquil, because the country was engaging in what Sigmund Skard describes as "the greatest turning point in modern Norwegian history."[2] Internationally, the Second World War had torn the country away from its state of innocence, and it shed any pretext of neutrality and aligned itself unabashedly with the so-called North Atlantic Treaty nations.

Internally, the Norwegians, who had identified themselves as a nation of farmers and rural dwellers, recognized for the first time in 1946 that people in densely populated areas now outnumbered those in sparsely populated areas. In the next two decades, the town and city population would continue to expand and almost double, while the population in the rural areas would decline.[3] Consequently, in 1952 a revolutionary change in the political process was instituted. A clause in the constitution that mandated a two-thirds representation in the *Storting* from specified rural constituencies, was replaced by a representation process in rough accordance with the size of county populations.[4] Proportional representation was also adopted at the local level, both for counties and communities.

Culturally, the country also had become a full fledged consumer society striving for spiritual, industrial and technological, as well as recreational aims and products. Consumer ideals mandated that every household should own a car, a radio, a television set, an indoor bathroom. Recreational ideals dictated that all working adults should receive an extended vacation period each year. Of course, there were peculiar expressions of this civilization in Norway, including the aim of each family to have ready access to one or more of the hundreds of thousands of cabins on the coast or in the mountains, or the claim to having a "people's king," who was more nearly of the people than above the people.

Intellectually, Norway accepted the broad notion of the scientist, the technologist, the expert in decision making. Decisions, political and otherwise, would thenceforth be made, at least in part, based on research, scientific inquiry, and experimentation.

Economically, Norway had become competitive with other Western countries. Growth was most marked after World War II in the industrial sector, which had come to employ more wage earners than all other sectors of the economy combined. The sectors to suffer constant decreases in the work force were agriculture, forestry and hunting.[5]

With national prosperity came a resolve on the part of policy makers to assist those more destitute and poor in society so that they might also enjoy the growing wealth. The poorest strata of society came from the farming and fishing industries. These sectors were not only given benefits through subsidies to their products, and through social welfare programs. Enormous efforts were made to insure health, rehabilitation, skills training, and retirement opportunities for all people.

Some of the impetus for these policies came from the government, which was dominated by the political Left. However, the divisions between Right and Left remained minimal with regard to social welfare commitments as evidenced by the far-reaching program for retirement, passed in 1966, at a time when the Left did not rule the *Storting*.

One of the major social welfare agendas was education. In those first years following the war, Minister of Church and Education, Kåre Fostervoll was mainly interested in expanding the existing schooling enterprise at every level. In higher education, for example, the *Storting* approved, in 1946, a second university at Bergen, and plans were soon under way to transform the Technical College at Trondheim into a comprehensive university, and even to extend higher education into the far North of Norway where a fourth university would be established in 1969 at Tromsø. Fostervoll was replaced in 1948 by Lars Moen, who had served, as had Fostervoll, in a German prison camp. Moen was a good man, open to new ideas, but he remained committed to implementing the programs adopted by the Labor Party prior to the war. It was not until Birger Bergersen took over the reigns as Minister of Church and Education in 1953 that educational politics once again became infused with a new type of reform thinking. Bergersen had served as ambassador to Sweden and he brought back novel ideas toward reform that would set a whole new reform cycle in motion, which would alter the structure of schooling, and it would bring this about through a new mode of innovation: reliance on research and development.

THE COUNCIL FOR INNOVATION IN EDUCATION

Consistent with the spirit of cooperation and unity, all segments of the educational enterprise and all political parties joined together to proclaim that any further developments in education ought to be based on experimentation with new school types and forms. In fact, a law providing for the establishment of an independent, consultative educational research body in the Department of Church and Education, was passed on 8 July 1954 without opposition.[6] For the next quarter of a century the Council for Innovation in Education *(Forsøksrådet)* would be the focal point of educational research and development.[7]

Research and technology had entered into education as never before. Policy makers claimed that new forms must be demonstrably better than old forms if they were to be incorporated into the system. No longer was pedagogy simply to be an expression of some ideological bias or to be based on the particular political faction. The leaders in education would have assurance that proposals are based on experimental proof.

This belief was naive in certain respects. First, there was the assumption that research and scholarly inquiry had not guided reform work in the past. In fact, Norway had a rich tradition of modeling new school forms and programs after successful, real endeavors, albeit usually forms and programs that existed in foreign environments outside Norway. The standard set by Frederik Moltke Bugge in his three volume report of the school systems of Europe had been emulated by almost every commission that set to work on some Norwegian reform endeavor. Norwegians were intimately aware of developments elsewhere, and usually incorporated innovative practices found in particular institutions outside Norway on a general scale in Norway. Even the desire to adopt a National Council for Innovation in Education grew, in large measure, from a desire to emulate that which was found to be worthy elsewhere. The Norwegians recognized the importance of a law, passed in 1950 in Sweden providing for the organization of a Bureau of School Experimentation within the Swedish National Board of Education.[8]

Of course, there is a great difference in maintaining a borrowing mode and experimenting with new school forms within Norway itself. However, experimentation had also enjoyed a long tradition in the country. Even prior to the time of independence in 1814, the Christiania Cathedral School had served as one of four experimental schools which contributed mightily to the far-reaching secondary school ordinance of 1809.[9]

The major new feature of the 1954 act was that experimentation would be driven by a well funded government sponsored center specifically designed to try out new school forms and educational methods before these would be mandated by law. The personnel of this center would be social and behavioral scientists devoting their energies to help in solving problems confronting the government pertaining to structural issues, curriculum, and methods of instruction.

Experimentation as an appropriate mode of inquiry had become generally popular following World War II both by professionals and politicians. The Coordinating Committee for Schooling, which had operated from 1947 to 1952, had noted in its final report, that the existence of the Swedish Bureau of School Experimentation was worthy of emulation and suggested that the Norwegians ought to follow suit.[10] In that same year the Secondary Teachers Association sent a proposal to the Department of Church and Education that a research council be established to conduct systematic research on matters related to instruction.[11] In 1954 the Department submitted what was to become a hallmark document, Proposal Nr. Nine, to the *Storting* endorsing, among other things, the concept of a coordinated research endeavor.[12]

With the Council for Innovation in Education now in place, it was clear what the initial experiments would concentrate on, because the Department had already declared what its priority would be. The two most common school forms beyond the seven year folk school were the academic oriented *realskole* and the more practical continuation school.

On the one hand, there was sentiment from the minority parties and the old guard of the Labor Party, such as Fostervoll and Ribsskog, that these two school forms ought to remain, but that the continuation school be made compulsory to all who did not attend the *realskole* and be extended so that all youth would be in school until the age of sixteen or seventeen years. On the other hand, there was growing sentiment, especially among the new leaders of the Labor Party, that these two school forms ought to be integrated into a single comprehensive "youth school" (*ungdomsskole*), which would have theoretical and practical tracks.[13]

A genuine research mode would have been to experiment with the newly proposed form then compare it with the old form. To cast "experimentation" in such a manner quickly brings into focus the limitations of social experimentation. It would have been impossible to prove the value of one form over the other. The Council was inevitably cast as a political creature, and it was used by the new Minister Bergersen to publicize his new agenda. Even though the Council was a rather small operation in those first years, Bergerson turned to the media to publicize its work and use it as a vehicle for his political ambitions. Through all of this, experimentation was being used in a more restricted sense in that the Council tried out new forms with the intention of working out the snags in them.

In the fall of 1955, three schools in Malm, Sykkylven, and Ørsta, were designated to experiment with a two year comprehensive program beyond the seven year folk school. These were called "ad interim experiments," because they were quite modest in nature, consisting of a two year continuation school and the first two years of the *realskole*, under one roof. That is, they functioned under the same administration and with a single teaching staff. Two years later seven additional schools began to experiment and by 1959 eleven schools and 1400 pupils were involved in experiments.[14] A significant aspect of the experiments was the finding that fifteen percent of the *realskole* pupils and forty-five percent of the continuation pupils did not remain in the class they started with, suggesting the value of a combined school.[15]

A second model of experimentation was also under consideration from the very beginning of the Council, which would reduce the folk school to six years then build a three year youth school on top of that. Such a model eventually succeeded the old form, but it would wait until the climate was ripe for such an innovation.[16] Even as these experiments were moving forward, it was painfully apparent that great restrictions were being placed on attempts to expand the number of schools involved, because (1) few countryside schools could be included in the experiments, and (2) there were no legal provisions for widespread adoption of these newer school types. Minister Bergerson would not tolerate such hindrance, and he broke all precedence by having his Department of Church and Education draw up a full proposal for a new school law rather than turning to the traditional route of requesting the naming of a commission, whose work might take years.

On 17 January 1958 the Department submitted its proposal to the *Storting*.[17] The proposal set off a stormy debate in the news media, the professional organizations and the political arena. Over 1400 statements of protest arrived at the Education Committee of the *Storting* during the next year.[18] The very first paragraph of the proposed law is indicative of the problems it was creating. After noting that the purpose of the school is "to work to make the pupils become good members of the community," and "help to give the pupils a Christian and moral upbringing," the discussion section for this paragraph actually notes, in good technocratic style, that it would have been more appropriate not to make a statement of general goals at all. The Christian world rose up in arms on two accounts. First, the goals of an institution must be clarified; otherwise it is difficult to determine if the institution is doing what it is intended to do. Second, it was clear that Christian and moral upbringing were now being subordinated to broader social goals.

The proposed new folk school law led, as much as anything, to a split between the political Left and Right. The period of reconciliation between the various political factions in Norway was again ruptured and the coming decades would be characterized by hardened political party positions regarding the purposes and practices of schools. After a year of stormy debate a new school law was passed on 10 April 1959.[19]

THE FOLK SCHOOL LAW OF 1959

The aim of the folk school, was that the school should assist the home in helping pupils become good members of society.[20] From the Left point of view, such an aim was not at all radical. Still missing from the law would be any reference to citizenship or expressions about devotion to the nation, that characterizes so much of modern state schooling elsewhere. Schools remained a partner with the parents in rearing children, and in fact, homemaking became a mandatory subject in the new law, because it was felt that it could help instill in the youth a positive attitude toward home and family life.[21]

From the Right point of view, however, such a declared aim was clear evidence that Labor was politicizing schools. Per Lønning, Right member of the Education Committee in the Department of Church and Education, challenged the "socialistic" language in the proposal, suggesting that it reflected the partisan ideology of the government. According to Lønning, schools were not intended to mold the young to be obedient, compliant members of society; their goal ought to be to educate toward free and independent adults.[22]

Another stated aim of the schools was to help give pupils a Christian and moral upbringing.[23] We see that Norwegian schools had not yet entirely broken away from the church and become a secular institution, although, as we shall see below, formal school administration ties with the church were finally broken.

The greatest change intended in the law was the attempt to achieve parity between countryside and town schools. In spite of numerous amendments that had been made over the years to the 1936 folk school law, prior to 1959 there remained, in actuality, two laws: a town and a countryside folk school law. Much of Norway remained not just rural, but isolated. Families still lived on farms tucked away from the rest of society, and it would be difficult to provide an equal educational opportunity for them. The new law dictated a minimum size that a school could be, and set guidelines for how school districts could be established and combined. Provision was also made for children who would have to travel great distances of live away from home in order to satisfy the law.[24]

However, the greatest change in the law for the countryside had to do with the length of the school week and year. In 1954, the youth in the towns were receiving 6,400 hours of instruction over a seven year period as opposed to 4,500 hours of instruction in the countryside.[25] In fact, countryside youth were still attending school only three days a week.

In 1955, the Department had resolved to eliminate the three day school week in countryside schools, and a subsequent law was instituted which declared that over the next four years a full five day week should be implemented and the number of school weeks should be extended from 20 to 38 weeks each year in all schools. The new law confirmed that all schools would extend their programs to 39 weeks a year and even six days a week.[26]

In terms of the internal structure of the school, certain minimums were set for small institutions. No longer was it possible to have undivided or one-room schools;[27] and while two, three, four and five division schools remained possible, it was clear that the two and three division schools were much less desirable than the more fully graded institutions. Another great shift in the law was provision to have the state carry the financial burden of expanding the countryside schools, at least so that enough funds would be available for countryside schools to be financially competitive with town schools.[28]

The 1959 law also redefined the administrative structure of schooling. Each community would have two bodies. The general school board (*skolestyret*) would oversee all schools run by the community.[29] The community school council would consist of the inspector, all principals and teachers in full-time posts, and be responsible for such professional matters as the school plan, instruction and school books.[30] At the local school level, a supervisory committee (*tilsynsnemnd*) would exist to deal with school-home relations,[31] and a teachers' council would also be constituted.[32]

In this streamlining, two important trends become apparent. First, schools are seen as civic and professional institutions, they have long since ceased coming under the direct authority of the church. Second, the trend toward centralization continues unabated. Individual schools are now an integral part of a broader system and are unable to exercise the autonomy that was once taken for granted. While greater central funding was necessary to rectify disparities between town and countryside, it also brought with it clear constraints and directives. Even while there was essentially no change in the formal role of the Department of Church and Education with regard to the seven year folk school, it would play a central role in the experiments with the nine year unified school.

The 1959 law contained a number of provisions relating to the possibility that a community (i.e. municipality) may experiment with a nine year unified school. Article 10 stipulates, for example, that any community, "on the recommendation of the school board and by agreement with the Department, might decide to oblige pupils to attend a unified school for 9 years."[33] The insertion of this provision did not come without a good deal of debate and negotiation. The original proposal from the Department had failed to stipulate that the Department would be consulted,[34] but some anxiety was expressed about the possibility that too many communities would opt for the new model and the Department was needed to monitor the experiments.

Still another problem connected with the nine year school, was the concern expressed by some that a community might want to participate but retain some of its other schools, and so a further provision was inserted into the law that would allow a community to introduce a voluntary unified school.[35]

Even if a community opted to experiment, certain guidelines were necessary. The typical option would likely be to retain the seven year school and simply add two more years of theoretical and practical study. However, the option was given to experiment with a 6-3 school model.[36] Other directives also spelled out the terms of curriculum and teachers.

The 1959 law provided the legal mechanism for the Council for Innovation in Education to construct a nine year school and put it in place. In fact, by the time a general law on basic education was adopted in 1969, mandating a nine year school, only 60-70 of the 451 municipalities had not adopted such schools at least to some degree. Over half of the ninth graders in the country, and many more seventh and eighth graders were receiving instruction in a nine year school.[37]

The Right took strong issue with any provision that would mandate a nine year school. Hartvig C. Christie, Education Committee member of the *Storting*, claimed that such a provision went too far, because it defined what was to be before genuine experiments could be conducted to determine what the form should actually look like.[38]

It would be a mistake, however, to assume that the final form of the nine year school was more political than experimental. Indeed, a variety of structural and programmatic alterations were tried in the 1960s before the final version was adopted. Of course, these alterations reflected an interplay between politics, research, and professional interests. It is to these alterations that we turn in the next chapter.

16 The Nine Year Basic School

The one guiding principle that would ultimately dictate the final form of the basic school was the idea of unity (*enhet*). Within that concept, each school and each class in the school should reflect the various levels, interests and social background of the members of society. The strongest education for each child would be to help him/her live together and work with other members of society. Though unity was the ultimate principle, it certainly had not been the starting point in the experiments of the schools. Tradition continued to dictate divisions, levels and ranks within and between the schools, even when society itself had come to take for granted the principle of cooperation, unity, and democracy.

One of the major educational traditions to overcome in Norway was the notion that all pupils in a particular type of school would have the same program. The elective tradition, taken for granted in the United States, has no place in Norwegian tradition. Cafeteria style education in a school is foreign to the Norwegian mentality. Of course, within the European and Norwegian tradition, it was taken for granted, that different types of schools would offer quite different programs, but traditionally all students in a given type of school were expected to take the same program of studies as all other students. Consequently, attempts to join the continuation school and the *realskole* would present major problems.

EXPERIMENTATION CONTINUES

As we noted in the previous chapter, the first experimental step taken by the Council for Innovation in Education was simply to put the two schools under the same roof. This idea continued to be reflected in the first major Council plan issued in 1960, which called for two so-called "lines of study:" a general theoretical line and a general practical line.[1] The major distinction between the two lines of study in that combined school would be foreign language. The theoretical line (*realskole*) would offer English and possibly one other language. The practical line (continuation school) would offer no language or possibly English, then divert the time to other subjects, usually of a practical nature.

A more striking deviation from Norwegian tradition was a division within the core subjects of study themselves. Norwegian, mathematics and English were envisioned to be differentiated into a, b, and c levels of difficulty. Those pupils in the theoretical line would enroll in more taxing b or c levels of difficulty, while those in the practical line would enroll in the easier a or b levels. The subjects of German, natural science, and social science would each maintain two levels of difficulty.

In grade nine even greater differentiation was envisioned by the Council. As in grade eight, the theoretical line would have one or two foreign languages while the practical line would have none or one, and that at a lower level of difficulty. In addition, the practical line would be divided into a number of specializations: work shop, domestic science, office and business, agriculture, and fishing and seamanship. Pupils in those practical studies would also study mathematics that was appropriate to a practical field rather than mathematics having a more academic, theoretical orientation.

The above plan was debated far into the night in the *Storting* on 8 June 1961, and it became so heated that the president was compelled to request that the members return to a tone befitting parliament. There was no vote but the whole discussion centered around a few central issues.[2] In the first place, the Council was inclined toward a 6-3 structural variation and the instructional plan would, therefore, begin in the seventh year. The differentiation envisioned by the Council would, consequently, take place at an earlier stage than was taking place in the 7-2 plan. Many members of the *Storting* declared that such a notion was tantamount to pushing back the clock and robbing the nation of the victories it had won by adopting the seven year unified school.

Closely related was the fact that differences between the two lines of study were seen to be too great. In fact, differences appeared to be as great, if not greater, than between the old *realskole* and continuation school. Such retrogressive notions would certainly not be tolerated in Norway.

The issue was not so much the retention of the seven year school, but the prevention of early differentiation. In fact, the 6-3 model was popular on a number of grounds. For example, university lecturer Eva Nordland and Primary/Secondary Education chief Helge Sivertsen argued in a proposition before the *Storting* at the time that the 6-3 model be adopted on human development grounds. "With 13 years of age, pupils normally enter a new period of psychological development, filled with an urge and a need toward independence, greater maturity and new interests. . ." A three year school could address this period in their lives more adequately than could a two year school, because it could create a milieu and an atmosphere that would foster the pupils initiative and personality. It could help the young person feel a part of a social environment and a sense of responsibility to the school.[3] The Council for Innovation in Education reacted quickly to the *Storting* debate and reinstituted most of the program that had existed in the old seventh year.

In 1963 the Council came out with a completely revised experimentation proposal. Because the new scheme was published in a little brochure having a blue cover, it came to be known as the "Blue Plan."[4] The major change in the new proposal was to eliminate the two lines of study. Norway would take a dramatic step in this action, because it signaled a move away from the old notion that students in a certain type of school must all take the same curriculum. The new differentiation model would allow students in their eighth year to opt for course plans each having 27 hours of required study (out of a total of 36 hours), but students would also be able to choose some optional courses, which were open to all students regardless of the course plan they had selected. Students in the theoretical plan might even be able to opt for practical courses.

In the ninth year students would move into one of six plans of study, one of which would remain essentially the theoretical line, but the number of hours in each plan would be reduced to 16 so that all students would be able to select an even greater array of optional courses than in the eighth year.

This plan was not intended to supersede the 1960 plan. Rather, communities could continue following the older plan, but new programs could go in the direction of either the 1960 or the 1963 plan. Reaction in the *Storting* to the new plan was positive, and signaled permission on the part of the Council to move completely away from the idea of differentiated lines of study.[5]

The following year the Council came out with still another experimental design, known as the "Red Plan," because of the red cover of the publicity brochure.[6] The major characteristic of the new plan was to integrate the theoretical and practical plans of study. In fact, grades seven and eight possessed the same obligatory core courses of study, and continuity was further enhanced in that the instructors remained the same in the core courses of these two grades. The three levels of difficulty in Norwegian, mathematics and English were retained, but the number of required hours in the Red Plan was extended to 31 as opposed to 27 hours in the Blue Plan.

In grade nine the notion of extensive optional courses was retained, but reduced, allowing 15 of 36 weekly hours to be taken by student choice, rather than 18 as had been the case in the Blue Plan. The remaining 21 hours were taken in revised subject groupings with the one stipulation that each student have a 7 hour main subject field.

The Blue and Red Plans were soon joined by a Green Plan, which further integrated the program of studies in the schools.[7] At least 25 communities were working with the Green Plan by the fall, 1966. The number of optional courses was reduced from 15 to 12 in grade nine, and students were also heterogeneously grouped in their Norwegian courses. Two years later, the same was done in mathematics, with the notion that individual differences of students would be accounted for within the classroom itself rather than between classes providing for different levels of difficulty.[8]

The movement was clear; each new plan signaled a step toward a single course of studies for all pupils through the nine years. Of course, some optional courses were being retained, but the number of hours allowed for them was continually reduced. Unity was paramount, but that unity pertained to the composition of classrooms. Differences in student background and ability were recognized, but those differences were to be accounted for within the classroom itself.

While the Council for Innovation in Education was engaged in an active and expanding experimental process, the governmental wheels were slowly turning to effect a general law for the basic school. On 1 March 1963, a Royal Commission, consisting of 15 members was named, including a school superintendent, members of the *Storting*, school inspectors, headmasters, and scholars. The Commission submitted a preliminary report to the Department in 1965, which became the basis for a formal proposal by the Department to the *Storting* on 7 April 1967.[9] In this proposal the Department reviewed the experiments that had been under way, discussed some of the transition problems, and proposed a preliminary draft of a law concerning a unified nine year basic school. After two years of debate and deliberation, a comprehensive law was finally passed on 12 June 1969.[10]

THE BASIC SCHOOL LAW OF 1969

It would be superfluous to reiterate the exact elements of the new law, because they are clear within the framework of the developments that have been described through the previous decade. A summary of the situation might be helpful. The general aims of the basic school remained somewhat consistent with the 1959 law although a clearer incorporation of the Right into the aims is noted. The 1959 law was castigated for stressing social ideology while remaining silent about free and independent adults. The new law was tempered in that it stressed the making of "self-reliant human beings," who possess "mental freedom and tolerance."[11]

The child attends a junior school for six years followed by a three year youth school. Through the first seven years, all children take the same subjects and in the eighth grade five hours a week of optional studies are taken. This is expanded to ten hours a week in grade nine.[12] No more than 30 pupils may be assigned to any one classroom.[13] Some account is taken of remote areas where pupils from several grades must join together.[14]

One of the innovations of the law is that a special social-pedagogic advisory body is set up to decide whether a pupil needs special education.[15] Administratively, local school authorities are responsible for carrying out education. The supreme authority remains the community school board;[16] however, the parent and professional bodies defined in the 1959 law remain. Costs connected with the basic school are covered by the local authorities, but a good deal of state aid is ensured to cover many of the expenses, including running costs.[17]

Two of the more difficult issues surrounding the new law had to do with the subjects to be taught, and the qualifications of the teachers. In the next section, we deal with the *Normalplan* for the new school, which came into effect in 1974.[18]

THE *MØNSTERPLAN* FOR BASIC SCHOOLS

The 1969 law stipulates that "the subjects taught in school shall normally comprise religious instruction, Norwegian, mathematics, foreign languages, physical training, home studies, social studies, nature study and aesthetic, practical and social training."[19] It then explains that "the Department shall lay down a model plan of studies, which shall provide a full account of the aims set for the school, of the allocation of subjects and lessons, and of teaching programs for all subjects and at all class levels."[20]

At the time the Department was preparing its *Storting* proposition, it moved to begin the task of developing a Normal Plan appropriate to the new school. On 27 June 1967 a commission was named with Hans-Jørgen Dokka as its chair. Remaining in harmony with the 1939 Normal Plan, the name given the group was the Normal Plan Commission (*Normalplanutvalget*) of 1967. Curiously, none of the members of this Commission was associated with any political ideology; each was a highly regarded professional;[21] however, the work of the Commission soon led to extensive partisan debates and hardened points of view.

The controversy was not just political, but professional. Norway has a recent tradition of organizing national councils responsible for primary education, secondary education, teacher education, vocational education, etc. It was thought by many that the National Council for Primary Education would be the appropriate body to engage in the professional task of developing the curriculum for the new schools. Others, including the teacher organizations and Department leaders, maintained that the Department should name its own commission. A compromise plan emerged in which the Department would name its commission, but that the National Council would make a substantial contribution to the final report.[22] With two groups working on one plan, it was destined for trouble from the very beginning.

Other factors would also spell trouble. The plans of the past had treated town and countryside separately, and they had not been required to deal with a unified curriculum in the eighth, ninth and tenth grades. Of course the plans of the Council for Innovation in Education would assist the Commission, but we recall that the only fully developed plan of the Council for Innovation in Education was that which came out in 1960, which had not yet joined the practical and theoretical lines of study.[23]

Even the name of the Commission raised problems. The 1936 law for the countryside schools had mandated the development of a Model Plan (*Mønsterplan*) while the 1936 law for the town schools had mandated a Normal Plan (*Normalplan*). The resulting plans had taken the name Normal Plan, and the 1967 Commission was also given that name. Then the 1969 law used the name Model Plan as it mandated the formation of a Normal Plan Commission.[24]

On the positive side was the existence of the 1939 Normal Plan, which remained highly respected among professional educators. It would serve as a valuable model, at least for the first seven grades of study. Many of the problems confronted by the Commission were identified by its Chair, Hans-Jørgen Dokka, in an article published in 1977.[25] One of the major problems, had to do with the issue of differentiation, an issue that had plagued the work of the Council for Innovation in Education for the past decade and one half, and it had not yet been resolved beyond basic statements of principle. Two facets of the problem were identified. On the one hand, the choice of optional courses would have some effect on further choices in secondary school, particularly the selection of a second foreign language. On the other hand, the core subjects that all students enrolled in presented serious competence, interest and ability problems.

Norwegian educational politics had finally transcended the structural issue of schooling and was now facing the problem of student differences as they presented themselves within the inner life of the school. It was clear to everyone that the problem could only be resolved within the context of a program that accounted for individualized instruction of some kind, or at least some sort of grouping process within the classroom itself. However, the Primary Education Council wanted to resolve the issue in its report of 16 June 1971, by recommending that a transition policy be adopted placing children into different ability groups.[26] This was not really a part of the charge, and only led to heightened controversy.

Closely related to these differentiation problems was the issue of standards. There was sentiment in the Commission that no minimal standard ought to be set, so that maximum flexibility could be insured in developing the subjects for the new unity school. To the contrary, there was great sentiment that the new school would result in lessened standards.

Another of the major problems facing the Commission was the charge of the 1969 law that their plan would "provide a full account of the aims set by the school. . ."[27] Dokka provides a fascinating account of the difficulties this presented with the specific course on religious instruction. It was a no-win situation, because anything more specific than was in the original law would come under attack by some faction of society. If

Dokka had taken a stand on a strong religious program, he would have been attacked by the less religious oriented people. If he had taken a stand for a more neutral position, he would have been attacked by the strong Christian community.[28]

Still another problem had to do with the assignment of time to the various subjects. This was particularly thorny because the number of hours of instruction each week was probably going to be reduced from 36 to 30 hours as Norway moved from a six day week to a five day week. Given this development, subjects such as religion were particularly vulnerable. The 1963 Council for Innovation in Education plan had recommended two hours a week in each of the nine grade levels or 18 hours, while the Department was inclined toward 21 hours.[29] When the Commission actually recommended 16 hours, great cries of outrage were heard.

The proposal of the Council for Primary Schooling only added to the controversy. That body recommended reducing an "hour of instruction" from 45 minutes to 40 minutes so that more "hours of instruction" could be given in the various subjects.

A final problem facing the Commission was the openness in which it was expected to work. The previous Normal Plans had been worked out by small committees of people and simply published as finished products. The new plan was subjected to public discussion at every step and included dozens of consultants working on one or another aspect of the plan. From the beginning it was a highly charged political process,[30] and it is remarkable that it every became a finished product.

An interim product did emerge in 1971, which was sent to the *Storting*.[31] It was 1974, however, before the Model Plan was finalized.[32] In accordance with the 1969 law, it would be binding on all schools,[33] although the model plan actually stipulates in its forward that it is presented as a "guidance giving structural plan."[34]

The plan might conveniently be divided into two major sections. In the first section are more general comments about the purposes of the school, the school as a community, subject matter, differentiation, methods of teaching, etc. Emphasis is placed on the fact that content is not specified in detail in order that the school boards, the local school, and even the teacher might try things out and draw from local materials and information. The beginnings of a reorientation in education is here beginning to take form. The centralization process has finally begun to be called seriously into question. Responsibility and authority are beginning to be delegated to the local level. In fact, the entire plan only provides a guiding framework and is not to be taken as a compulsory minimum requirement to be met by all children.

All classes in the basic school are to be undifferentiated, and individual differences are to be accounted for in the classroom itself. The teacher would be given aids and materials to help in dealing with differences, but the classrooms would not be divided into ability groups. Within this context, the student would be encouraged to learn to make choices, in the earlier grades these choices would be made within subject areas, and at the upper grades, choices would even extend to the selection of certain courses themselves. The Plan also took the position that a specific line of studies would not be necessary to gain admission to further study in upper secondary school.

The Model Plan reiterates the basic goals of the school as laid down by the 1969 school law, but goes into specific detail about those aspects of the law that are relatively new, particularly as they relate to such traits as creativity, self-reliance, freedom, tolerance, learning how to learn, cooperation, etc.

The School as a community is also stressed, not only in its own right, but as a part of the larger society. Consequently, young people would be exposed to that broader community. The Plan shows strong evidence of being influenced by the old 1939 Normal Plan, with its progressive education, activity school orientation. School is not to be seen as an institution where students sit passively. They ought to be active learners, they ought to be taken on excursions and engage in work experience, they ought to be engaged in groups of differing sizes, they ought to have individual attention and individual challenges. The school community does not discriminate on the basis of sex, requiring that all classes be open to both sexes.

A major aspect of the Plan has to do with the distribution of subjects and periods. Weekly teaching periods allocated to specific subjects is 123 in the first six years, with a minimum number of 129. Local authorities may increase the number of hours to 138 hours of state supported hours and they may add another 9 hours at their own cost.

The last three years take a total of 90 hours, 30 each year. In grade eight, five hours are in optional subjects, and in grade nine, seven hours are optional. Otherwise the courses and the hours in these courses are strictly defined.

The major portion of the report is devoted to instruction in the different subjects. Each subject is typically treated in five ways: 1. the goals, 2. the content, 3. the working modes, 4. the teaching materials, and 5. evaluation.

Because religion occupied such a central place in the debates, we shall only mention that it was decided that religion would receive eighteen hours of instruction, or two hours each week in each of the nine grades. A comprehensive syllabus is developed for each subject, although, as we have mentioned, the content it not compulsory; however, within the compulsory courses, there are also compulsory topics that must be taught, including traffic studies, alcohol, narcotics, tobacco, career guidance, family education, nutrition, first aid, and dental care.

Other important issues in schooling also were incorporated into the Plan, including special education, education of the Lapps and other minority groups. All of this had important implications for the kinds of people who were becoming teachers and the kind of training they would receive. Teacher training would be central to the success of the new school.

TEACHER EDUCATION AND THE BASIC SCHOOL

The new basic school would place great responsibility on the teacher of that school, who typically had been trained to work in a different type of school carrying out quite a different type of instructional program. Teachers of the past had been prepared to act as a source of knowledge and an evaluator, but the teacher of the basic school was viewed as one who would act as "a guide, a source of inspiration and an organizer of knowledge for the students."[35] Few were trained to help students become creative, self-reliant, cooperative learners.

One of the major problems with the educational system in Norway was that training colleges fell within a different division of the Department than did the basic schools. Consequently, as the basic school took form, there remained the problem of changing the training program to correspond with the new regulations. This would be no easy task. Before the nine-year school was put into effect, various types of teacher education were taking place in different institutions. The university had been responsible for the education of *realskole* teachers, special teacher training colleges for continuation and vocational school teachers, and general teacher training colleges for primary and continuation school teachers.[36] It would be necessary to integrate these responsibilities, but a clear understanding of the situation requires a brief comment about the traditions that had emerged in each institution.

The university had not seen fit to become involved in pedagogical studies throughout the nineteenth century. The 1896 school law on higher common schools provided the first major legal incentive for the universities to provide some pedagogical study for teachers of the higher schools. In 1905 a law on teacher examinations provided the basis for the establishment of a seminar at Oslo. The names of Otto Anderssen and Herman Ruge are vital reminders that the seminar served students preparing to become secondary school teachers at the university. That preparation was highly academic, taken during one semester and consisted of the study of historical and philosophical issues surrounding schooling in the country. It had almost no practical dimensions connected with it.

Over the decades a number of committees and proposals were drawn up, but little had been accomplished in a formal sense prior to the emergence of the basic school. Even then, the university took almost no interest surrounding the preparation of teachers for the new youth school. In contrast, a number of teacher colleges were actively involved in questions of teacher preparation.[37] Of course, it would be a great boon to the colleges to take on that responsibility, in addition to preparing primary school teachers, which had always been their responsibility.

The general teacher colleges had provided, since the early 1930s, two major forms of primary teacher preparation. Students, who had graduated from the *gymnasium*, were expected to take a two year course of studies, while those who had graduated from the seven year folk school, were expected to take a four year course of studies. With the emergence of the experimental mode in Norway in the mid-1950s, the teacher colleges began to engage in a host of experimental programs.

Because the basic schools in the earliest experiments were based on special lines of study, the colleges also began to orient their experiments toward specialized study, particularly extending their two year program one extra year and offering subject based studies in such concentrations as music, domestic studies, English, Norwegian, mathematics, social studies, etc. The notion was that the teacher training colleges would take over the training of teachers for the youth school. These trends were formally recognized when the *Storting* passed an interim or provisional law on teacher training in 1961.[38] In that law a major shift in the definition of a teacher's qualifications took place. Whereas, in the past, teachers had been trained and qualified to teach in specific types of schools, they were now qualified according to a particular category: primary, *adjunkt*, and *lektor*. The certified primary teacher could become a qualified *adjunkt* teacher, which might simplistically be thought of as a teacher qualified to teach in lower secondary school, by taking two additional years of specialized training either at the university or a teacher training college. In other words, lower secondary teachers, who had previously been trained at the university, and who had been trained as subject specialists, could now be trained at an institution which had until then only trained primary teachers. In the process, these colleges began orienting themselves toward specialist training.

However, the basic school was reoriented during the 1960s toward an undifferentiated and unified school, which had dramatic implications for the type of training the basic school teachers ought to have. It was evident that teachers would be required to have a far greater general pedagogical education and they would become more and more responsible for the selection of content, the way it was organized, and the process of transmission.[39] In an effort to take advantage of these changes, the teacher colleges tended toward experimental more than conventional teacher training institutions. According to Telhaug, by 1971, approximately 70% of all the classes taught at the teacher training colleges could be labeled experimental.[40]

The situation had reached the point by 1967 that the Department charged the National Council on Teacher Education to draw up a proposal for a new law related to teacher education. After one year of deliberation, a proposal was submitted to the Department,[41] including the following: (1) teacher education candidates shall be drawn from those having taken the *examen artium*, (2) basic training should take three years, (3) those wishing to teach specialized subjects must engage in a further year at the university or a college, (4) students who have specialized in a subject at an institution of higher learning must take an extra year of pedagogical training at a teacher training institution.

While the Council was working, the Secondary Teachers Association set up its own committee to come up with a proposal, chaired by the original director of the National Council on Innovation in Education, Tønnes Sirevåg. That committee was still working when the Teacher Education Council proposal came out, and its structure was such that it presented a genuine alternative to the original proposal. That proposal recommended that the training also be three years, but that the last year be taken over by an institute that divides its time between theory and practice. Those students who have not taken the teacher college route would be subject to one half year pedagogical training at the institute, which would also have responsibility for assessing the candidates and recognizing them as qualified teachers.[42]

Other proposals also came into being at the time, which were considered by the Department as it drew up its final proposal, which was sent to the *Storting* in 1971.[43] Because there was a change in the government, with the Labor Party loosing its hold on the *Storting*, it could not consider the proposal in that session, so still another proposal was submitted the following year.[44] In that proposal the notion that primary teachers would have three years of normal study and that youth school teachers would have primary training plus an extra year, either at the university or the training college, was maintained. One other dramatic shift in identity was noted. Not only would the students come to the institution with an *examen artium*, but that institution would be recognized as an institution of higher learning, with the same rights as other institutions of higher learning, including the right to engage in advanced studies and research. The teacher education law was passed on 8 June 1973,[45] thus completing the major revisions necessary to implement the full basic school into the system.

17 Reform at the Upper Secondary School

The upper secondary school in Norway encompasses that education intended primarily for those between the ages of sixteen and nineteen years of age. It includes traditional theoretical education, vocational education and the first forms of adult education. The higher common school law of 1935 and the vocational education law of 1940 had set the pattern for secondary schooling during the first decades after World War II. Those laws were joined by still another law, enacted in 1949, concerning the folk high schools,[1] which also service large numbers of secondary school age youth.

The laws for these three types of schools held rather firmly until the 1960s, when it became apparent that they would soon no longer be valid because of the changes taking place in the basic school. Early postwar projections had largely settled certain issues regarding the nature of the future upper secondary school. For example, the Coordinating Committee for Schooling, in its Thirteenth Report on Secondary Schooling, in 1950, reinforced the notion that a comprehensive three year upper secondary school would eventually become the standard.[2]

However, most issues remained unresolved and they gave special focus to the debates that evolved out of a host of committees that were named between 1960 and the passage of a comprehensive secondary school law in 1974.[3] The first committee during this period of time to issue its report was a so-called *Samlegymnaskomite*, which raised the problem of central vs. local control of upper secondary education. It was the sense of the committee members that since the communities had become responsible for the basic school, educational planning and development at the upper secondary level would also be better served if it took place at the community level.[4]

The next select committee, named in 1962 and taking the name of its chair, rector Agvald Gjelsvik (*Gjelsvikutvalget*), was charged with the task of making recommendations concerning the subject matter content and the internal structure of the *gymnas*, including instructional methods and teaching plans within the individual subject areas.[5] The committee claimed that the *gymnas* ought to consist of approximately two years of core courses, including Norwegian, religion or philosophy, two foreign languages, social sciences, natural sciences, mathematics and physical education, and one year of optional or specialized courses of a general, vocational or aesthetic nature. The first year of study would be devoted to those core courses and the second and third years be divided between core and optional courses. A few members suggested that the *gymnas* be divided into lines of study, but that was a definite minority. The committee did foresee the clustering of specialized courses under three major divisions: social sciences, natural sciences, and foreign languages.

The Gjelsvik Committee had a limited charge that did not allow for basic considerations of the entire spectrum of upper secondary education. That task fell on the so-called Steen Committee, which was formally named the School Committee (*skolekomite*), but which was known widely by the name of its foreman, Reiulf Steen, a journalist. Its charge was "to assess questions related to higher schools for general education and vocational education." In addition, the committee would develop a plan for a school system that would accommodate all young people within the 16-19 age group from the perspective of the new situation being created by the nine year basic school.[6]

The Steen Committee ultimately submitted three reports, the first published in 1967 and focussed "On the Needs for Training and Educating in the Age Group from 16-19."[7] The recommendations in this report coincided in large measure with the Gjelsvik report, at least insofar as it opted for a set of core courses with optional specialized courses. The significance of this report was much greater, however, because the Steen Committee was referring to all upper secondary schooling, not just the *gymnas*.

The Steen Committee attempted to accommodate to the present reality by suggesting, at least as a temporary measure, that all schools not have to provide a full set of core courses immediately, but that they adopt a middle way program. On the one hand, pupils could engage in a *gymnas* type program that consisted almost entirely of general courses. On the other hand, they could engage in a vocational course of studies, with a small number of core or general courses thrown in each year. A third option would be for students to take a mixed program consisting of about half general and half vocational courses for two years, after which they could transfer either to a *gymnas* type program or a vocational school type program for the third year.

The second report was published in 1969, and focused on the "Experimental Plans for Study Lines: Technical and Industrial Subjects, Commercial and Clerical Subjects, Home Economics, Maritime Studies, Aesthetic Studies and Art Education, Physical Training and Sport Education, and General Studies."[8] The third report was published in 1970, and focused on the "Experimental Plans for Study Lines: Agriculture, Fishing, Apprenticeship and Vocational Schools, Higher Schools for the Functionally Problematic, and Adult Education." The last proposal also addressed issues connected with a general law for all upper secondary schools.[9]

A number of other committees dealing with special aspects of education, such as private schooling, apprenticeship training, special education, and examinations, were also named during this time period. We shall deal with the work of many of these committees before our story has been concluded.

The national educational councils also planned and proposed changes. This included not only the Council for Secondary Education, but the Council for Innovation in Education, which continued to assert itself by initiating experimental programs. The first upper secondary experiments initiated by the Council for Innovation in Education came in 1968 and were mainly an outgrowth of the Gjelsvik Committee recommendations having to do with the study of new working arrangements and cooperative learning modes in the *gymnas*. The next year experiments were undertaken which dealt with the Steen Committee recommendations, the first being rather modest in nature, but dealing with structural adjustments. At Narvik, for example, the *gymnas* students in the science line experimented with one year of science and one year of vocational education.[10]

In 1970, a series of two year foundation courses for crafts and industry, as well as commerce and secretarial training, were set in motion, with others in agriculture coming a year later. About half the students' time was devoted to general studies and the other half to vocational studies. In 1971, still another set of experiments were under way. These dealt with the total upper secondary situation, and they typically involved combining different kinds of schools in a region and restructuring them so that they constituted a somewhat integrated institution providing a full three year course of studies. By 1973, a total of 13 *gymnas* and 31 vocationally oriented schools were engaged in some form of experimental work.[11]

The Department of Church and Education continued acting as the clearing house of petitions and reports, usually sending them to a wide range of organizations in the country. For example, *Instilling III* of the Steen Committee was sent to no less than 106 organizations in addition to all universities, *gymnas*, folk high schools, and vocational schools in Norway.[12] The Department would then prepare reports and recommendations to the *Storting*; these reports attempted to draw together the reactions coming from the various sources. The consequence was a multitude of reports and proposals that would have only complicated the process of decision-making regarding the new school in most countries. Outside of Norway, the involvement of so many bodies with so many vested interests, would certainly have spelled trouble for the future of a meaningful comprehensive upper secondary school law, but the consensus orientation of Norway would somehow allow the process to work. Even in Norway, however, whereas there was general consensus among political factions regarding the nature of the basic school, divisions continued about the nature of the upper secondary school. Even its name was a point of controversy. In its charge to the Steen Committee, the Department had used the term "higher" school, but the use of the term "high" or "higher" school would have created difficulties with tertiary level schools which had adopted variants of these terms to identify institutions of higher learning.[13] The Labor Party advocated the use of *gymnas*, because it was generally recognized and respected. The Right challenged its use because the term *gymnas* symbolized a special type of program for a small segment of the population, and recommended the more general term "further school" (*videregående skole*), because the school would serve every segment of the population and provide all education beyond the basic school.[14]

The political situation had also become more complicated. The last time the Labor Party held a clear majority in the *Storting* had been 1957. Although Labor was by far the largest single party, the number of delegates in the *Storting* stood at forty-nine percent in 1961, forty-five percent in 1965, forty-nine percent in 1969, and forty percent in 1971.[15] Because no single party was able to gain a majority, the country was governed by coalitions throughout the 1960s and 1970s. For certain periods of time, these coalitions did not even include the Labor Party.[16] Any law on upper secondary education would be a product of various points of view. It would represent a product of a broad consensus building process, which was, fortunately, not foreign to Norwegian political thinking.

Reidar Myhre suggests fourteen major issues surrounding the debates on the upper secondary school law, including the school's name, its formal goals and objectives, its organizational structure, administrative arrangements, admissions criteria, instructional schedule, teaching requirements, curriculum, differentiation issues, marks and evaluation, instructional modes, and special education provisions.[17] However, these issues were discussed within a broader context that must be understood by anyone not entirely familiar with Norway. In the next sections we shall draw attention to but two facets of Norwegian schooling that might assist the reader in understanding part of this context. These facets are: (1) the rapid expansion of upper secondary students, and (2) the public-private school context.

EXPANSION OF SECONDARY EDUCATIONAL ENROLLMENTS

In past decades, especially after the Labor Party came into power, it has been the policy of the government to equalize educational opportunities among all classes of people in the country.[18] In spite of the concerted efforts on the part of the Norwegians to provide equal educational opportunities to all the youth of the country, there has remained enormous differences in terms of the kinds of educational experiences the young people in Norway have received, particularly at the secondary level. The Norwegians have been acutely aware of the differences, particularly as social science research information, has come into the public eye.[19]

The first major study after World War II was conducted by Vidkunn Coucheron Jarl, who determined the highest school attendance levels of 8,000 young men between the ages of nineteen and twenty-two years of age in the years 1947-49.[20] He found enormous differences remained between the countryside and towns. At the time fifty-one percent of all the population had been attending some kind of schooling beyond the folk school. He found that the percentage of town youth to attend the *gymnas* was double that of the countryside youth (14% to 7%). The *gymnas* program had not only remained within the traditional mode, but the number of students completing the program had remained highly limited and biased toward the town. Of course, attendance figures in upper secondary schools had begun to change, but those changes were not substantial. Whereas a total of eight percent of the youth were attending the *gymnas* when Coucheron Jarl did his study, by 1960, the percentage of youth had only risen to twelve percent.[21]

The difference between town and country was not just in the *gymnas*. Coucheron Jarl also found that a greater percentage of town youth had attended all other forms of post-folk school institutions than countryside youth.[22] He found that a higher percentage of countryside youth attended at the lowest levels of vocational training, while far greater percentages of youth in the towns were attending the higher levels of technical, crafts, commercial, agricultural, and maritime studies.[23]

In 1961, Natalie Ramsøy published a study showing the social background of young people who attended schooling beyond lower secondary school. Predictably, she found that over sixty percent of the youth whose fathers were in academic work or acting as higher functionaries in society, had gone beyond that level. Thirty-five percent of those whose fathers were in commercial or office work had also gone beyond lower secondary school, whereas only fifteen percent of the crafts worker, six percent of unskilled worker, and five percent of agricultural worker children had gone so far in school.[24]

When breaking these figures down between town and countryside, she also found that the countryside children were disadvantaged in comparison with the town children in all social categories. For example, whereas from sixty-four to seventy-two percent of the children of academics and higher functionaries in the different towns attended some form of schooling beyond lower secondary school, only forty to fifty-nine percent of those in similar occupations in the countryside did. Whereas seventeen to thirty percent of those children of town commercial workers attended school beyond lower secondary school, only five to seventeen percent of the children of commercial workers in the countryside did so.[25]

The most vivid breakdown of the situation at the *gymnas* came in a study by Sigmund Vangsnes, who provided social class data on those receiving *examen artium* marks in 1950. Almost half (47.9%) of all holders of the *artium* turned out to be children of academics or middle level functionaries. Another 25% were children of lower level functionaries. The figures for children of those in agriculture and forestry (4.9%), crafts (6.1%), fishing (1.6%), and foreman for workers (3.5%) were relatively insignificant.[26]

The Norwegians had long been aware of sex differences and attendance. Census data and Department of Church and Education statistics had always provided sex differences, so the recognition of inequalities of opportunity were more attitudinal that informational. At the folk school level, girls had attended school in numbers equal to the boys from the time the folk school had became a genuine common school. Even at the *realskole* level, the number of girls had been roughly equivalent to the boys since Norway had gained independence from Sweden in 1905. The *gymnas* situation had remained a different story. As late as 1960, almost fifty-eight percent of all *gymnas* students were boys, though it began to decline in the late 1960s and had reached a fifty-four percent level for the boys by 1970. In the 1970s girls finally gained parity with the boys, at least in terms of numbers, at the upper secondary level.[27]

There was general consensus that the upper secondary school required fundamental changes if the situation were to be rectified. We turn now to still another broader context issue: private schooling.

PRIVATE SCHOOLING

Private schooling played a vital role in nineteenth century Norway, although state schools eventually came to dominate the scene with most of the private schools either becoming public institutions or ceasing to exist altogether. By 1965/66 less than one percent of all primary school youth remained in private schools, while the percentage of those in secondary schools was somewhat larger.[28] In other words, the private school issue was almost entirely a secondary school issue. A number of explanations can be given to explain the existence of such a small private school population. Religion has been the major factor leading to the establishment of private schooling throughout Europe. It is only in nation states such as the Netherlands and Belgium, which have strong religious cleavages that one finds a strong commitment to private schools.[29] Norway remains a fairly homogeneous culture, particularly with regard to religion. Even in countries which do not have religious cleavages, such as in France, a significant division often exists between those in favor of a religious based school and those in favor of purely secular institutions. Here again, while the private school issue has always been a source of lively debate, almost everyone in Norway accepts the fact that the public school ought to reflect the dominant religious tone of the country, at least to some degree. Consequently, religious schools play a rather insignificant role in the educational drama of Norway, even though there are three schools which cater to the small Catholic population, and even though there are a few religious oriented schools that seek to stress religion more than can be found in the public schools.

In addition to religious schools, some schools exist which emerged out of the New Education Movement. The most popular form is the Waldorf Schools, which rely on the anthroposophical notions laid down by Rudolf Steiner. In addition there are a small number of international schools, which cater to the foreign population in business, NATO headquarters, diplomatic corps, etc.

Private schools have long been given some form of public support on an *ad hoc* basis, and it required continual effort on the part of those involved in the private schools. However the situation had deteriorated dramatically since the time that the Labor Party had gained control of the government, and by the 1950s relatively few schools were receiving any support, and even that support was minimal. The advocates of the political Left were quite satisfied to allow the situation to continue, and they would not have been unhappy to see private schooling die out altogether. In fact, they sympathized with the efforts of the socialist countries in Eastern Europe, which had systematically eliminated private schooling altogether.

On the other hand, the Conservatives were determined to bolster the support of the private schools, particularly the schools that stressed a firm commitment to religion. In 1959 the issue of private support was raised anew, when the *Kristelig Gymnasium* and the Sand *realskole* made application for funds, having never received such support in the past. There was some sympathy, and they were given some assistance. The issue with these schools was not controversial, but in 1961 the Seventh Day Adventists made application for support, and this application required a general assessment of policy.[30]

The Gjelsvik Commission addressed the issue in its report, but there remained strong resistance to general support of private schools. When the Conservatives came into power in 1965, action began which eventuated in the establishment of a commission which would deal with the issue of general support for private schools, and the financial consequences this would have on the government. This body issued four reports in 1967,[31] and in 1968 a firm proposal was formulated and submitted to the *Storting*. In that paper, it was made clear that private schools would not be able to exist without state support. The report also pointed out that much of the vocational education of the country depends on private initiative, that they constitute an important human right, that is vital to democracy.[32]

On 6 March 1970, a law was finally passed which allowed private schools to receive grants of up to 85% of all running costs if they: (1) have as an objective a plan to carry out pedagogical experiments, (2) have been established for religious or ethical reasons, or (3) meet a quantitative educational need not sufficiently cared for by the public authorities.[33]

It was clear that the public relied a bit on the private sector to satisfy some of its upper secondary school needs, but most of schooling would continue to take place in the public schools.

UPPER SECONDARY SCHOOL ISSUES

We turn now to the specific issues that policy makers were constrained to deal with as they struggled to design a new upper secondary education policy. The major concern had to do with the old dualistic frame of mind that had characterized Western civilization and Western education from the time of the Greeks, and which had remained firmly entrenched in the higher schooling tradition of Norway. In spite of the dramatic adjustments that had been made in the movement toward a unified school and in the curriculum, the *gymnas* had remained somewhat immune to modernizing trends, at least insofar as it continued to focus on academic, general, and liberal studies, while it relegated the more utilitarian, practical, and vocational studies to the less valued, vocational schools, continuation schools, and apprenticeship programs. What would be the relationship between general and vocational subjects in the schools providing upper secondary education? Would the different school types be collapsed, as had happened with the *realskole* and the continuation school? Would the *gymnas* remain distinct and be a rather exclusive enclave for the brighter students?

In the old *gymnas*, it was taken for granted that a student would come into the school with a similar level of competence as all other students, but a major reason why three, four, and five year schools existed having A and B forms was to provide for various backgrounds as the starting point of the school. It had already been decided that the basic school would cease designing its program in such a way as to insure that each student had attained a minimum competence level. How would the upper secondary school provide for varying backgrounds of students? How would it become a school for a more heterogeneous population of students? What level of differentiation was to exist in the school?

Still another programmatic problem had to do with the tradition in Norway that all students in a school would take, by and large, the same program of studies. Some inroads toward optional courses had been made in the basic school. To what extent would general courses be required and optional courses be made available to students at the upper secondary level? What would the ratio be of required and optional courses within each grade level?

These kinds of questions were raise repeatedly in the committees that considered the future of upper secondary schooling, but the major conceptual design for the school was actually set by the Steen Committee. It perceived the requirements of the upper secondary school to provide (1) vocational training, (2) university and other higher education preparation, and (3) general education.[34] The committee saw these three requirements being actually tightly intertwined. The nature of the work world was such that those going into the vocations required general education and the opportunity to continue their education beyond the elementary training provided in upper secondary school. The new law would give equal status to practical and to general education. On the one hand, those engaged in preparation for higher studies would require studies outside their narrow theoretical program. This would include exposure to the world of work, the aesthetic world, sport, free time, and democratic living. On the other hand, those in practical studies would sit side by side with the general studies students, and they would receive a good general education.

The Committee decided that a typical program of studies would consist of a one year foundation course, followed by a second and third year of specialized study. Any student who was preparing for university studies ought to devote approximately two of the three years to general, theoretical study. The remaining one third of the time would be for those studies such as vocational exposure. The Committee determined that those who would engage in a vocational program could either concentrate on a foundation vocational program during the first year, or they might combine the foundation vocational program with a foundation general studies program over a two year period, gaining one year of vocational experience and one year of general experience in the process. The third year could be taken either in a combined course or a vocational course of studies. What this amounted to was a school that provided all sixteen to nineteen year olds with a variety of educational opportunities for a three year period.

The school would provide a number of different study paths. Each study path would allow students to attain specific competence in a one, two or three year sequence. The type of educational path would be open to individual student choice. The choice of study path would not disadvantage any student in terms of access to higher education study. In other words, vocational tracks would provide legitimate university preparation.

One of the starting assumptions of the Labor Party was that the physical structure of the new upper secondary school would be a comprehensive unified school. The naive assumption was that all the educational paths being provided would be found in every upper secondary school. It was only possible, so they reasoned, to bring about equality of education and reinforce social leveling by adopting such a comprehensive unified school. This position was, of course, challenged by the Right, both on pedagogical and social grounds. In the first place, the Right saw little social consequence to a unified school. It simply did not have the social leveling effect so desired by the Left. Second, it would be unpractical to unify everything under one roof. Norway did not have a tradition of especially large schools, and a fully comprehensive unified school would lead inevitably to such institutions. Sound pedagogy would dictate that some division of labor be found between different schools.[35]

The Steen Committee acknowledged the comprehensive unified design as one of the options. It also acknowledged that another option would be to retain the *status quo* in terms of structure, but that the *gymnas* and vocational schools would each provide a similar foundation course of studies. A third option, the option recognized by the Steen Committee as a transition mode, was that the *gymnas* and vocational schools work together so that most of the students would probably take the foundation course at the *gymnas*. Though a minority of the Committee advocated a unified form, the majority decided it would be premature to advocate one of the options over another.[36]

However, consensus was coming into focus on a number of the issues. In its political platform in 1969, the Right was unequivocal that the new school must provide a general education, but with "a clear work orientation." It would consist of three years of study, each year being built on the previous year, but simultaneously consisting of a defined level of competence that would allow the student to move in various directions with further schooling, vocational training, or work.[37]

The Department of Church and Education prepared its first major proposal about upper secondary schooling in 1969.[38] That proposal was based on the *Gjelsvikutvalget* and the first two reports of the Steen Committee. The *Storting*'s Education Committee submitted its own recommendations for the first time in 1971.[39] It concurred with the notion that a typical program of studies would consist of a foundation course followed by a further course of studies. It further recommended that a school could have one or more lines of study, even to the point that a school provide all lines available, but the general plan would be to provide a general theoretical line in each school and selected vocational lines along with that general line.

Eventually, the Department took the position that a comprehensive, unified school did not have to be in one location. A cluster of schools within a relatively short distance from each other could constitute a total upper secondary school program of studies. That notion represented a new concept of unity (*enhet*), and allowed for the multiplication of vocational lines that are necessary in an advanced industrial state.[40]

THE UPPER SECONDARY SCHOOL LAW OF 1974

The Upper Secondary School Law was finally passed in June, 1974, with the provision that it take effect on 1 January 1976. The principles laid down by the Steen Committee were accepted with little modification: All young people have the opportunity to attend upper secondary school for at least three years; the choice of educational course of studies is, in principle, free; vocational and general courses may be combined; instruction must begin at the level the students have come to through the nine-year basic school.[41]

Nine branches of study exist in the upper secondary school. They are:

General Education
Manual and Industrial Studies
Arts and Crafts
Fishing and Maritime Studies
Sports
Clerical and Commercial Studies
Domestic Arts and Sciences
Social and Health Studies

All branches of study have the same structure, consisting of one or two year foundation courses and continuation studies (I and II), each lasting one complete year. The two year foundation course combines the one year vocational course with another year of general education.

Each vocational branch of studies is broken down into specialized courses of study. For example, Manual and Industrial Studies includes the general vocational subjects such as metal work, carpentry, and plumbing, but also special courses in piano tuning and repairs, upholstery, flower decoration, barber, and clock repair. These add up to hundreds of programs of study, almost all of which have a foundation course and advanced courses of one or two years.

The upper schools are so organized that some schools attempt to offer a general program as well as a wide range of vocational courses. It simply is not possible to offer all vocational courses in any one school, so a community usually has a coordinated system so that a young person is able to find a special course of studies somewhere. Of course, in the rural areas, even this is not possible, even where communities cooperate with each other. A number of other features have entered into the picture, and we shall address these as we turn to our final section.

Section VI

Norwegian School Reform — Consequences and Problems

18 Equality of Educational Opportunity

A major purpose of the four structural reform cycles discussed in this study, has been to ensure that people of all backgrounds, all social groups, both sexes, and all occupational orientations, were provided with equality of educational opportunity. The term "equality of educational opportunity" was popularized in the 1960s and 1970s, when social scientists began trying to find meaningful norms by which they could measure the degree to which various sub-populations in Europe and the United States had achieved equal educational opportunity. All of the standards they established were related directly to social status and social mobility. Coleman, for example, outlines what he feels are the major historical concepts of the term, suggesting that the first genuine notion was to give the youth of different social classes an education appropriate for them. Then, the class struggle forced Europe to begin moving away from the class-stratified system toward equal exposure to a curriculum. The final step in the evolution of the concept, according to Coleman, had to do with the school becoming responsible for helping each child achieve a minimal level of educational competence.[1] Torsten Husen concurs, by and large, with Coleman's notions, but categorizes the variety of concepts in terms of Liberal and Conservative orientations. However, he takes the issue one step further, suggesting that a radical concept of equality of educational opportunity includes the notion of equity in terms of life chances and social mobility.[2] Henry Levin recently summarized the various standards being used by those involved in the issue, maintaining that four classes of criteria dominate the literature:

    (1) equal access to the educational system;

(2) equal participation in the educational system;
(3) equal educational results; and
(4) equal educational effects on life chances.[3]

The early phases of education in Norway focus on equality of educational opportunity, but of quite a different nature than those projected by contemporary social scientists. In Norway, the first major purpose of schooling for the masses was based on the assumption that all God's children possessed the capacity to be saved and an equal right to salvation. Families and clerics had an obligation to provide the youth with the tools necessary to gain access to the word of God. Norway was as successful as any European country, even prior to the entrance of the state school system, in providing the youth with the ability to read the scriptures and other materials that would ensure a basic understanding of Christianity. The drive for equal spiritual opportunity for salvation was not simply a matter of individual choice. The family and the church were obliged to provide a minimum level of education, otherwise an individual was not allowed to participate as a full member of society. However, this imperative had little to do with social equity, as expounded by social scientists, it had more to do with otherworldly opportunities.

The second major purpose of mass schooling, emerging during the period of romantic nationalism, included not only a spiritual aim, but a mental, rational, and aesthetic aim. All Norwegians were seen to possess the capacity to think, to learn, to grow as human beings, regardless of social background. In this context, equality of educational opportunity also had little to do with breaking down social class differences. It was related to the belief that some appropriate form of schooling should be provided to all people, and that the common person could find fulfillment as a human being by striving toward enlightenment, by becoming a self-sufficient thinker, by overcoming the chains of ignorance. Enlightenment should not be reserved for the better classes, it should be available to everyone, and common schools would provide access to this world.

Social scientists have been prone to connect the concept of equal opportunity closely with industrialism and social mobility. Certainly, changing economic conditions played a major role in the first educational reform cycle outlined in this study, but religious and enlightenment interests far overshadowed these considerations, at least in Norway. Indicative of the subordinate role economics played in schooling considerations is the fact that vocational education was not even under the jurisdiction of the Department of Church and Education until the second reform cycle was under way, and it was not fully integrated into the national system of education until just prior to World War II.

The third major purpose of Norwegian mass education finally was attached to social class and mobility imperatives. The conventional concepts of equal educational opportunity begin to emerge; however, spiritual and enlightenment impulses toward education, continued to exist, and persist even today. The second, third and fourth reform cycles discussed in this study were based on the intention that schools ought to model social integration.

The major social equity standard of the Norwegian folk school, toward the end of the nineteenth century, was to provide an institution that everyone, not already involved in some other form of schooling, could attend. The intention of reformers was to ensure that everyone was given equal access to the educational system, and to provide options sufficient to ensure that young people could learn and progress even into adulthood. Even in adulthood, options were to remain available for individuals to pursue general educational ends. In this context the folk high schools came to play a central role. There was some sentiment toward equality of educational experience at this point in time, but that would be better realized during the time the third reform cycle was under way after the turn of the twentieth century.

A fourth standard of equality of opportunity was projected during the movement toward the unified school, shortly after the turn of this century. Equality of opportunity, could only be achieved by creating one school for all learners, requiring everyone to participate in a very similar course of studies, at least through some basic school period. Equality, in this respect, had a special meaning: sameness.[4] Everyone was to receive the same basic education. Even though the principle of *enhet* (unity or oneness) pertained mainly to structural changes, it was also recognized that a number of internal elements in any system advantage certain segments of a population and disadvantage others. This leads to still another equity standard, that of equal performance in schooling. These last three standards, access to the system, participation in the same curriculum, and equal performance, form the basis of our discussion of equality.

GENERAL EDUCATIONAL EXPANSION

Norway has become one of the model Western European countries in terms of its commitment to education for all. In terms of enrollments alone, in 1870, the average young person entering the work world had attained much less than six years of schooling. Over time, the number of years Norwegian youth attended school rose steadily. Even though the great upturn in European secondary enrollments took place after World War II, the percentage of certified Norwegian school leavers from secondary school in 1950/51 was already 9.0% of the appropriate age level, considerably higher than Austria (3.5%), Denmark (4.7%), Finland (7.7%), Germany (4.9%), Italy (3.0%), the Netherlands (5.5%), Sweden (5.4%), Switzerland (3.2%), and the United Kingdom (4.0%). At that time, the average young person was attending nine years of school before entering the work world.[5]

By 1965, the average person was attending eleven years of schooling. Even though compulsory education ended at age 14, 97.5% of the school population was remaining in school for at least one additional year, 78.4% for another year, and 62.7% for a third year. This is in stark contrast to other European countries.

By 1982, the average adult in Norway had attended almost thirteen years of schooling,[6] and 79% of all 13-18 year olds were attending school, which represented an attendance achievement better than or comparable to countries such as Sweden, the Netherlands, France, Denmark and Belgium.

Impressive as these figures are, it remains to be seen if the rapid growth of students has eliminated or appreciably reduced access, participation and achievement differences between the sexes, minority groups, special needs children, and social classes.

SOCIAL CLASS DIFFERENCES IN SCHOOL

Liv Mjelde recently noted that an assumption of school integration efforts has been "that equality of education would give working class children the possibility of moving out of this social class and into the middle class..." She then notes: "Research has shown that these efforts have failed."[7] Actually, research has shown that distinctions remain in terms of different groups in society, but the answer as to the system's success or failure is rather complex.

We can say, unequivocally, that all social classes now complete the basic school, and that they all take about the same curriculum, which satisfies two equality standards mentioned above. However, there is some evidence that internal achievement distinctions remain, at least during the last three years of basic education. In the early 1970s, pupils in the upper section of the basic school were allowed to select syllabuses having three degrees of difficulty in the major subjects of Norwegian, English, and mathematics. The Institute of Applied Social Research in Oslo found that the higher the social group, the greater was the tendency to select the highest curriculum, and the lower the social group, the greater was the tendency to select the lowest curriculum. Figures for 1974 are found in Table 18.1.[8]

Table 18.1

The Percentage of Basic School Leavers in 1974, Broken Down by Social Class and Curriculum Level

| | Percentage of Social Group | | | |
	I	II	III	IV
Highest Curriculum	77.4	59.4	39.7	35.1
Middle Curriculum	11.0	16.8	16.3	15.2
Lowest Curriculum	11.0	23.1	43.1	48.6

The school reformers ultimately stopped dividing pupils into difficulty groups, but we can assume that internal divisions continue to be made in the classrooms of the basic school.

Social class participation in the upper secondary school at the time the reforms were being implemented were also clearly evident. The number of pupils to opt for one, two, or three years of upper secondary schooling is clearly related to social class origins. In Table 18.2,[9] we find that whereas almost 87% of the highest social group continued into some form of upper secondary school, only 59% of the lowest social group continued. All groups experienced some attrition with increasing age levels, but over half of the highest social group remained in school at age 19, whereas only 21% of the lowest social group remained in school.

How do we explain these social class differences? One of the fuller explorations of this matter has been engaged in by Hernes and Knudsen, who have attributed the differences mainly to resources available to the

Table 18.2

Percentage of Pupils from Ages 16 through 19 within the Four
Social Groups Attending School in 1975

	Ages of Pupils			
	16	17	18	19
Social Group I	86.6	84.7	75.3	51.2
Social Group II	79.6	73.2	60.7	39.5
Social Group III	66.6	56.8	41.8	25.7
Social Group IV	59.2	49.2	33.9	20.8

individual child. Resources come from three sources: (1) individual or private sources connected with family, (2) collective resources connected with the neighborhood or circle of friends, and (3) public resources. They found that family factors, particularly father's education and family income, were closely associated with choices being made in terms of course of studies and upper secondary school participation. The authors theorized that this association was related mainly to interests, stimulation, and motivation.[10] The youth from higher social levels were recruited more actively and pressed more diligently to opt for higher educational levels.

While the above observation is consistent with the findings of most of the developed world, it remains significant, because Norway is a progressive social democracy, and it has consciously attempted to ameliorate social class distinctions within its broad social structure. For example, salary differences are relatively uniform across occupations. Not only are the beginning salaries of workers quite high and the final salaries quite low, but the salary differences between skilled professions and unskilled workers are also minimal.[11]

Hernes and Knudsen also found that educational choices were closely associated with collective resources tied to neighborhood and friends.[12] In spite of attempts to overcome urban advantages, differences remain in terms of participation in schooling. Whereas 71.1% of all 17 year olds were in school in Oslo in 1982, only 53.5% were in school in the far North county of Finnmark. While 73.4% of that age group in Oppland remained in school, only 61.6% were attending in Troms.[13]

Even when we control for social class in the various regions, differences remain still. For example, in Oslo the four social groups noted above claimed 84.1%, 72.9%, 53.4%, and 44.2% of the 16-18 year olds in 1975, respectively, while only 73.0%, 59.1%, 43.7%, and 35.0% of the youth in the four groups were in school in Finnmark.[14] Not only do private resources make a difference, but neighborhood and community resources are associated with attendance differences.

Is it any wonder, then, that attempts to equalize public education resources would not result in equality of educational choices being made. However, they ought to reduce to some degree, the level of differences that exist, and it is encouraging that the number of 17 year olds attending school increased by almost 10% between 1975 and 1982, and most of the increase was noted in the rural areas (see note above). Formal schooling has come to play a greater role in social advancement than it has in the past. In terms of social mobility, it was not as necessary in previous eras to participate in school as it is today in terms of social mobility. Consequently, schools do not serve simply to reproduce social inequalities, but they have greater potential than in past times of providing access to social station based on merit and performance.[15]

Consequently, it is important to enquire whether schools have contributed to greater educational equality over time. Among the schooling indicators, probably the most important is participation in the matriculation examination at the end of upper secondary school. Beginning in 1946, the Central Bureau of Statistics of Norway has collected data on persons who passed their examination along with information on their social background. It is impossible to compare the data directly, because of structural changes over time, but it is possible to arrive at relatively equal data with some frequency adjustments after 1951, which we show in Table 18.3.[16]

While the percentage of young people in each group increased, some increased dramatically. The children of fishermen increased by a factor of 8.4, workers and foremen by a factor of 5.9, craftsmen by a factor of 5.2. On the other hand, the children of "superior employees, professionals and teachers" increased by a factor of 1.3, self-employed in manufacturing, trade, shipping, financing, by a factor of 2.3. It is clear that greater and greater numbers of children from the lower classes are leaving upper secondary school and taking the matriculation examination, even though there remains a large discrepancy between many of the groups.

MALE/FEMALE DIFFERENCES IN SCHOOL

During the basic school period, the period when essentially the entire age level is in school, girls achieve at a much higher level than boys.

Illustrative of this situation was the period when pupils could opt for three levels of difficulty, during the early 1970s. On Table 18.4[17] we find a breakdown of the options selected by boys and girls in 1974.

Table 18.3

Frequency of Matriculation Examination from 1951 to 1978 in Groups for Breadwinner's/Father's Occupation in Terms of Percentages

	1951	1958	1963	1974	1978
Self Employed in Agr. and Forestry	4.9	6.1	8.1	22.3	26.8
Fishery	1.6	2.3	3.0	11.3	13.4
Self Employed in Manuf., Trade, Shipping, Finance	18.2	29.0	37.5	40.8	41.9
Craftsmen	6.1	12.8	21.7	27.0	31.9
Superior Employees, Professionals, Teachers	47.9	49.8	60.0	57.3	62.1
Subordinate Employees	25.0	21.1	24.9	35.8	41.8
Workers and Foremen	3.5	4.3	7.6	17.7	20.8

Table 18.4

Basic School Leavers in 1974 in the Different Social Groups in Terms of Curriculum Difficulty Selected

		Social Groups			
		I	II	III	IV
Most Difficult	(M)	75.2	54.8	35.0	31.6
	(F)	79.7	64.2	44.6	38.7
Middle Difficulty	(M)	12.2	18.2	15.7	14.8
	(F)	9.9	15.5	16.8	15.7
Lowest Difficulty	(M)	12.6	26.3	48.0	52.5
	(F)	9.9	19.8	38.0	44.6

A greater percentage of girls in every social level selected the most difficult curriculum, while a greater percentage of boys in every social level selected the curriculum having the lowest difficulty. Not only did girls select more difficult curricula, but they attained higher marks than boys in every social group.[18]

Throughout most of the history of Norwegian education, boys have held the edge in terms of those passing the *examen artium*, although the differences have narrowed through the years. Finally, in 1975, more girls than boys passed the examination, and they have maintained parity with the boys since then.[19]

Because upper secondary education is now vocationally oriented, it is crucial to enquire as to the choices young girls make in terms of the branch of the curriculum they choose. Their choices are more complicated than the choices boys make, because they grow up receiving a double message that defines females as homemakers and mothers, but it also says that females are able to assume any role that males have. In other words, equality of the sexes has taken on a specific meaning. On the one hand, some have tried to define it in such a way that women would continue to maintain different roles but these roles might come to carry high status and provide attractive economic remuneration. On the other hand, differences in roles between males and females could simply be abolished. The second alternative is that practiced almost exclusively, not only in Norway, but throughout Scandinavia.[20] This orientation was actually put into Norwegian law in 1978, confirming legal equality between the sexes.[21] Consequently, females are now accepted without equivocation into the work world. The major problem they face is that they are also expected to continue playing the role of housewife and mother, either part-time or full-time.

The choices girls make are varied. Some drop out of school altogether after compulsory education. Some attempt to combine work preparation with home management, by specializing in fields of study such as home economics, sewing, hair dressing, arts and crafts, and nursing. Some take subjects that are traditionally low paying, requiring little training, allowing them to enter quickly into the work force but also allowing them to stop work as soon as they begin to establish a family. These include waitressing, working as a receptionist, or file clerking. Some are now choosing to move into sectors formerly occupied by men, although certain sectors have not yet witnessed greater equity. In the trade and industrial sectors, for example, Mjelde found that 80% of the female industrial workers are in the unskilled category and receive low wages, while only 12% of the male workers fall into this category.[22]

There are bright spots in the occupational landscape. By 1980, goldsmiths, traditionally male dominated, were 80% female.[23] Opticians were 46% females, clock-makers 37% female. A startling finding is that there is not a single occupational category that does not have some female representation, including fishing and whaling, crude petroleum production, motor power working, smelting and metallurgical working, auto mechanics, and plumbing.[24]

In spite of these advances, by 1980, two thirds of the girls continued preparing for lower paying, traditionally female oriented occupations: textile industries, sewing, and home economics. And those girls, who were engaged in professionally oriented occupations, were most interested in being nurses, child care workers, social workers, medical secretaries, etc.[25] This has implications for issues related to general vs. vocational schooling, which we turn to next. However, a growing number of the brighter young people are opting for branches which only a generation ago were the preserve of those who could not make it school. Vocational programs are becoming increasingly popular, and the competition is exceedingly keen for many of the streams, which means that only the brightest are able to gain admission to them.

VOCATIONAL VS. GENERAL SECONDARY SCHOOLING

The *gymnas* and other types of post-basic schools were combined in the 1974 Upper Secondary School Law to form a differentiated comprehensive school. One of the fundamental aims of the new law was to ensure equal status to practical and theoretical education. Throughout the country, general studies now exists side by side with practical studies; in theory, any young person can choose from the various branches of study that exist.

The immediate impact of the 1974 law was a sudden threefold jump in general education enrollments. By 1977, 57% of all upper secondary students were in the general branch. In an unexpected turn of the situation, these enrollments quickly began to decline. By 1980, they had dropped to 53% of all students, and by 1983 to 47% of all students. To speak of an overall enrollment level is somewhat misleading, however, because the initial enrollments in general studies in 1983 were only 33% of the total first year upper secondary school enrollments, but they hold steady through the three years of upper secondary school, while all other branches experienced an enormous attrition rate. For example, in the manual and industrial branch, 23,800 students were enrolled in the first year in 1983, while the figure dropped to 8,400 students in the second year and a meagre 2,070 the third year. Only one student in ten remains in the manual and industrial branch through the three years. This is rather typical of all vocational branches, and because the general branch holds steady, the percentage of students in general education skyrockets during the second (51%) and third (74%) years.[26]

Two major factors explain the decline in enrollments in the manual and industrial branch. First, many of the courses in the branch require only one year in order for young people to qualify for semiskilled jobs, so many drop out and go to work. In contrast, the general branch provides no job preparation so the only option available is usually to continue in school. Second, the government provides far fewer vocational places at the more advanced level, because they are decidedly more expensive than general education.[27]

The government is making efforts to rectify the situation. Whereas the general education branch increased by 8,960 (11%) students between 1977 and 1983, the vocational branches increased by 34,970 (40%) students. In spite of this, the study places that are not meeting student demand remain in the vocational branches. Most students, who complete the nine year compulsory school are able to find a place in the general education branch, and their ability to proceed through the continuation studies is by and large assured. In contrast, those seeking vocational training usually engage in great competition for a place. Once that place is gained, the students must excel if they wish to go beyond the foundation course and be admitted to a specialized vocational training course at the continuation I and II levels.[28]

The admissions standards to the general education branch are minimal. The few students who are denied admission usually have been denied because a school does not have sufficient places for them. The low admissions standard should not imply that only the dull student applies. The general branch leads most directly to university and other higher education study, and many of the brightest young people continue to go that route. However, a growing number of the brighter young people are opting for branches which only a generation ago were the preserve of those who could not make it school. Vocational programs are becoming increasingly popular, and the competition is exceedingly keen for many of the streams, which means that only the brightest are able to gain admission to them.

Because general education demand is by and large being met, its utilitarian or personal vocational value is diminished, and it retains only its general social value for a large share of the student population. A lowered status is coming to be attached to it as it takes on a commonplace value. There is no great occupational reward attached to gaining general education, unless the student goes on to higher education studies, although there is some incentive for the individual to remain in general education, because it is detrimental to the individual if an upper secondary education of some kind is not obtained.[29]

Still another factor that comes to play is the policy that all streams of education lead to the possibility for further education. A bright young person can prepare for a vocation and also look forward to a future place at the university if he/she so wishes. It appears to the student to be the best of all worlds, for he/she can always change directions without very much loss of time. Consequently, the high achieving student often chooses a vocational track rather than the general education branch.

The tendency of bright students to opt for vocational education will be greeted with some applause by those who have worked to equalize the general and the practical branches of learning. However, this policy has also begun to create severe difficulties for those who have a history of low achievement in school. In the past, vocational education was a means for personal advancement and development of those who did not do well in school. Today, these students are systematically being excluded from this opportunity because their places are now being taken by students who have excelled in school.

The only options open to low achieving students are to drop out of school or to enter general education. Of course, general education study provides them with the possibility of going on to higher education, which for most is rather remote, and it also provides the opportunity of going into an apprenticeship program. Most apprentices are expected to attend general education for two years before going into training. To require them to continue in a school type where they have not succeeded is certainly not a sound solution to their problem. Even at the upper level of the basic school, a growing portion of the school population are characterized as "school tired youth," because the process is not motivating for them. It is not interesting and relevant to many young people's lives. They require a different type of educational experience, including that which stimulates tactile and kinesthetic senses, such as field-based learning.[30] It is reasonable to project that many lower achieving students will not be able to take advantage of the apprenticeship or higher education options open to them. Consequently, they will end up having no vocational skills at all.

SPECIAL EDUCATION

The 1969 Basic School Law states simply that pupils in the basic school who are judged to require particular help, may receive special education, "either within or outside the school."[31] Such a statement glosses over the veritable revolution that was taking place in special education and highlights, as no other issue can highlight, the commitment of the Norwegians to equal access and participation within a single school designed for all. Earlier laws and regulations in Norway, such as the law of 1951, reflected the general tendency to place special needs children in separate institutions, away from the rest of the school population. In fact, most of these institutions were boarding schools.[32] This would soon change, however, and the basic position of the Norwegians was set as the government considered special education within the framework of the 1969 Basic School Law. Their commitment was unequivocal: special education should work toward the same aims as for ordinary education, and this can only take place if special needs children are integrated as far as possible with normal children in the school and classroom.[33] Every effort must be made to prepare special needs children for further education, so that they might become productive citizens of Norwegian society.

If special education were to receive its rightful place in the basic school scheme, the special education law would have to be modified. The *Storting* had this in mind, when it established a select committee in 1969 to accomplish this goal. In fact, even before the Basic School Law had been passed, the fundamental commitment of the government had been clearly stated by another select committee, which declared:

> no unnecessary lines of division should be drawn between handicapped persons and others in matters concerning medical and social treatment, upbringing, education, work, and welfare.[34]

Such a policy was by no means established without opposition. In fact, it was resisted by broad segments of the population, including members of the Right, Center and Left parties. The teachers of special schools worried that they would loose their positions, if programs were integrated with the general schools. Teachers of the basic schools complained that special needs children would create a severe burden that would only hinder the instructional process. Parents of special needs children were actually concerned that their children would not receive adequate assistance if they were placed in regular classrooms.[35]

In spite of this, however, the principle of *enhet* would have little meaning if exceptions were made for large segments of the population, and the Norwegians had been very generous in defining who a special needs child was. Over ten percent of all pupils were being defined in such a way that they would require special help.[36] With the revision of the Basic School Law in 1975, the Special Education Law of 1951 was abolished and provisions were incorporated into the Basic School Law.[37] Consequently, Norway was one of the first nations in the world to adopt a policy of mainstreaming at the basic school level. That policy became standard for all institutions, including nursery schools, the basic school, and secondary schools.

Prior to the 1975 revised Basic School Law, secondary schools had also gained a good deal of attention by those considering special education policy. In 1965, for example, the Department of Church and Education actually combined special education concerns with vocational education, when it named the so-called Kjølner Select Committee to consider the "Vocational Training of Physically Handicapped."[38] The committee was charged with the responsibility of identifying the population under question, appropriate instructional plans, the relationship between theoretical and practical studies, and their ultimate role in the work world.

In 1968 two other committees were named, one by the Council on Special Education and the other by the Department of Church and Education. The Council committee, called the Kiil Committee, was to consider the kind of education necessary to ensure that mentally deficient young people would be able to function in some meaningful manner in the work world.[39] A Department committee, called the Søbye Select Committee, also considered the mentally deficient, but specifically within the commercial and business sector. Probably the most important of these committees, the Blom Select Committee, was named in 1969 and given the charge to draw up a law concerning special education, including provisions for secondary education. Their report was published in 1970, and it stressed, among other things, the right of mentally retarded to secondary level training.[40]

By the late 1970s, Norway had passed a point of no return. The opposition had been sufficiently silenced and political consensus for integration had been won. Not only had the notion of special schools been overcome, but some were even claiming that special education experts were no longer appropriate. With mainstreaming, it was necessary that all teachers have some background with special education, while experts would be antithetical to the interests of *enhet*.[41]

Such an extreme position was actually never acted upon, In fact, almost all of the special schools that existed remained into the 1980s, and the number of pupils in most special school categories, including hard of hearing, visually handicapped, and speech difficulties, actually increased slightly in number by 1982. The major reductions in student numbers at special schools was found in the categories of mentally retarded and socially maladjusted.[42]

The decision to retain the special schools has resulted, in part, because of political pressure, but also because of the emergence of new thinking on the part of experts in the field, who have begun to question whether the *enhet* policy may, in certain cases, be detrimental to the interests of the individual child.

A new wave of thinking, going beyond mainstreaming, is presently captivating the attention of those interested in Norwegian special education. Giving it the label, The Norwegian Flexible Model, special education experts are now advocating a new form of education for special needs children.[43] The old dichotomy between special schools vs. regular schools has been found to be faulty, because the focus on special needs children should not be on the institutional setting so much as on the needs of the child. Those needs might well require a special school, they might require mainstreaming, they might require a combination of special school and normal school, they might require work with an ordinary teacher and work with an expert coming into the school.

It is true that the special schools will probably be kept, but they are undergoing a transformation so that they will be integrated into the system and work with individual schools. New models are already being developed. Madlavoll School, in Stavanger, is actually a special education school that is combined with a normal school in one building, while Kalbakken School, in Oslo, is a special school that serves as an educational resource center for 14 surrounding normal schools. At this latter school, children may only be enrolled on a full-time basis for a maximum of two years, to ensure that most of their experience is in a regular institution.

Of course, some resistance is being encountered to this new idea. The young Labor Party members, for example, argue that mainstreaming has not been fully implemented. They argue that this new thinking is little more than a rationalization for retaining those special education schools still in existence. Bureaucrats in the Department and at the local level worry about the costs involved in the new scheme.[44] In spite of this controversy, the commitment to unity and equality for special needs children is never questioned.

EQUITY ISSUES AND MINORITY GROUPS

One of the distinguishing features of the country is its homogeneity. Only about 3.0% of the population would identify themselves as members of some minority group. The largest part of this population would be migrants, who have lived for a short time in Norway, having basic roots in some other Northern European or North American country. Two major minority groups must receive special consideration in this study: Lapps and Pakistanis.

Lapps represent the most important indigenous population of Norway, having lived in Northern Norway for thousands of years. Even though Norwegian Lapps constitute almost half of all the Lapps in the northern countries, numbering approximately 25,000 people, they constitute only about 0.5% of the Norwegian population. Pakistanis are a very recent group to arrive in Norway, and although their numbers are less than half that of the Lapps, they are a visible minority in cities such as Oslo, and their numbers and cultural background pose special problems for school officials. These two minority groups provide a dramatic symbolic test of the policies of equity and unity in the country.

The Lapps

The Lapps now enjoy full judicial equity given to other Norwegians, although this has been relatively slow in coming. Only after World War II were laws abolished, placing Lapps in a less favorable position, but even today some of their nomadic cultural practices come in conflict with Norwegian tendencies to establish firm land boundaries and restrictive farming provisions.

Historically, if a policy existed at all regarding the Lapps, it was usually based on the assumption that they ought to be assimilated into the mainstream of Norwegian society. For hundreds of years, Norwegians have attempted to root out the animistic religious practices of the Lapps. Special Christian boarding schools were set for them as early as the sixteenth century. Assimilation endeavors are nowhere better illustrated than with the early language of instruction policies of the Norwegian government. In 1880, the regional office at Tromsø, in the far north, issued a directive that Norwegian be the language of instruction in all schools and that Lappish only be used to assist the instructional process.[45] In 1898, the Department of Church and Education applied this policy throughout Norway, adding that even where the majority of the children were Lapps, the Lappish language only be used when "absolutely necessary."[46]

Such a policy was challenged from time to time during the next half century, but it generally held firm. The Folk School Law of 1936 reiterated the position that Lappish could only be used as an instructional aid.[47] Following World War II, the Coordinating Committee for Schooling issued an important report on the Lapps, recommending that parallel classes be set up in the first years of school, so that Lappish speaking children be given the basics in their own language, before learning Norwegian. Textbooks and teacher training was to accompany these provisions. In addition, a continuation school and a folk high school was recommended, which would serve to focus on Lapp vocational and cultural needs.[48]

In spite of such overtures, the 1889 policy remained, by and large, in force until a special commission on the Lapps issued its report in 1959, although matters were to begin changing in that same year. The School Law of 1959 stipulated that Norwegian should be employed as the language of instruction, but that "in oral work, school children shall use the method of speaking employed in the home, and the teacher shall, as far as possible, adjust his own language to that of the children."[49]

Finally, in the 1960s, the seriousness of the situation began to become public. Anton Hoem undertook studies of Lapp children at the basic school level and found that only about half as many Lapp children were choosing the most demanding course plan as were other Norwegian children.[50] In terms of Norwegian language, twice as many Lapp children were found in the lowest level as other children. At the same time, Hoem provided solid evidence that the marks the Lapp children were receiving were much lower than the general school population.

Such findings only reinforced the notion that cultural assimilation might not be the answer, and as Norway joined nations throughout the world in becoming more sensitive to minority needs, assimilation policies began to give way to other alternatives. The Lappish language began to be used in certain schools, and a number of other measures came into force.

Teachers were encouraged to study Lappish by being given a leave of absence with pay; study fellowships for Lapp youth were instituted; special secondary schools having Lapp oriented courses of study were established; special transportation and salary supplements were provided to teachers working in northern Norway; textbook preparation in Lappish was intensified at all levels of schooling.[51]

The school laws also reflected greater sensitivity to Lapp interests. The 1969 Basic School Law stipulated that in the Lapp district, instruction would be provided in Lappish for those who speak the language, upon request of the parents. The 1975 revision went even further, mandating that any parents may request Lappish instruction for their child in the Lapp district.[52]

The language issue only reflected the general tendency to recognize that equality, in terms of sameness, was not the solution for the Lapps. The concept of equality would have to undergo a change. An OECD evaluation team in Norway suggested equality for minority groups must "include the right to have an influence on the standards according to which equality is being measured."[53] That is, equality has been defined in Norway by mainstream groups, but that definition may not be acceptable to other groups in society. Provision must be made to allow these other groups to chart their own course, to define their highest aspirations, to realize their own unique quality of life.

The Pakistanis

In the past two decades, Norway has experienced, for the first time in its history, the influx of growing numbers of immigrants from countries sharply different from themselves. Refugees from Vietnam and so-called "guestworkers" from Turkey and Pakistan are posing great problems of a practical and theoretical nature; so far the Norwegians have been unable to determine just what should be done. The largest single group is from Pakistan, and their numbers shift so dramatically, that it is difficult to know what to do in terms of educational provisions. In 1982, for example, a total of 608 Pakistanis arrived in the country, while another 488 emigrated, leaving a net increase of 120 people.[54] At the time there were already over 7,000 Pakistanis in the country, and in the next five years the figure would rise to over 9,000, at least 2,000 of whom were school age.[55]

Having already become somewhat sensitized to minority problems, the Norwegians were willing to accommodate when the first children started school in the early 1970s, but the new immigrants posed a genuine dilemma. Their population was so unstable that it might have been prudent to allow them to maintain their own value system and cultural mores within the schooling framework. On the other hand, they were in Norway, and some reasoned that they live according to Norwegian standards.

The first course of action taken was to try and integrate the children to school by teaching them Norwegian. However, this was a practical expediency and was not intended to lead to assimilation in any fundamental way. Little had changed when a 1980 *Storting* report provided some clue as to government policy. "It is not necessary," reads the report, "that immigrants become as Norwegian as possible (assimilated), but it is necessary for immigrants to adjust as far as possible to Norwegian norms.[56] This seems rather rational on the part of the host society, but for the guests, the intent appears to be, that Pakistani children be socialized to Norwegian values.

Mohammed Awan, a Pakistani scholar in Norway points out the contradictions this approach creates for the Pakistani parents, who quickly recognize that Norway stresses equality between the sexes in every field of life, with girls enjoying the same educational facilities, women enjoying an independent life even in marriage, the modern "househusband" sharing housewife work even though ready-made food is available, sex education being promoted in schools, as well as rural and urban people living a standard life.[57]

In his studies, Awan confirms that Pakistani children are undergoing a complex process of socialization that leaves nothing unaffected. Emotions, thought processes, and values are all shifting. The solutions are not as easily identified as the problems, but the presence of Pakistani children are requiring the Norwegians to recognize the insularity with which they have approached educational policy in their country.

SUMMARY

To the question of who shall benefit from the educational process, the simplistic Norwegian answer has been that everyone deserves an equal educational opportunity. The issue of equity has long been the major priority of policy makers, who have been intent on providing all segments of the population with a more just and equitable allocation of the available educational goods. Earlier equity issues focused on spiritual and internal human rewards, while more recent efforts have centered on social status and mobility. Equity priorities have left an indelible mark on the kinds of programs being made available, intended to reduce differences associated with social class, sex, and occupational orientation. Norwegians recognize that in many respects they have been unsuccessful in overcoming the distinctions that occur in society. In this respect, their schools continue to replicate those distinctions, at least to some degree. The challenge of the future is to find ways to further erode and overcome the legacy of divisions and differences.

19 Control Issues in Education

In the early days of independent Norway, the introduction of local self-government actually marked a major step toward full democratic rule in the country. For much of the remainder of the nineteenth century, local rule was strongly guarded, though financial requirements often dictated that the central government take over a limited number of educational functions. For the past century, however, the country has witnessed an inexorable movement toward centralized rule, at least in educational matters. The emergence of the Labor government, which dominated politics from the mid-1930s until the 1970s, only accelerated the process.[1]

Actually, signs of the decline of Labor domination were already apparent in the 1961 elections, when certain members of the Party split away to form the Socialist People's Party, and Labor lost its absolute majority in the *Storting*, even though the powerful Labor prime minister, Gerhardsen, continued to serve until 1965, except for a brief ouster in 1963. In 1965, a coalition of non-Labor parties took over and ruled until 1971, when Labor leader Trygve Bratteli became prime minister, but only because the coalition leaders were unable to maintain solidarity because they could not agree on what appropriate action to take regarding membership in the European Economic Community. In spite of the fact that the Labor government remained in power, the number of representatives in the *Storting* had declined to barely 40% in 1973, and the number of people voting Labor was no more than 35%, the lowest percentage since 1930. With the aid of the Socialists, however, Bratteli remained in power until 1976, and was replaced by still another Labor leader Odvar Nordli, who was able to remain in office when Labor picked up greater strength in the 1977 election. When Nordli resigned in 1981, the first woman Prime Minister in Norway's history, Gro Harlem Brundtland, briefly assumed office, only to be eliminated in the election that year that witnessed another sharp drop in popular support of the Labor Party (37%).

The Conservatives, who had gained only 34% of the seats, were able to form a coalition government in 1983, to include the Christian People's Party and the Center Party. Thus, the past two decades has witnessed Norway moving away from Labor Party domination toward its more conventional "consensual" decision making process, which means that decisions would reflect a broad spectrum of sentiment.[2]

Within this context has come a growing sentiment that the centralized form of decision making has little place in contemporary education. The broad spectrum of political voices have granted that the structural reform process required a high degree of centralized authority and control. Now that structural issues are finally being laid to rest, voices have been raised demanding a new type of input into education. "Local freedom" and "local initiative" became key phrases as critics exclaimed that schools had become distant, professional, machine-like institutions.[3]

The cause of local control was actually fought on both ends of the political spectrum. During the 1960s, the more radical political parties, the Socialists and the Communists, were energetic in speaking for a greater voice on the part of and students in local school affairs.[4] Ultimately, however, it was the Conservatives, who would use local control as a means of distinguishing themselves from the old Labor dominated policies. Whereas Labor had exercised a centralizing influence, the new politics, so claimed the Conservatives, demanded decentralized influences.

The movement toward local control has been, in large measure, a consequence of Norway taking part of a broader international movement, initiated in the 1960s, for greater community, parent, and even student participation in school policy formation. There had long been some provision for parent participation in local schools. The old 1889 Folk School Law, for example, had stipulated that each school shall have a School Supervisory Committee, with three of the five members representing the parents.[5] Such an arrangement had not changed over the years, so that the 1959 School Law, had also designated that three of the five members of the Supervisory Committee organized at each compulsory school should be parents. The major tasks of this latter committee had been to bridge the gap between home and school and to give advice to those in authority.[6] However, this was not a satisfactory arrangement for large numbers of parents. In the first place, the members of this committee were chosen by the School Board located in each municipality. In the second place, the actual powers of the committee were highly restricted. After a decade of debate on the issue, the 1969 School Law would make extensive provision for input into each school. There would be a "Parents' Council,"[7] a "Students' Council," and even "Class Councils" representing each grade level at the Basic School.[8] The original law provided only that these groups continue to play advisory and coordination roles, but the tenor of the times had moved beyond that point so that the 1975 revision of the law stipulated that these actually have legitimate authority to contribute to policy decisions in the school.

These activities coincided with the work of a select curriculum committee, which was deliberating on the form of the new Model Plan, that was passed by the *Storting* in 1974. The most significant guiding principle of the plan was that local school boards, the individual schools, and the individual teachers be given considerable authority to determine what is taught and how it is taught.[9]

Students would also become more participatory in the educational process, although the major input of students into decision-making would actually come at the secondary school level. The 1974 Secondary School Law mandated that student councils be organized,[10] but more symbolic of the activism of students was the establishment of a secondary school that was largely inspired by the students. At that time a wave of alternative schools was rolling across the Western world. In the United States, the free school movement and alternative school movement had come about largely from the initiative of concerned parents and educators, who were unhappy with the dehumanized manner in which their children were being educated.[11] In West Germany, the "anti-authoritarian" movement had been largely inspired by political radicals.[12] In Norway, students themselves demanded a new form of schooling that would allow them to take on greater responsibility for their educational experiences and define what was appropriate and relevant. This led to the establishment of the "Experimental *Gymnas*," that became an actual part of the Oslo school system and served as a model for other similar schools throughout Scandinavia.[13]

The movement for decentralization has touched a number of important spheres in education, including a shift toward locally defined schools, to locally oriented research and development activities, to locally determined resource allocations to locally educated and oriented teachers.

SCHOOL DEVELOPMENT

With the completion of the structural reform process, greater attention could now be given to the inner life of the school, the quality of the educational process, the substance of the educational program. Such concerns could only be defined in terms of the quality of life in each individual school. Centralized mandates and provisions could only assist in this effort, a creative, innovative, vital school life must be maintained by the school itself. Focus on the individual school was consistent with the shifting political climate, and it was consistent with the laws and the Model Plan under which schools were operating. These provided, among other things, for schools to define certain courses of study and time arrangements; much of the content and working arrangements, particularly the inclusion of local subject matter and the use of the local milieu as a resource in instruction; and flexibility in managing, organizing and allocating teacher resources.[14]

The new thrust presented a genuine dilemma for the school, which had become habituated to direction from central authorities. Local innovation, institutional creativity, and individual school development posed as much a threat as it did an opportunity. School leaders and teachers were now being told they must take individual initiative, and they were trying desperately to comply with such a central mandate, but without much guidance or experience as to how to accomplish such a task.

A number of initiatives were undertaken, mainly by educators having some experience with school development processes, who recognized the need and set out to help schools learn how to redefine themselves. Specialists at the Work Research Institute, for example, obtained funds from the Department of Church and Education to initiate studies in internal organization of five secondary schools. This study, begun in 1971, was carried on over a five year period, and was based on certain concepts of the Director of the Institute, Einar Thorsrud, known worldwide for his work on industrial democracy, where workers themselves assume a great deal of authority and responsibility for the work they do.[15]

The most ambitious project in school development was initiated by an organization that had evolved out of an OECD project, headquartered in Oslo, to study how educational change could be better managed. Known initially as International Management Training for Educational Change (IMTEC), it conducted, among other things, international seminars on various change topics. In 1974, IMTEC organized such a seminar, entitled "Critical Processes of Educational Change," which brought together some of the best people in educational organization development work. One outgrowth of this work was the initiation of a school development project in Norway, to help basic schools engage in school development programs.[16]

The project was based on a survey feedback procedure, where school personnel filled out a detailed questionnaire about a number of spheres in their school, including: Values, Beliefs, and Goals; Instructional Goals; Instructional Practices; Institutional Climate; Norms and Expectations; Leadership; Decision-Making Strategies; Influence, Power and Control; Degree of Institutional Change; Task and time Structure; and Incentive and Reward Structure. From this data, profiles were developed so that staff members were able to see where they were in agreement about their institution and where they were dissatisfied with the existing situation and where their practices coincided with their own ideals. External consultants then assisted the various schools in redefining themselves so that some of their perceived weaknesses might be overcome. The IMTEC School Development project was initiated in over 100 Norwegian schools and served as a model for a number of other school development activities run by teachers colleges, school districts, and the Department of Church and Education itself.

OPEN SCHOOLS

One of the major local initiatives to occur throughout the country was the introduction of so-called open schools. Because these schools came largely through locally organized groups, it is difficult to define them in any explicit fashion. Fundamental to open schools was the notion that Norwegians were living in a society of continual change. The schools in such a society required quite different subject matter or content, new working styles, and innovative assistance from administrative authorities. Most of all, however, the school required enormous flexibility and the ability to adjust to ever changing needs and demands.

In 1968, the first school declared itself to have an open school format. Two years later approximately 10 schools were in the process of adopting an open school program and structure. In 1971 no less than 60 communities were engaged in some form of schooling that had broken from the traditional school plan and a year later the open schools numbered more than 100 throughout the country. These were, by and large, basic schools, most of which were primary schools, either separate or combined with lower middle schools.[17]

Almost all of the schools originated from local initiative. In some communities, parent groups formed to demand that action be taken. In other communities, the school superintendent or some other official took the initiative. In still other communities, teachers requested that they be given the resources to take on the burden of this new pedagogical style.

Open schools certainly did not originate in Norway. That country was participating in a wave that was rolling across Scandinavia, Great Britain and the United States. However, the sudden emergence and explosion of the movement could be attributed, in part, to the new climate for local activity and the growing tendency for decentralization of educational policy. It did benefit from some central activity. In 1970 the Council for Innovation in Education had taken on a project to experiment with open schools, with the intention of defining an appropriate content and instructional organization. That initiative was valuable in publicizing and extending open school activities, but it was also somewhat antithetical to the movement itself. Open schools thrived, in part, because they satisfied local needs and evolved out of the energies of people who wished to participate in designing appropriate working environments for themselves and the children. Centrally designed research and development activities represented a cooptation of that endeavor, and symbolized a general tendency to decentralize on many fronts, including educational experimentation.

DECENTRALIZED RESEARCH AND DEVELOPMENT

On 2 April 1982, a white paper was issued by the newly elected Conservative government, which declared that the National Council for Innovation in Education would be abolished. The major argument for this action was the following:

Local initiative from the school itself must be the most important starting point of any experimental activity. Centrally planned reform is discouraged and the NCIE is terminated.[18]

The NCIE had become a major symbol for central control and was to be gradually phased out between 8 December 1982 and 31 December 1984. The disestablishment process went very quickly, mainly because personnel left their posts as quickly as they could relocate themselves elsewhere in the system. It remains for us to detail why a national R&D center would be so quickly dismantled. We recall that NCIE had been established in 1954 with the intention of making "systematic research the basis for innovation in education." In fact, all proposals for research and experiments were to be evaluated by NCIE, and although the Department exercised ultimate control, the NCIE was given the authority to manage all experiments and development projects related to the schools.

During the first decade, the NCIE concentrated on the development of the nine year basic school, but in the 1960s the NCIE had stretched its influence into almost every sphere of education as its experiments and projects focused on teaching methods, grouping, remedial programs, optional courses, programmed learning, and individualized instruction, as well as structural changes taking place at the secondary level, vocational schooling and even teacher training.[19] Eventually, the NCIE also turned to educational work in sparsely populated areas.

There is common agreement that the NCIE exercised a substantial impact on educational reform. However, its work also began to run somewhat counter to the shifting sentiment that the centralized government had run its course. With the psychic shift taking place away from central control, the work of NCIE began to take on dinosaur-like qualities, as it continued to act as the broker and guide to almost every innovative educational undertaking in Norway. When policy shifted toward local control, it began to adjust its orientation, but it was unable to shake its centralizing reputation. In addition, the NCIE had become identified too closely with the past political aims of the Labor Party.

In 1981, during the national election campaign, the Right Party reaffirmed that its first principle in school politics would be that of individual choice, which was translated to mean local control.[20] Because the NCIE symbolized the major political instrument of centralized Labor educational reform activities, the victory of the Conservatives in 1981 doomed the continued existence of the National Council for Innovation in Education.

The major issue facing the government at present is the practical implementation of R&D to the local level. The national advisory boards for the various types of education are being allocated more resources for educational development, but that only shifts the process from one centralized entity to another. Teacher training institutions will also likely play a larger role in research and development. Finally, individual schools are being given greater scope for innovation.[21] A few examples are already available, but it is uncertain if they are providing any working model. One example would be the need to introduce computer education into the system.

The initial Norwegian computer education program was designed to run from 1984 until 1989. The program dictates that a good deal of responsibility be given to the district and local school.[22] According to the initial plan, a number of individual schools were selected to receive funds to implement computer education programs. Interested schools were notified that they must apply to an agency of the government for funds, satisfying specified criteria. First, the school provided evidence that it had engaged in a broad institutional self-assessment process in which it defined its own goals, norms and values. its organizational and role structure, and its ability to innovate. Second, the school would indicate how computer education would fit into this broad framework, including how the students would be introduced to the possibilities and limitations of computer technology, how students would learn what role computer technology was coming to play a role in society, and how the students would gain practical computer-use experience.

Over 300 schools made application for funds, although only a very small number were actually accepted. The intent was that they would serve as model schools for future applicants, so schools selected represented a broad spectrum of socioeconomic and ethnic environments, types and levels of education, and differing subject matters. A large number of services are being given to the schools, to help them realize their computer education aims.[23]

If the computer education program represents a model, it is clear that central personnel will continue to play a major role in educational innovation. In fact, it remains unclear what will take place, and the best guess is that only limited decentralized concrete R&D work will occur in the immediate future, although resources remain available. However, the resource structure has also been so decentralized that it is difficult to gain a grasp of the way funds will be used. That issue shall be our concluding task in this chapter.

DECENTRALIZED FUNDING POLICY

Norway has long maintained a shared resources policy in terms of primary schools. That is, the local municipality has covered some of the costs, while the central government has covered other costs. With the introduction of the basic school in 1969, the government was covering approximately 50% of all costs, based on a gliding scale which provided as little as 25% subsidy for some costs and as much as 85% subsidy for other costs. The government obligation to the local municipality was based on a formula which accounted for 138 teaching periods during the first six years of school. The actual minimum teaching periods added up to 129 periods, so there were cushion funds available for special assignments, head teacher responsibilities, secretarial work, etc.[24]

A similar arrangement was instituted for secondary schools. For example, at the upper secondary school, a minimum of 30 periods of 45 minute classes were required, adding up to 90 periods over three years. The actual grants were calculated on the basis of 112 periods, leaving money for counseling, advisement, etc.[25]

In a certain sense, government funding has always been decentralized in that the local community school office received a direct grant for the basic school funds, and the local county school office received a direct grant for the upper secondary schools. The funds were given to two separate levels because secondary schooling has always been administered on a more central basis than has primary education.

In the past two decades, however, a different kind of thinking has slowly begun to penetrate political thinking. On 29 Oct. 1971, a so-called 'Main Committee' (*Hovedkomiteen*) was established by the government to consider how local administrations, municipalities and counties, could be better coordinated and reformed. One of the major issues the committee faced had to do with revenue distribution between the central government, the county, and the municipality. The Committee worked for a decade, and finally issued a major proposal on revenue distribution to the country in 1979.[26] and a complementary proposal on the municipality in 1982.[27] The major intent of their proposals was that all government grants for specific operating expenses, including equalization funds, at the local level be eliminated. This would pertain not only to educational allocations, but to health, social, cultural and other grants. These funds amounted to approximately 30% of all income at the local level (30 billion Kroner) in 1985.

The funds in question would not be withdrawn, but they would be allocated as a single block grant. Then the decision would be made at the municipal or county level how the funds would be divided up and used. This meant that the educational office would be in competition with all other local offices for these funds, and it set up an entirely new set of political moves necessary to insure the continuation of adequate educational monies. School officials had become used to getting a fair share of the funds, and their only responsibility had been to use the funds effectively and wisely. Now they would be expected to make a case for the funds, along with officials representing various other sectors of the local environment.

Such a prospect represented a genuine threat to educators, who had never been expected to be quite so entrepreneurial. In 1983, hearings were conducted on the issue and invitations were requested from various parties. Educator groups were united in opposition to the proposal. The Norwegian *Lektorlag*, representing secondary teachers, claimed that most of the recommendations of the Main Committee were poorly documented or developed and were therefore not sound. They also claimed that the small, poor communities would not fair as well as the larger, wealthier communities.[28] The Norwegian *Lærerlag*, representing basic school teachers, argued that stable funding remain a part of the system, that education is a national responsibility and that equal education could only be insured if education remains a national enterprise.[29]

While officials representing other special interests responded in a fashion similar to educators, other responses from more general political interests were strongly in favor of the new proposal. The proposal was consistent with the desire to decentralize and realize genuine self-determination at the local level. It reduced the tendency to specialize and focus on special interests, and provided an opportunity for local bodies to gain a sense of the general funding picture. It relieved local bodies of being victimized by central mandates allowing them to solve recognized problems and address real needs.[30]

In 1985 the *Storting* approved the proposal and directed that it be implemented beginning 1 January 1986. It is too soon to suggest what kind of implementation difficulties will result from the new provisions.

20 Educational Reform in Norway

We have concluded our story of educational reform in Norway, but it is crucial that we reflect on the major focus of this study, which has been on structural reform, involving the establishment of a common school and incorporating new curricular spheres into the system. At the time of independence, Norway maintained a schooling tradition, albeit somewhat less developed, that replicated the dualistic school tradition found throughout Europe. On the one hand, so-called "higher" schools existed, which were closely tied to the family background and social status of the elites. The very nature of the school programs tended to reinforce the status and position of the elites of Norwegian society. On the other hand, the broader elements of society rarely participated in this world and the education which they received in the "lower" schools and elsewhere was of quite a different kind.

Their dualistic schooling tradition, however, was relatively weak and only partially responsible for the rather high level of general enlightenment that was to be found in the country at the time. In fact, at the time of independence, a wide array of educational forces were at play that confused and confounded the dualistic schooling tradition. In spite of this, Norway has faced a problem similar to the rest of Europe, in that educational reform has focused mainly on breaking down this dualistic school structure and replacing it with a comprehensive, unified school form. It has taken approximate one and one half centuries to accomplish this task. In spite of this extended time frame, Norway has been on the forefront in Europe in terms of its ability successfully to bring about fundamental structural change. Three major issues are of importance.

First, what types of changes take place? Second, what are the conditions for planned change? Third, what are the phases involved in the change process?

TYPES OF EDUCATIONAL CHANGE

Our study has concentrated on structural change within the context of national reform in Norway. This necessarily requires us to focus on long-term general reform rather than small, short-run changes that always occur within an educational system. We have followed four major reform cycles that have been carried through in the country as it moved methodically, but incrementally, toward an integrated school format. We found that each reform cycle analyzed was a complex, time-consuming process. The duration of any reform cycle would not even be measured in months or years, but in decades. The longest cycle consumed approximately half a century and even then it was not fully implemented before a new cycle had began.

In addition, each cycle was evolutionary or incremental in nature. It did not attempt to revolutionize the entire school structure, but represented a somewhat tempered shift in terms of the ultimate intentions of the reformers, many of whom possessed, in certain respects, a vision far in advance of the reforms they actually instituted. That vision was of an extended, unified, comprehensive educational structure. However, each reform cycle represented a relatively small, methodical, intentional progression toward that ultimate end. For example, reformers in the various reform cycles concentrated on the concept of a three year common schooling experience, while subsequent reformers pushed it to five years, then to seven years, and finally to nine years. The reforms also witnessed the gradual inclusion of ever greater populations within the system, such as females, special needs pupils, vocational students, and minority groups.

The first cycle consisted of an attempt to build a coordinated system of education. A number of political and economic factors contributed to this reform, but the major force for change came from the romantic nationalist movement that flowered within a generation after independence. By the end of the 1830s certain formal educational reform recommendations were already being made.

However, the formal school structure remained essentially in place. That is, a disparate number of school types existed, each serving its own population, each providing its own curriculum. The children of the official class were receiving a predominantly Latin language program in the lower level of the Latin school, and more than half of their time was devoted to Latin, Greek and Hebrew language study in the upper level. The children of the commercial class were learning modern languages as well as technical and science courses at the burgher schools in the cities. The children of the common classes were attending poor schools in the cities or *allmueskoler* in the countryside, mainly to receive some religious instruction in preparation for confirmation.

Even though structural differences existed in terms of schooling, Norwegians had long held to the belief in certain types of equality of educational opportunity, rarely recognized by contemporary social scientists, who connect the concept closely with social class and social mobility. Religious impulses led to universal schooling prior to the nineteenth century, because of the assumption Norwegians maintained that all God's children possessed the capacity for salvation. Schools and education were intended to provide all youth with an opportunity to qualify for salvation.

The romantic nationalist movement provided yet another equal opportunity concept, also rarely recognized by social scientists. This included the belief that all young people possessed the capacity for individual enlightenment, rational thought and aesthetic expression. While school reinforced social differences, they all intended to provide their learners with an opportunity for a certain level of enlightenment.

In spite of the fact that social class divisions were becoming less and less viable, the existing schooling structure could likely have been able to maintain itself as it was for several generations, simply because the schools did not differ much from those which existed well into the twentieth century in most European countries. To their credit, the Norwegians struck out into new territory, borrowing school models from other countries, where needed, while forging a school program more suitable to the needs of their incipient modern, democratic society.

In the second cycle, beginning soon after the 1869 Higher Common School Law, Norway would embark on an attempt to structure, not only a comprehensive school system, but the elements of a common school, which would include large segments of the population, previously excluded from its classrooms. By the turn of the century, when this second reform cycle came to its conclusion, the Norwegians could count themselves among the first to have realized the notion of universal common schooling and the beginnings of secondary schooling of one kind or another for most of the population. In the process, great strides were being made to include populations that had previously been excluded from the system, including females and the handicapped.

Major changes in the political structure had been necessary before the reform measures could be carried through the government. In 1884, political parties emerged on the scene, and the progressive reform activities were set, by and large, by the Liberal Party, which had gained control of the *Storting* in 1884. While political democratization, at least in terms of universal manhood suffrage, was still far in advance of other countries, including those in Scandinavia, it had not preceded these school reforms but accompanied them.[1]

In spite of the progress that had been made in the educational system, it remained limited in some respects. For example, the time young people spent in school, particularly in the countryside, was minimal. Also, vocational training was not yet conceived to be a part of the general system of schooling in any meaningful sense. Of course, schools existed that helped satisfy new economic demands, but, except for continuation schools in the towns, they were largely private endeavors outside the general system of education.

The third reform cycle consumed approximately half a century. Beginning toward the end of the first decade of this century, it took a single word as its label and slogan: unity (*enhet*). The first phase of that cycle was characterized by a number of commission reports, one of which was actually called the Unified School Committee, although the most important committee of this reform cycle was the Parliamentary Commission, which deliberated for almost an entire decade, between the two world wars.

Early in this century, Norway was experiencing a major shift in its economy. It was quickly becoming a modern industrial nation, with an urban, labor dominated work force. The recommendations of the Parliamentary Commission would wait until the Labor Party finally gained control of the government in the 1930s. Subsequently, a number of school laws were passed, that would have propelled Norway to the forefront of educational reforms taking place throughout Europe.

Before these education laws could be fully implemented, World War II interrupted the reform cycle, deflecting is purposes and delaying its full implementation. The first decade following World War II was dictated by the impact of the National Socialist occupation and was characterized by an overarching sentiment toward solidarity on the part of all political parties in Norway, at least with regard to education. Norway had experienced a traumatic sense of disorientation during the period of occupation by the Germans and the various groups resolved to neutralize the divisions that separated them in order to achieve a commonly agreed upon end in education. In terms of the direction education would take, the reform process was somewhat regressive, compared with countries such as Sweden, which had not suffered occupation during the war. While Sweden moved forward with its comprehensive school agenda, Norway remained closely linked with the reform process that had been under way during the prewar years.

The 1950s signaled the beginning of a new era of reform, an era characterized by experimentation with new school forms, centered on the idea of a compulsory nine year basic school. This basic school would extend the common school two more years by combining the first years of all the major secondary school forms that existed as a result of the school laws of the 1930s: the *realskole*, the *gymnas*, the continuation school, and the vocational school. It would also be uniform in both the town and countryside. In other words, a basic school law would emerge that would hold, for the first time, for the primary schools of all the country. As early as 1955 the first experimental schools were already being instituted and in 1959 a basic school law was passed, which made possible the systematic adoption of experimental nine year schools on the part of interested communities.

This entire period was characterized by a willingness on the part of all political parties to work in harmony with each other toward a common end. It was only in the 1960s that this harmony began to break down and Norway once again entered a period of partisan politics. Even then, the divisions represented more differences of opinion about how best to achieve commonly agreed upon educational goals than it did the goals themselves. The *Storting* remained dominated by Labor which was the major force in pushing for passage, in 1969, of another school law on basic education. That law mandated the adoption of compulsory, nine year basic schools throughout the country.

A number of parliamentary changes came about in the next years, that addressed various aspects of the basic school. A major focus of attention was on the type of teachers that would be necessary to staff the basic school. Extensive experiments with teacher education were initiated, culminating in a teacher education law in 1975 that included a redefinition of teacher education institutions into institutions of higher learning. Still another focus of attention was on the curriculum that would be appropriate for the basic school. The Normal Plan of 1939 was replaced by the so-called Model Plan (*Mønsterplan*) for all basic schools.

The adoption of a basic school had profound implications for secondary education. Secondary schools had until that time consisted of a number of different types, both at the lower and upper secondary school level. Now, lower secondary schooling would take place in the last three years of the basic school. The secondary school law of 1974 dictated that the different institutions offering upper secondary education would be collapsed into a three year comprehensive upper secondary school, having a number of different streams, being open to everyone, and giving equal status to practical and theoretical studies. By the beginning of the 1980s, the new school structure was in place. Norway had achieved a monumental victory over the traditional dualistic school structure. The schools had finally come to correspond more nearly to the society which cultivated them.

The story of reform, which has been outlined in this study, provides an opportunity to reflect on the process of change, within the context of planned national educational reforms.

One of our major tasks has been to explain why the Norwegians have been so successful in their structural reform endeavors, while most of Europe has lagged far behind. We empirically identified a number of conditions that helped us explain the change process that was at work in the various educational reform cycles in Norway.

CONDITIONS FOR EDUCATIONAL CHANGE

In this study we have relied on a general mobilization model to help us explain the reasons why Norway has been so successful in its reform endeavors. A basic assumption of this model would be that stable and enduring educational systems are those which closely mirror the social, economic, and political conditions of the society of which they are a part.[2] As we launched our study, we believed that a basic contradiction existed between Norway's broader social, economic and political conditions and its educational system, in that Norway's social situation was actually more integrated than its schools. In spite of the rhetoric found in the literature about the necessity of using the schools to break down social barriers, we suspected that the school reforms were rarely intended to bring about a fundamental change in social life. Rather, they were intended to bring schools in line with broader social conditions and economic demands.

However, it is not enough to suggest that contradictions exist between the educational system and broader social conditions. A country's political structure must be able to translate disparate educational conditions into public policy. Some polities possess a greater capacity than others to reform the educational systems in such a way as to temper these contradictions, to establish greater correspondence between social and economic conditions and the educational system. We would count Norway among those who possess this capacity, simply because it has been as successful as any country in Western Europe in its educational reform endeavors. The Norwegian structural reform process has highlighted certain important conditions that have been at work in all four reform cycles. These conditions have facilitated the change process that we believe to be necessary at various phases in the planned change process at the national level. We shall simply state these in categorical fashion and elaborate with examples in our later discussion. The conditions include the following:

External and Internal Adaptation Capacity. On the one hand, Norwegians have maintained a high degree of awareness of educational innovations taking place particularly in Europe and they have been highly responsive to these innovations. They have maintained a remarkable capacity to adapt these external innovations to their own needs. On the other hand, Norwegian educators and policy makers have maintained the capacity to identify their own educational requirements and adapt their system in such as way as to satisfy these requirements. The country has identified its own contradictions and has been able to derive solutions that are specific to its internally defined needs. In a comparative sense, we are able to identify some societies, which have a great capacity to borrow, to adopt innovations from abroad. Countries such as Brazil and Japan come readily to mind. We are also able to identify societies which at one time or another, have revealed a great capacity for internal innovation. The United States and the Netherlands come readily to mind. But a country that reflects the capacity to adapt ideas from abroad while at the same time having the capacity to develop a sense of genuine internal ownership of its reforms is more rare. The Norwegians have demonstrated that capacity in each of their reform cycles.

Access to the Political Process. Reformers must have access to those who are able to make politically binding decisions about education. In Norway, a remarkable openness exists, providing almost anyone, who wishes to expend the effort, access to those making decisions. This may be, in part, because the population is so small but also because education has been so central in the political process, that educators and others involved in education are accorded a voice and recognition not typically experienced in many countries. In addition, Norway has evolved what is described as political corporatism, which allows special interest groups, such as teacher organizations and school associations to be continuously and formally involved in political decisions.[3]

Leadership. The success of any reform depends, in large measure, on the leaders who are engaged in the process. However, our Norwegian experience emphasizes that leaders are not synonymous with those within the formal positions of power. Reforms have also depended on the initiative of leaders from the private sector and educators, who have no formal political power. At certain phases in the process, however, formal leaders must become involved and the reforms come to depend to some extent on these formal leaders bringing the reform through those particular phases.

A Sense of Ownership. The reform process must ultimately be structured so that those who are expected to carry out the mandates of the reform have some sense of ownership of the reform. Teachers must believe that the new arrangements support their basic orientation toward teaching and learning. Administrators must believe that the reforms are consistent with their basic value system and administrative styles. Parents must trust that the new reform will not deprive their children of opportunities and privileges. This does not suggest that the reform will be initiated by teachers, administrators, or even parents, but at some point in the process they must be given the opportunity to participate in the deliberations and feel that their input can alter, if necessary, the direction of the reform.

Willingness to Compromise. At critical phases in the process, leaders and professionals must be so disposed that they are able to submerge their own perceptions of what ought to be done and allow the perceptions of others a degree of credibility. Basic commitments can be held, but an orientation toward a win-win situation in relationship with those who have differing points of view must be maintained, rather than a position of win-loose in the reform process, which is necessarily a political process.

Existence of a Tangible Reform Model. The reform process must, at an appropriate phase in the process, provide a tangible model of the reform endeavor. Structural reform requires different institutional configurations. That new configuration must be available and appear to demonstrate its viability, if it is be accepted by decision makers and actors in the educational program.

All of the above conditions are not necessary at every phase in the reform process, but each must exist at certain crucial phases in the process. Norway has maintained a consistent and regularized procedure for reform. These have come in the form of specific steps, which typically have included legislative mandates. A detailed assessment of this procedure provides an opportunity inductively to illuminate a sense of the way intentional reform is accomplished at the macro-level, at least in Norway. We have endeavored empirically to derive a consistent set of phases in the reform process based on the successful reform cycles studied in Norway. These include (1) an initiation phase, (2) a study phase, (3) a consensus building phase, (4) a legal framework phase, and (5) an implementation phase.

THE PHASES OF EDUCATIONAL REFORM
1. Initiation Phase

As we have stressed earlier in this chapter, educational reform has been an outcome of various social, political, and economic forces operating in Norway. However, individuals or specific groups must eventually move to begin defining an appropriate educational response to these forces. We have found that this initiative has come from professional educators both in the public and the private sectors, from professionals outside the system of primary and secondary schooling, and from those politicians, who have included educational change on their political agenda. For example, people such as Frederik M. Bugge, a cathedral school head, and Hartvig Nissen, a private school owner, spearheaded the first educational reform cycle, while Johan Sverdrup, the Prime Minister, played a crucial role in the initiation of the second cycle. Birger Bergersen, Head of the Ministry of Church and Education, was instrumental in initiating the final reform cycle. Leaders such as these informed themselves deeply and acutely of conditions in Norway and in other countries, and then exercised exceptional insight in making a case for change and moving decision makers to engage in formal assessment of the possibility of change. The major outcome of the initiation phase is a commitment to enter a formal study phase for reform.

2. Study Phase

The study phase in Norway, at least until very recently, has generally consisted of the establishment of one or more commissions consisting of a broad representation of points of view to assess the situation and come up with recommendations for change. Only on rare occasions was that not the case. We recall, for example, that the Great School Commission of 1920 was rendered inoperative, because it was considered to be biased against certain segments of society. The major recent breach of this tradition was the request of Minister Bergersen, that the Department of Church and Education draw up a proposal for what would become the 1959 School Law, rather than appoint a balanced commission to undertake the study and arrive and appropriate recommendations.

Some of these commissions have deliberated for up to a decade before coming to a final set of recommendations. Their recommendations have almost always consisted of what has been termed a "mutual adaptation and development process,"[4] which has included extensive reviews of conditions outside Norway, broad social and economic conditions in Norway, and the perspectives of those in the educational community itself.

The recommendations made by the commissions have also been expected to present a tangible model. In earlier years those models were adapted from foreign countries, from the private educational sector in Norway, or from public institutions which had not yet become generally available. We recall, for example, Hartvig Nissen's impact on schooling in the nineteenth century, and his indebtedness to pedagogical thinking and programs in France, Germany, and Great Britain for his own private school model and his proposals for reform. However, a number of reform proposals are unique to Norway. Thus, the Norwegians debated for several decades the possibility of substituting an Old Norse curricular line for the classical Latin line, which was deemed inappropriate and unconnected with Norwegian history and culture. As experimental science entered the picture after World War II, structural models were actually developed experimentally with the expectation that they would come to serve as demonstration institutions for more general reform.

3. Consensus Building Phase

The recommendations that have emerged from Norwegian commission activities have rarely been acted on directly. Rather, they have been subjected to an extensive review process which encouraged input from the most diverse segments of society and the educational establishment. This process does not just allow differences to be aired, but has usually led to adjustments in the original recommendations. In the process, greater consensus is arrived at on the part of diverse segments of society.

It is this particular phase that sets Norway and a few other consensual democracies apart from conventional models of change. Certain social scientists explain how a consensual democracy operates by noting that there is usually no single power block strong enough to override the opposition with the consequence that change requires compromise.[5] In a limited sense, this may be the case in education, but a certain ideological orientation is also at work. Implicit in Norway's reform activities is an awareness that education cannot function as a national enterprise unless there is a general commitment to it by participants, by the broad citizenry, who must gain some sense of ownership of any educational reform endeavor. Otherwise, they will subvert its success and deflect its intentions.

One of the striking observations we have made in this study has been the willingness on the part of reformers to back away from proposals that would alienate or antagonize certain segments of the educational establishment and society. The Latin language issue represents a classic case of sensitive politicians choosing to allow what was generally agreed as an obsolete curriculum activity to die a natural death rather than overly antagonize opponents by killing it outright. Of course, Norwegians have not always operated on the basis of their own proven reform design. We suspect the stormy protest against various segments of the 1958 Department of Church and Education reform proposal was, in part, because Minister Bergersen had not respected the tradition of appointing a broad-based commission to study the issues of reform and draw up the proposal that would reflect various values operating at the time.

Each of the reform cycles reviewed in this study has included an extensive attempt to allow the broadest possible input from every institution and organization that is remotely connected with the educational enterprise. Literally hundreds of organizations, institutions, and individuals were usually invited to respond to reform proposals. The general process has necessitated a willingness on the part of the framers of recommendations to compromise and shift directions, and it has contributed to a shift in attitude of groups negatively disposed to the recommendations. Indicative of this type of shift was the extensive review given to the Parliamentary Commission recommendations on higher common schools. The Department had been quite negative toward the proposals of the Commission, but was persuaded toward support by additional input by the teacher organizations.

At times, this diverse input has had a profound impact on the direction deliberations have taken, and has led to the modification of the original recommendations as the process moves toward the establishment of educational law. We recall, for example, the counter proposal of Hartvig Nissen, which actually replaced the formal commission proposal leading to the 1860 School Law.

4. Legal Framework Phase

The entire educational reform process in each of the cycles has been directed toward the establishment of one or more educational laws. In a certain respect, Norwegian laws rarely change conditions in a fundamental way. They more typically simply confirm and formalize what is taking place in a less formalized manner, and they suggest the direction in which education is already moving. For example, the 1860 school law established the policy of permanent primary schools rather than travelling schools. However, it took more than three decades for this objective to be realized. The translation of the preparatory phases into law actually represents a continuation of the consensus building process. In fact, even though there is often bitter debate and deliberation as the process moves toward completion, most political groups have ended up trying to assume credit for the ultimate legal outcome. All political parties today express pride in the basic school and the success of the educational reform cycles.

5. Implementation Phase

If any school law, that has been established, is to be implemented, it requires expert professional leadership, a sense of ownership on the part of the users, and a perception that it satisfies the needs of Norwegian society and especially Norwegian children. While most structural change activities in certain areas outside Norway founder because the earlier phases have been carried out almost exclusively by leaders and decision makers, the change process in Norway has built into it corrective mechanisms that prevent radical opposition from occurring. A further advantage of the Norwegian reform process has been that while implementation activities typically tend to contribute to issues and problems that have set a new reform cycle in process, Norway has actually thrived on its own success. That is, once a reform cycle has been on the way toward general implementation, the reformers have begun to suggest that new initiatives could be undertaken that would further the vision of a unified schooling structure.

Of course, not all implementation efforts have been successful. If a tangible model has not been at the base of reform endeavors, unanticipated difficulties have begun to develop that have required adjustments. We noted, for example, a number of these difficulties in our discussion of problems Norway presently confronts regarding vocational education, special education, and minority education endeavors that were based more on ideology than practice. These problems may prove to be severe enough to bring about yet another general reform cycle, although it is unlikely that such a cycle would focus on structural reform, because structural reform is now essentially complete. There is little sentiment to suggest something like extending common schooling from nine to eleven years, although there is clear sentiment to include further populations of students, including preschool children and various adult learners into the school structure. In spite of this, structural reform has taken on diminished importance and given way to other issues that occupy Norway's attention.

NORWAY FACES THE FUTURE

During the past decade, Norway has struggled with a number of educational issues. These might be broken down into three distinct categories. First, there are a number of problems the country faces that are very similar to those of all mature modern nations. These include the development of a system of preschool education, the possibility of extending the age of compulsory education, the incorporation of new vocational subjects into the upper secondary school and the expansion of post-compulsory schooling enrollments, the integration of upper secondary, tertiary and adult education, and a clear definition of the notion of recurrent education. Because these trends are so common, we choose not to discuss them.

Second, there are the problems Norway faces that are similar to those problems faced by the few Western European countries that have completed their comprehensive reform programs. In this regard, Sweden comes immediately to mind, and it is clear that the two countries face certain very similar issues, most of which continue to center around unity and equity.[6] It has been found in both countries that structural adjustments are unable to solve the remaining issues connected with equity. Other courses of action are necessary, and in both countries, the solution has been defined in such a way that it rests with some form of local initiative. In terms of governance, local, community authorities are becoming more and more responsible for the way personnel are assigned, the manner in which programs are run, and the way money is spent. A striking deviation from tradition in this regard is the tendency to allow local authorities greater flexibility with regard to curriculum planning and implementation.

Local control has also extended to the individual school, which has been given the responsibility to define how it will operate and how it will enhance and improve the quality of life within the school.[7] Quality of life pertains not only to children but the professional staff as well.

Local control has also extended to the classroom level and the way each individual child is to be treated. The classroom teacher has been given greater and greater responsibility to ensure that each child be given the kind of educational program appropriate to that child. Each teacher is being charged with the responsibility to resolve the remaining problems of injustice and inequality that the structural adjustment are unable to deal with. Two revisions of the 1974 model curriculum plan have been adopted (M85 and M87), and the most recent has been compared with the pre-Labor Party period when almost no central involvement in the curriculum was expected.

As this imperative has become a part of the common wisdom, three major challenges to that aim have begun to solidify. Critics point out that the policy places so much responsibility on the local level that they are unable to deliver. The teacher associations claim that the teachers are already overburdened and they cannot be expected to take on such overwhelming responsibility without enormous resources and pay for the work they are expected to do. Teachers complain that local communities are expecting them to become local historians and social scientists, for which most have little training. The government expects the teachers to be researchers, but their training has not prepared them for the task. Many critics also worry that the firm ideals of national unity now seem to be confused. Professionals and politicians of every political orientation wonder how the ideals of unity can be maintained. Even Conservatives, such as Steinar Riksaasen, Superintendent of Schools in Oslo, lament the loss of national curriculum content, compulsory subjects, stable student groupings, firm time schedules, the loss of the inner unity of subject matter, etc.[8]

There is rising concern that because there is so much flexibility, conventional course labels no longer have general meaning. The time allotted to a course in one community may be quite different from the time allotted in another community. The content covered in a course in one school may be quite different from the content covered in another school. In spite of these voices of protest, the advocates of change, who are dominating the new curricular studies, continue to accentuate the trend to local initiative and responsibility.

The third category of problems Norway is facing are those rather unique to the way that country has defined its comprehensive structure. There remain internal contradictions in the structure, such as the mechanism established to equalize vocational and general education, which at the present time actually disadvantages large numbers of youth, who have no other real option but vocational training.

Somewhat more remote from actual schooling, but just as crucial in terms of long-term developments is the interest on the part of authorities to encourage educational development at the grass roots level. Such an R&D model has enormous potential, but lacks any historical foundation and may never really materialize. The few projects that have been undertaken, such as computer education, still require a substantial centralized input.

Decentralized funding policies also may be too young to make any judgment about their potential. They certainly place school people in a different role as they must learn to compete with other agencies for resources. Time alone will determine if they possess the ability to justify the resources which they feel they require.

There is also the growing recognition that certain groups in society do not benefit fully from policies of "equal access" and "equal treatment" in the educational process. It is here that some distinction between equality and social welfare must be made. Equality in Norway is typically equated with the right of individuals and groups to their share of the resources society, the opportunity to compete with others without disadvantage. However, equal opportunity must be supplemented, in certain cases, by programs and resources that compensate for inherent disadvantages that equal access and participation would never provide. This is particularly the case with regard to special needs children and certain ethnic minorities. Adjustments are being made, but no solution has yet been found to those in need of social welfare considerations in education.

The "post-comprehensive era" in Norway is still very young. It is difficult to define where the nation will turn its energies and direct its attention. If the past two centuries is any indicator, we can be assured that it will be successful in its endeavors.

Notes

Preface
1. Henry M. Levin, "The Dilemma of Comprehensive Secondary School Reforms in Western Europe," *Comparative Education Review* (October, 1978), p. 435.
2. Val D. Rust, "The Common School Issue — A Case of Cultural Borrowing," in W. Correll and F. Süllwold (eds.), *Forschung und Erziehung* (Donauworth: Auer, 1968), p. 93.
3. Karl Deutsch discusses the notion within the context of cybernetics in *The Nerves of Government* (London: The Free Press of Glencoe, 1953), but does an actual study in "Social Mobilization and Political Development," *American Political Science Review*, vol. 60 (Sept., 1961), pp. 493-514.
4. B. G. Peters, "The Development of Social Policy in France, Sweden and the United Kingdom," in Martin 0. Heisler (ed.), *Politics in Europe* (New York: David McKay, 1974), pp. 257-292.
5. An example of comparative studies between Sweden and West Germany is Robert H. Beck, "Chapter Eight: A Contrast in European School Reform: West Germany and Sweden," *Change and Harmonization in European Education* (Minneapolis: University of Minnesota Press, 1971).
6. James Coleman, "The Concept of Equality of Educational Opportunity," *Harvard Educational Review*, vol. 38, no. 1 (Winter, 1968), pp. 7-22.; Torsten Husen, *Social Background and Educational Career* (Paris: OECD, 1972).

Chapter One: Democracy and Education in Pre-Independent Norway
1. Neil Elder, Alastair H. Thomas, and David Arter, *The Consensual Democracies? The Government and Politics of the Scandinavian States* (Oxford: Martin Robertson, 1982), p. 3.
2. Article 108.
3. Stein Kuhnle, *Patterns of Social and Political Mobilization: A Historical Analysis of the Nordic Countries* (London: Sage, 1978).
4. Stein Rokkan, "Geography, Religion, and Social Class: Crosscutting Cleavages in Norwegian Politics," in Seymour M. Lipset and Stein Rokkan (eds.), *Party Systems and Voter Alignments: Cross-National Perspectives* (New York: Free Press, 1967), p. 368.
5. John Dewey, *Democracy and Education* (New York: Macmillan, 1916), pp. 101-102.
6. Joseph A. Lauwerys (ed.), *Scandinavian Democracy: Development of Democratic Thought and Institutions in Denmark, Norway and Sweden* (Copenhagen: Danish Institute, Norwegian Office of Cultural Relations, and Swedish Institute, 1958); Wilhelm Keilhau, *Norway in World History* (London: Macdonald and Co., 1944; Thomas K. Derry, *A Short History of Norway* (London: Allen & Unwin, 1968); reprinted ed. (Westport, Conn.: Greenwood Press, 1979); Hjalmar H. Boyesen, *The Story of Norway* (New York: G.P. Putnam's Sons, 1886).
7. Derry, Chapter 5.

8. Keilhau, Chapter 9.
9. Boyesen, Chapter 15.
10. Halvdan Koht and Sigmund Skard, *The Voice of Norway* (Morningside Heights, New York: Columbia University Press, 1944), p. 12.
11. Keilhau, p. 31.
12. Rokkan, p. 369; Vilhelm Aubert, "Norske jurister: En yrkesgruppe gjennom 150 år," *Tidsskrift for Rettsvitenskap*, vol. 77 (1964).
13. Andreas Holmsen, *Norges historie: Fra de eldste tider til 1660*, 3de ed. (Oslo: Universitetsforlaget, 1961); J. R. Christianson, "The Reconstruction of the Scandinavian Aristocracy, 1350-1660," *Scandinavian Studies*, vol. 53 (Spring, 1981), pp. 289-301.
14. Otto Hellevik, *Stortinget-En sosial elite? En undersøkelse av sammenhengen mellom sosial bakgrunn og politisk karriere* (Oslo: Pax forlag, 1969), p. 37.
15. James A. Storing, *Norwegian Democracy* (Boston: Houghton Mifflin Co, 1963), p. 16.
16. Peter Christian Asbjørnsen, and Jørgen Moe, *Norwegian Folk Tales*, translated from the Norwegian by Carl Norman and Pat Shaw Iversen (Oslo: Dreyers forlag, 1960), p. 6.
17. Raymond E. Lindgren, *Norway-Sweden: Union Disunion and Scandinavian Integration* (Princeton: Princeton University Press, 1959), p. 20.
18. Aubert, p. 109.
19. Boyesen, p. 475.
20. Louis Hartz, *The Liberal Tradition in America: An Interpretation of American Political Thought since the Revolution* (New York: Harcourt, Brace & World, 1955).
21. Elder, Thomas and Arter.
22. Rokkan, p. 379.
23. Kuhnle, pp. 17-18.
24. Rokkan, p. 379.
25. For a full account of his life, see Halfdan Olaus Christophersen, *Niels Treschow, 1751-1833* (Oslo: Grøndahl & søn forlag, 1977).
26. Quote of Hesselberg in Ibid.
27. Einar Høigård og Herman Ruge, *Den Norske skoles historie: En oversikt* (Oslo: J. W. Cappelens forlag, 1947), p. 62.
28. Carl Johan Fredrik Wisløff, *Norsk kirkehistorie*, 2 vols. (Oslo: Lutherstiftelsen, 1966), vol. 1, p. 191.
29. For an account of the schools see: Jan Berggrav, *Oslo katedralskole gjennom 800 år* (Oslo: Gyldendal Norsk forlag, 1953); Einar Aas, *Stavanger katedralskoles historie: 1243-1826* (Stavanger: Johns. Floors forlag, 1925); Einar Aas, *Kristiansands katedralskoles historie: 1642-1908* (Oslo: Gyldendal Norsk forlag, 1932); Asbjørn Øverås, A. E. Erichsen, and Johan Due, *Trondheim katedralskoles historie: 1152-1952* (Trondheim: F. Brun forlag, 1952); Harald Bergh, *Hamar katedralskoles historie* (Hamar: Hamar Arbeidersblads trykkeri, 1953).

30. H. Glarbo, "Studier over danske adelsmønds udenlandsrejser i tiden 1560-1660," *Historisk Tidsskrift*, 9th series, vol. 4 (1926), pp. 221-74; Birte Andersen, *Adelig opfostring: Adelsbørns opdragelse i Danmark: 1536-1660* (Copenhagen: G.E.C. Gad, 1971).
31. Wisløff, vol. 1, p. 305.
32. Bergh, pp. 45-47.
33. J.R. Christianson, "The Reconstruction of the Scandinavian Aristocracy, 1350-1660," *Scandinavian Studies*, vol. 53 (Spring, 1981), p. 296.
34. Willis Dixon, *Education in Denmark* (Copenhagen: Centraltrykkeriet, 1958), p. 12.
35. Martin Dehli, *Fredrikstad bys historie*, 2 vols. (Fredrikstad: Fredrikstad kommune, 1960), vol. 1, pp. 83-87.
36. Ibid., p. 345.
37. Nicolai Wergeland, *Christiansands beskrivelse* (Oslo: Universitetsforlaget, 1963), pp. 182-209.
38. Reidar Myhre, *Den Norske skoles utvikling: Ide og virkelighet* (Oslo: Fabritius forlag, 1976), p. 17.
39. "Forordning om skolerne paa landet i Norge, og hvad klokkerne og skoleholderne derfor maa nyde," Friderichsberg den 23 Januar, Anno 1739.
40. Høigård og Ruge, p. 48.
41. Dixon, p. 48.
42. Øverås, Erichsen and Due, p. 277.
43. Michael Drake, *Population and Society in Norway: 1735-1865* (Cambridge: The University Press, 1969), p. 10.
44. Wergeland, pp. 207-208.
45. "Forordning om skolerne paa landet," 1739, Article 37.
46. Article 38.
47. Unesco, *World Survey of Education: Volume II: Primary Education* (Paris: Unesco, 1958).
48. "Placat og nærmere anordning angaaende skolerne paa landet i Norge," Christiansborg slot udi Kjøbenhavn, den 5te Maji, 1741.
49. Olav Kolltveit, *Odda, Ullensvang og Kinsarvik i gamal og ny tid*, 2 vols. (Odda, Ullensvang og Kinsarvik bygdeboknemnd, 1963) vol. 2, p. 586.
50. Anders Ohnstad, *Aurland bygdebok: Fram til om lag 1920* (Aurland: Aurland sogelag, 1962), pp. 275-76.
51. Ibid., p. 165.
52. Knut Tveit "School and Literacy: Introduction of the Elementary School in Norway in the 1730s and 1740s," unpublished manuscript from the University of Oslo, undated.
53. Wergeland, pp. 209-10.
54. Haagen Krog Steffens, *Kragerø bys historie: 1666-1916* (Christiania: Grøndahl & søn, 1916), p. 210.
55. Bull, et al., vol. 4, p. 340.
56. Wergeland, p. 214.
57. Bull, et al., vol. 4, p. 40.

58. Edward D. Clarke, *Travels in Various Countries of Scandinavia: Denmark, Sweden, Norway, Lapland, and Finland* (London: Cadell and W. Davies, 1838), p. 378.
59. Martin Luther, *Three Treatises* (Philadelphia, 1960), reprint of 1520 document.

Chapter Two: Educational Alternatives at the Time of Independence

1. The constitutional convention was held at the mansion of Carsten Tank Anker at Eidsvoll in 1814. Of the 112 delegates, 54 were from rural districts, 25 from cities and towns, and 33 from the military. More than half were from the official class (59 delegates , including 14 active priests), 16 were business-men and 37 were farmers; James A. Storing, *Norwegian Democracy* (Boston: Houghton Mifflin Co., 1963), p. 23; Andreas Aarflot, *Norsk kirkehistorie*, 2 vols. (Oslo: Lutherstiftelsen, 1967), vol. 2, p. 288.
2. Anna-Liisa Sysiharju, "Primary Education and Secondary Schools," in Folmer Wisti et al. (eds.), *Nordic Democracy: Ideas, Issues, and Institutions in Politics, Economy, Education, and Cultural Affairs of Denmark, Finland, Iceland, Norway, and Sweden* (Copenhagen: Det Danske selskab, 1981), p. 420.
3. Anders Bure, *Regni Suecie geographica et politica descriptio* (1631), pp. 36-37, cited in Carlo M. Cipolla, *Literacy and Development in the West* (Baltimore: Penguin Books, 1969), p. 54.
4. Edvard Bull, Wilhelm Keilhau, Haakon Shetelig, og Sverre Steen, *Det Norske folks liv og historie: Gjennem tidene*, 11 vols. (Oslo: H. Aschehoug & Co., 1929-38), vol. 7, p. 233.
5. John Patterson, *The Book of Every Loud: Reminiscences of Labour and Adventure in the Work of Bible Circulation in the North of Europe and in Russia* (London: 1858), pp. 51-52.
6. Aarflot, vol. 2, p. 236.
7. Cipola, p. 63.
8. Knut Tveit, "School and Literacy. Introduction of the Elementary School in Norway in the 1730s and 1740s," unpublished manuscript from the University of Oslo, undated.
9. Knut Tveit. "Skrivekyndighet i Norden i det 18. og 19. århundre," unpublished manuscript from the University of Oslo, undated.
10. Bull, et al., vol. 4, pp. 339-40.
11. Michael Drake, *Population and Society in Norway: 1735-1865* (Cambridge: The University Press, 1969), p. 164.
12. Only 4 registers from 108 parishes in Akershus diocese still remain, Johannes Helgheim, "Biskop Peder Herslebs arbeid med sjeleregister," *Norsk Pedagogisk Tidskrift*, vol. 64, no. 9 (1980), pp. 350-51.
13. Bull, et al., vol. 6, pp. 339-40.
14. Tveit, "School and Literacy," pp. 5-6.
15. Ibid.
16. Ibid., p. 10.
17. Johannes Helgheim, *Allmugeskolen på bygdene* (Oslo: Universitetsforlaget, 1980), p. 212.
18. Tveit, "Skrivekyndighet," p. 7.

19. Most of the biographical data in this chapter is taken from Einar Jansen (ed.), *Norsk biografisk leksikon*, 18 vols. (Oslo: H. Aschehoug & Co., 1934); Additional reference has been made, though not cited, to works such as Jens E. Krafft, *Norsk forfatter-lexicon: 1814-1856* (Oslo: Johan Dahls forlag, 1863).

20. Kjell Ivar Vannebo, *En nasjon av skriveføre: Om utviklinga fram mot allmenn skriveferdighet på 1800 — tallet* (Oslo: Novus forlag, 1984).

21. *Statistical Abstract* (Washington, D.C.: U.S. Government Printing Office, 1984); *Statistisk årbok* (Oslo: Sentralbyrå, 1984).

22. Val D. Rust and Francis Reed, "Home Teaching and Herbart," *Educational Horizons*, vol. 58 (1979/80), pp. 75-81.

23. Jansen, vol. 10, pp. 487-89.

24. Ibid., vol. 11, pp. 369-72.

25. Kenneth Charlton, *Education in Renaissance England* (London: Routledge and Kegan Paul, 1965), p. 213.

26. Egil Johansson, "The History of Literacy in Sweden in Comparison with Some Other Countries," *Educational Reports Umeå*, no. 12, 1977, p. 87.

27. Jansen, vol. 11, pp. 20-21.

28. Ibid., vol. 2, pp. 36-40.

29. Ibid., vol. 13, pp. 322-78.

30. Ibid., vol. 2, pp. 490-92.

31. Ibid., vol. 6, pp. 404-05.

32. Ibid., vol. 11, pp. 278-79.

33. Val D. Rust, *Alternatives in Education: Theoretical and Historical Perspectives* (London: Sage, 1977), pp. 16-17.

34. Trygve Dokk, *Oppsedinga: Det gamle arbeidslivet* (Oslo: Johan Grundt Tanum forlag, 1953), pp. 95-97.

35. Jansen, vol. 2, p. 288.

36. Ibid., vol. 3, pp. 186-87.

37. Ibid., vol. 9, pp. 558-59.

38. Hilkka Kauppi, "Public Libraries in the Nordic Countries," in Folmer Wisti, et al. (eds.), *Nordic Democracy: Ideas, Issues, and Institutions in Politics, Economy, Education, Social and Cultural Affairs of Denmark, Finland, Iceland, Norway, and Sweden* (Copenhagen: Det Danske selskab, 1981), p. 495.

39. E. D. Johnson and H. M. Harris, *History of Libraries in the Western World* (New York: Scarecrow Press, 1976).

40. Edward D. Clarke, *Travels in Various Countries of Scandinavia including Denmark, Sweden, Norway, Lapland, Finland*, 2 vols. (London: T. Cadell and W. Davies, 1838), vol. 2, p. 378.

41. Bull, et al., vol. 7, p. 232.

42. Knut Gjerset, *History of the Norwegian People*, 2 vols. (New York: Macmillan Co., 1915), vol. 2, pp. 347-48.

43. Sigvald Hasund and Ivar Nesheim, *Landbruks undervisningen i Norge gjennem hundre år: 1825-1925* (Oslo: J. W. Cappelens forlag, 1926).

44. Jansen, vol. 3, pp. 48-49.

45. Gjerset, vol. 2, pp. 399-400.

46. Ingrid Semmingsen, et al. (eds.), *Norges kulturhistorie*, 8 vols. (Oslo: H. Aschehoug & Co., 1979), vol. 4, p. 185.
47. Jansen, vol. 18, pp. 472-76.
48. Gjerset, p. 401.
49. Jansen, vol. 9, pp. 44-45.
50. Hans-Jørgen Dokka, *Fra allmueskole til folkeskole: Studier i den Norske folkeskoles historie i det 19. hundreåret* (Oslo: Universitetsforlaget, 1967), p. 60.
51. Einar Høigård og Herman Ruge, *Den Norske skoles historie: En oversikt* (Oslo: J. W. Cappelens forlag, 1947), p. 49; Wergeland, p. 49.
52. Wergeland, p. 209.
53. Dokka, p. 17.
54. Bull, et al., vol. 7, pp. 230-31.
55. Per Kviberg (ed.), *Kristiania og skipsfarten* (Kristiania: Alb. Cammermeyer, 1917), p. 38.
56. Ibid., pp. 48-56.
57. Ibid., pp. 48-74.
58. Ingrid Pedersen, *Litt om tegne- og arkitektundervisning i Norge før høiskolens tid* (Trondheim: F. Brun forlag, 1935), pp. 19-23, 55-61.
59. Dokk, pp. 100-02.
60. Clarke, vol. 2, p. 443.
61. Jansen, vol. 6, pp. 94-96.
62. Ibid., vol. 14, pp. 450-53.
63. Ibid., vol. 4, p. 172.
64. Carl Wille Schnitler, "Christianias Første kunstskole: Et bidrag til vor kunsthistorie," *Historisk Tidskrift*, vol. 5 (1909), pp. 121-153.
65. Cipola, pp. 117-18.
66. Clarke, vol. 2, p. 376.
67. Jansen, vol. 7, pp. 564-65.
68. Ibid., vol. 9, pp. 364-66.
69. Ibid., vol. 13, pp. 280-85.
70. Ibid., vol. 14, pp. 360-61.
71. Ibid., vol. 5, pp. 559-61.
72. Ibid., vol. 2, pp. 36-40.
73. Ibid., vol. 8, pp. 600-07.
74. Ibid., vol. 11, pp. 548-50.
75. Ibid., vol. 8, p. 476.
76. Charlton, p. 216.
77. Jansen, vol. 1, pp. 173-77.

Chapter Three: Educational Imperatives in Independent Norway

1. Sigmund Skard, *Classical Tradition in Norway* (Oslo: Universitetsforlaget, 1980), p. 83.
2. Hans-Jørgen Dokka, *Fra allmueskole til folkeskole: Studier i den Norske folkeskoles historie i det 19. hundreåret* (Oslo: Universitetsforlaget, 1967), pp. 87-104; Reidar Myhre, *Den Norske skoles utvikling: Ide og virkelighet* (Oslo: Fabritius forlag, 1976).

3. Paul Barth, *Die Geschichte der Erziehung* (0. R. Reisland, 1911); reprinted ed. (Darmstadt: Wissenschaftliche Buchgesellschaft, 1967), p. 464.

4. Willis Dixon, *Education in Denmark* (Copenhagen: Centraltrykkeriet, 1958).

5. Samuel Laing, *Journal of a Residence in Norway during the Years 1834, 1835 and 1836* (London: Longman, Rice, 1840), pp. 479-80.

6. Frederik Julius Bech, "Forslag til at danne almuens ungdoms lærere, samt ideer og vink til de paa landet i Norge omgaaende almue-skolelæreres hensigtsvarende dannelse," *Hist. Phil. Saml.* III, 1 (1812).

7. H. 0. Christophersen, *Niels Treschow: 1751-1833* (Oslo: Grøndahl & søn, 1977), pp. 119-127, 209-213.

8. Tønnes Sirevåg, "Utsyn over Norsk videregående skole i 175 år," draft manuscript, p. 5.

9. Edvard Bull, Wilhelm Keilhau, Haakon Shetelig, og Sverre Steen, *Det Norske folks liv og historie: Gjennem tidene*, 11 vols. (Oslo: H. Aschehoug & Co., 1929-38), vol. 8, p. 340.

10. Ibid., pp. 341-42.

11. Knut Nygaard, "Nordmenns syn på Danmark og danskene i 1814 og de første selvstendighetsår," *Norske videnskaps-akademi i Oslo, Historisk-filosofisk klasse*, vol. 1 (Oslo: H. Aschehoug & Co., 1960), p. 405.

12. *Norges Offisielle Statistikk, Historisk statistikk 1978* (Oslo: Statistisk Sentralbyrå, 1978), p. 623.

13. "Lov angaaende de lærde skoler og examen artium ved universitet, *Stortings-forhandlinger* (1815-16), Sept. 1815, pp. 206-07, March, 1816, pp. 28-29, 106.

14. Einar Høigård og Herman Ruge, *Den Norske skoles historie: En oversikt* (Oslo: J. W. Cappelens forlag, 1947), p. 77; Christophersen, p. 371.

15. Johann Friedrich Herbart, "Über Erziehung unter öffentlicher Mitwirkung," in Walter Asmus (ed.), *Johann Friedrich Herbart: Pädagogische Schriften*, vol. 3 (Düsseldorf: Helmut Kuepper, 1965).

16. Oscar J. Falnes, *National Romanticism in Norway* (New York: Columbia University Press, 1933), p. 109.

17. *Historisk statistikk 1978*, p. 623.

18. Øverås, Erichsen and Due, p. 300.

19. Høigård og Ruge, p. 91.

20. Dokka, p. 25.

21. Fritz K. Ringer, *Education and Society in Modern Europe* (Bloomington: Indiana University Press, 1979), p. 133.

22. Martin Dehli, *Fredrikstad bys historie*, 2 vols. (Fredrikstad: Fredrikstad kommune, 1964), vol. 2, p. 264.

23. Johannes Tews, *Ein Jahrhundert preussischer Schulgeschichte* (Leipzig: Quelle und Meyer, 1914).

24. Articles 1 and 2.

25. According to Karen Larsen, the speciedaler at the time had approximately the same value as the American dollar ($1.08), see *A History of Norway* (Princeton: Princeton University Press, 1974), p. 399.

26. Anders Ohnstad, *Aurland bygdebok: Fram til om lag 1920* (Aurland: Aurland sogelag, 1962), p. 282.

27. Olav Kolltveit, *Odda, Ullensvang og Kinsarvik i gamal og ny tid*, 2 vols. (Odda, Ullensvang og Kinsarvik bygdeboknemnd, 1963), vol. 2, p. 161.
28. For example, Ibid., p. 162.
29. Quoted in Bull, et al., vol. 8, p. 342.
30. Nikolai Wergeland, "Kirke og undervisnings-væsenet vedkommende," printed in *Statsborgeren*, 3. hefte (1832), p. 73.
31. Kolltveit, pp. 160-161.
32. A. 0. Vinje, *Skrifter i samling* (Oslo: J. W. Cappelens forlag, 1943), p. 150.
33. Helge Dahl, *Norsk lærerutdanning fra 1814 til i dag* (Oslo: Universitetsforlaget, 1959), pp. 2-5.
34. Høigård og Ruge, p. 82.
35. *Lov angaaende almue-skolevæsenet paa landet*, 14de Juli 1827, Article 23.
36. Ibid., Article 3.
37. Ibid., Article 14.
38. Ola Høyland, *Stord bygdebok* (Stord: Stord herad, 1973), p. 106.
39. Ohnstad, p. 285.
40. *Statistiske tabeller vedkommende undervisningsvæsenets tilstand i Norge ved udgangen af aaret 1837* (Christiania: Christian Holst, 1840).
41. Val D. Rust, *Alternatives in Education: Theoretical and Historical Perspectives* (London: Sage, 1977).
42. Richard A. Easterlin, "A Note on the Evidence of History," in C. Arnold Anderson and Mary Jean Bowman (eds.), *Education and Economic Development* (Chicago: Aldine Publishing, 1965).
43. Høigård og Ruge, p. 90.
44. Dokka, p. 46.
45. Rolv Straume, *Bø bygdebok,* 3 vols. (Tromsø: Bø kommune, 1964), vol. 3, p. 348.
46. *Historisk statistikk 1978*, p. 619.
47. Rust, p. 35.
48. *Historisk statistikk 1978*, p. 619; Dokka, p. 48.
49. Dokka, pp. 51-52.
50. *Lov* (1827), Article 7.
51. Dokka, p. 52.
52. Dokka, pp. 51-52.

Chapter Four: Educational Overtones in Romantic Nationalism
1. Theodore Jorgenson, *History of Norwegian Literature* (New York: Haskell House, 1970).
2. Einar Jansen, *Norsk biografisk leksikon*, 18 vols. (Oslo: H. Aschehoug & Co., 1934), vol. 18, pp. 401 & 477.
3. "Blodstenen," printed on 17 Juli 1821, and reprinted in *Henrik Wergelands skrifter*, vol. 1 (Oslo: J. W. Cappelens forlag, 1958), pp. 295-297.
4. "For almuen," reprinted in *Henrik Wergelands skrifter*, vol. 1, pp. 271-280.
5. "For almuen: Andet hefte," reprinted in *Henrik Wergelands skrifter*, vol. 1, pp. 281-294.

6. "For almuen: Sjette hefte: Normandens katechisme," reprinted in *Henrik Wergelands skrifter*, vol. 2, pp. 243-252.
7. Henrik Wergeland, vol. 1.
8. Eilert Sundt, *Om Piperviken og Ruseløkbakken*, (Christiania: P. T. Mallings bogtrykkeri, 1858), pp. 43-47, also published in *Morgenbladet* (1858), no. 96.
9. In *Folkevennen*, 1852, pp. 39-40.
10. Hans-Jørgen Dokka, *Fra allmueskole til folkeskole: Studier i den Norske folkeskoles historie i det 19. hundreåret* (Oslo: Universitetsforlaget, 1967), p. 91.
11. Ola Høyland, *Stord bygdebok* (Stord: Stord herad, 1973), p. 106.
12. "For almuen," reprinted in *Henrik Wergelands skrifter*, vol. 1, p. 268.
13. Agnes Mathilde Wergeland, *Leaders in Norway and Other Essays* (Menasha, Wisconsin: George Banta, 1916), p. 55.
14. Bjørnstjerne Bjørnson, *Arne and Early Tales and Sketches*, translated by Rasmus B. Anderson (New York: Doubleday, Page & Co.,1881), pp. 203-247; for a list of specific books in one library, see, Eilert Sundt, "Om selv-undervisning og almue-biblioteker," *Folkevennen*, vol. 8 (1850), pp. 123-127.
15. Haakon Nyhuus, "De Norske statsunderstøttede folkebogsamlinger," in *Bibliotek og samfunn* (Oslo: J. Petlitz bogtrykkeri, 1963).
16. Dokka, p. 95.
17. Nyhuus, p. 36.
18. Martin Dehli, *Fredrikstad bys historie*, 2 vols. (Fredrikstad: Fredrikstad kommune, 1964), vol. 2, p. 396.
19. Henrik Wergeland, "Videnskabelighedens udbredelse i Norge," *Morgenbladet*, vol. 28 (Jan. 1835).
20. For the writings of Welhaven on Wergeland, refer to Johan S. Welhaven, *Samlede digterverker*, vols. 1 & 2 (Oslo: Gyldendal Norsk forlag, 1943).
21. Jorgensen, p. 195.
22. Welhaven, vol. 1, pp. 123-159.
23. *Norsk sagn, samlede og udgivne* (Arendal, 1833).
24. Peter Andreas Munch, *Det Norske folks historie*, 8 vols. (Christiania, 1851-1859).
25. Oscar J. Falnes, *National Romanticism in Norway* (New York: Columbia University Press, 1933), p. 82.
26. The first volume of Norwegian Folk Tales (*Norske folke-eventyr*) was published in Christiania in 1841-44, with the second edition in 1851-52.
27. Falnes, p. 240.
28. Sverre Mortensen and Per Vogt, *One Hundred Norwegians* (Oslo: Johan Grundt Tanum, 1955), p. 94.
29. Didrik Arup Seip, *Norskhet i sproget hos Wergeland og hans samtid* (Kristiania: H. Aschehoug & Co., 1914), p. 11.
30. Perfect because they were more archaic, more like Old Norse, Falnes, p. 306.
31. *Dølen* was published from 1858 until Vinje's death in 1870.
32. *Dølen*, p. 264.
33. Falnes, p. 237.

34. Halvdan Koht, *Johan Sverdrup, 1816-1869*, vol. 1 (Christiania: H. Aschehoug & Co., 1918), p. 30.
35. Sigvald Hasund og Ivar Nesheim, *Landbruks undervisningen i Norge gjennem hundre år: 1825-1925* (Oslo: J. W. Cappelens forlag, 1926), pp. 25-34.
36. Translated from the Norwegian by Rasmus B. Anderson (New York: Doubleday, Page & Co., 1881).
37. Einar Høigård og Herman Ruge, *Den Norske skoles historie: En oversikt* (Oslo: J. W. Cappelens forlag, 1947), p. 124.
38. Thomas K. Derry, *A History of Modern Norway: 1814-1972* (Oxford: Clarendon Press, 1973).
39. *Dølen*, no. 3 (1858).
40. Bjørnson, p. 35.
41. Falnes, p. 291.
42. Norges Offisielle Statistikk, *Historisk statistikk 1978* (Oslo: Statistisk sentralbyrå, 1978), p. 623.
43. Halvdan Koht, *Life of Ibsen*, translated by Einar Haugen and A. E. Santaniello (New York: Benjamin Blom, 1971), p. 57.

Chapter Five: The Winds of Educational Reform

1. Thomas K. Derry, *A History of Modern Norway: 1814-1972* (Oxford: Clarendon Press, 1973), Chapter 4.
2. Edvard Bull, *Sozialgeschichte der norwegischen Demokratie* (Stuttgart: Ernst Klett Verlag, 1969), p. 29.
3. Ibid., p. 36.
4. Ibid., p. 37.
5. Johan S. Welhaven, "Om nødvendigheten av at indskrænke sprogstudiets omfang i den lærde undervisning," *Vidar*, 5. Aug., 1832.
6. For a complete discussion of the debate see Otto Anderssen, *Realisme eller klassicisme: Et kapitel av 1830-aarenes kulturkamp* (Christiania: H. Aschehaug & Co., 1921); Helge Dahl, *Klassicisme og realisme: Den høgre skolen i Norge 1809-1869* (Oslo: Universitetsforlaget, 1976).
7. "Bemerkninger angaaende sprogstudiets omfang i vår lærde gjenstand i dette Blads no. 1 og 2."
8. Einar Jansen, *Norsk biografisk leksikon*, 18 vols. (Oslo: H. Aschehoug & Co., 1934).
9. Dahl, p. 19.
10. Jansen, vol. 13, p. 38.
11. Asbjørn Øverås, A. E. Erichsen, and Johan Due, *Trondheim katedralskoles historie: 1152-1952* (Trondheim: F. Bruns bokhandel, 1952), pp. 328-29.
12. Jansen, vol. 2, pp. 341-45.
13. Friedrich Wilhelm Thiersch, *Über den gegenwertigen Zustand des öffentlichen Unterrichts in den westlichen Staaten von Deutschland, Holland, Frankreich und Belgien*, 3 vols. (Stuttgart: J. G. Cotta, 1838).
14. Ibid., vol. 2, p. 379.

15. Frederik Moltke Bugge, *Det offentlige skolevæsens forfatning i adskillige tyske stater tillikemed ideer til en reorganisation af det offentlige skolevæsen i kongeriget Norge* (Christiania: Chr. Grøndahl & søn, 1839).
16. Ibid., vol. 3, pp. 4-44.
17. Ibid., vol. 3, pp. 45-81.
18. Ibid., vol. 3, p. 21.
19. Ibid., vol. 3, pp. 81-86.
20. Ibid., vol. 3, pp. 86-92.
21. Johannes J. Helgheim, *Allmugeskolen i byane* (Oslo: Universitetsforlaget, 1981), p. 56.
22. Einar Høigård og Herman Ruge, *Den Norske skoles historie: En oversikt* (Oslo: J. W. Cappelens forlag, 1947), pp. 87-88.
23. The Commission developed a number of draft proposals, along the way, including *Udkast til lov angaaende de lærde skoler* (Christiania: Chr. Grøndahl & søn, 1841), *Udkast til love om almueskolevæsenet* (1842).
24. *Statistiske tabeller vedkommende undervisningsvæsenets tilstand i Norge ved udgangen af aaret 1837* (Christiania: Christian Holst, 1840).
25. Helge Dahl, "Søren Jaabæk og folkeopplysningen," *Norsk Pedagogisk Tidskrift*, vol. 50, no. 3 (1966), p. 84.
26. Ibid., p. 82.
27. *Lov om almueskolevæsenet i kjøbstæderne* (Christiania: Chr. Grøndahl & søn, 1848), Article 1.
28. Val D. Rust, *Alternatives in Education: Theoretical and Historical Perspectives* (London: Sage, 1977), pp. 25-27.
29. Article 1.
30. Article 4.
31. Hartvig Nissen, "The School System of Norway," *Journal of the Society of Arts*, vol. 2, no. 98 (October 6, 1854), p. 766.
32. Rust, pp. 29-35.
33. Article 25.
34. *Statistiske tabeller, 1837.*
35. Article 2.

Chapter Six: Social Reform Impulses at Mid-Century

1. Quote of W. A. Wexels in Einar Molland, *Church Life in Norway: 1800-1950*, translated by Harris Kaasa (Westport, Conn.: Greenwood Press, 1978), p. 60.
2. Ingeborg Lyche, *Adult Education in Norway* (Oslo: Universitetsforlaget, 1964), p. 9.
3. Byron J. Nordstrom (ed.), *Dictionary of Scandinavian History* (Westport, Conn.: Greenwood Press, 1986), pp. 471-72.
4. *Sandhed til Gudfrygtighed* in 1737.
5. Nordstrom, p. 472.
6. Molland, pp. 32-33.
7. Ibid., p. 34.
8. Ibid., p. 39.

304 Notes

9. Edvard Bull, Wilhelm Keilhau, Haakon Shetelig, og Sverre Steen, *Det Norske folks liv og historie: Gjennem tidene*, 11 vols. (Oslo: H. Aschehoug & Co., 1929-38), vol. 6, p. 55.
10. Arthur Spencer, *The Lapps* (New York: Crane, Russak & Co., 1978), p. 35.
11. Ibid., p. 36.
12. Ibid.
13. For an overview of the labor movement, see Einhart Lorenz, *Arbeiderbevegelsens historie*, 2 vols. (Oslo: Pax forlag A.S., 1972).
14. Einar Jansen, *Norsk biografisk leksikon*, 18 vols. (Oslo: H. Aschehoug & Co., 1934), vol. 16, p. 305.
15. Thomas K. Derry, *A History of Modern Norway: 1814-1972* (Oxford: Clarendon Press, 1973), p. 42.
16. Jansen, vol. 16, p. 305.
17. "Arbeider-foreningenes petition til Hans Majestæt Kong Oscar I," *Arbeider-Foreningenes Blad*, nr. 27, 1849.
18. Derry, p. 43.
19. Einar Høigård og Herman Ruge, *Den Norske skoles historie: En oversikt* (Oslo: J. W. Cappelens forlag, 1947), pp. 98-99.
20. Martin Samuel Allwood, *Eilert Sundt, A Pioneer in Sociology and Social Anthropology* (Oslo: 0. Norlis, 1957).
21. (Christiania: Nordisk forlag, 1907).
22. Theodore Jorgenson, *History of Norwegian Literature* (New York: Haskell House, 1970), pp. 296-98.
23. A discussion of early girls schooling is found in Helen Englestad, "Håndarbeid i Norge før 1875," in Astrid Bugge, Helen Engelstad og Valborg Kvaal, *Statens kvinnelige industriskole: 1875-1950* (Oslo: H. Aschehoug & Co., 1950), pp. 18-42.
24. Article 2.
25. Agnes Mathilde Wergeland, *Leaders in Norway and Other Essays* (Menashe, Wisconsin: George Banta, 1916).
26. Ibid., p. 80.
27. Therese Bertheau, "Kvinder i den høiere skoles tjeneste," in Marie Høgh, *Norske kvinder: En oversigt over deres stilling og livsvilkaar i hundredeaaret 1814-1914*, 3 vols. (Christiania: Berg & Høghs forlag, 1914), pp. 161-187.
28. Otto Anderssen, "Norwegisches Schulwesen," in Wilhelm Rein (ed.), *Encyklopädisches Handbuch der Pädagogik*, 2. Aufl., 10 vols. (Langensalza, 1902-11), vol. 6, p. 307.
29. Hartvig Nissen, *Om kvindelige dannelse og kvindelige undervisnings anstalter* (Christiania: P. T. Mallings bogtrykkeri, 1849), p. 24.
30. For an account of the school see Nils Andreas Ytreberg, *Nissens pikeskole: 1849-1949* (Oslo: Kirstes boktrykkeri, 1949).
31. Ellisiv Steen, *Camilla Collett* (Oslo: Grøndahl & søn, 1963), pp. 10-11.
32. Betty Selid, *Women in Norway: Their Position in Family Life, Employment and Society* (Oslo: Department of Cultural Relations, Royal Ministry of Foreign Affairs, 1970), p. 11.

33. Jonas Lie, *The Family at Gilje*, translated by Samuel Corrin Eastman (Garden City, N.J.: Doubleday, Page & Co., 1923), p. 73.

Chapter Seven: Hartvig Nissen and the Foundation of Modern Schooling
1. For a full account of his life and works, see Einar Boyesen, *Hartvig Nissen: 1815-1874 og det Norske skolevæsens reform*, 2 vols. (Oslo: Johan Grundt Tanum, 1947).
2. Einar Jansen, *Norsk biografisk leksikon*, 18 vols. (Oslo: H. Aschehoug & Co., 1934), vol. 10, p. 140.
3. Otto Anderssen, *Kulturgang og skole i Norge* (Stockholm: P. A. Norstedt & søners forlag, 1917), p. 29.
4. Jansen, vol. 10, p. 140.
5. Ibid., vol. 10, p. 143.
6. Boyesen, vols. 1 & 2.
7. Helge Dahl, *Klassisisme og realisme: Den høgre skolen i Norge: 1809-1869* (Oslo: Universitetsforlaget, 1976), p. 58.
8. Ibid., p. 58.
9. Hartvig Nissen, *Grundtrek af en plan for omdannelsen af almueskolevæsenet paa landet* (Christiania: P. T. Mallings Bogtrykkeri, 1851).
10. *Om almueskoler og almueopplysningen*.
11. Ottar Hellevik, *Stortinget-En sosial elite? En undersøkelse av sammenhengen mellom sosial bakgrunn og politisk karriere* (Oslo: Pax forlag, 1969), p. 37.
12. See Hartvig Nissen, *Beskrivelse over Skotlands almueskolevæsen* (Christiania: P. T. Mallings forlags-boghandel, 1856).
13. Ibid., a visual scheme for the towns is on page 288.
14. Hartvig Nissen, *Udkast til love om almueskolevæsenet paa landet og i kjøbstæderne* (Christiania: P. T. Mallings bogtrykkeri, 1856).
15. A number of publications had made reference to the preparation of females to become teachers. For example, Frederik M. Bugge. *Det offentlige skolevæsens forfatning i adskillige tyske statter tillikemed ideer til en reorganisation af det offentlige skolevæsen i kongeriget Norge* (Christiania: Chr. Grøndahl & søn, 1839); the Swedish educator Per Adam Siljestrom, *Om bildningsmedlen och bildningen i Forenta Staterna* (Stockholm: P. A. Norstedt & søner, 1852), and Nissens 1856 recommendation: *Udkast til en lov om almueskolevæsenet paa landet*, (1859), Article 12.
16. Nissen, 1856, Chapters 1-3.
17. Tønnes Sirevåg, *Innhogg og innsyn i skole og politikk: 1814-1884* (Oslo: Universitetsforlaget, 1985), p. 39.
18. Ibid., p. 39.
19. Article 70.
20. Johannes J. Helgheim, *Allmugeskole på bygdene* (Oslo: Universitetsforlaget, 1980).
21. Sirevåg, p. 42.
22. Martin Dehli, *Fredrikstad bys historie*, 2 vols. (Fredrikstad: Fredrikstad kommune, 1964), vol. 2, p. 263.

23. *Lov om almueskolevæsenet paa landet* (Christiania: Chr. Grøndahl & søn, 1860).
24. Articles 3 & 11.
25. Reidar Myhre, *Den Norske skoles utvikling: Ide og virkelighet* (Oslo: Fabritius forlag, 1976), p. 50.
26. Article 5.
27. P. A. Jensen, *Læsebog til brug for vore skolers nederste og mellemste klasser ved undervisningen i modersmaalet* (Bergen: 1843); K. D. Knutzen, *Læsebog for almueskolens øverste klasse* (Christiania: Johan Dahl, 1836).
28. H. J. Grøgaard, *Læsebog for barn* (Christiania: 1816).
29. P. A. Jensen, *Læsebog for folkeskolen og folkehjemmet* (Christiania: 1863).
30. Olav Kolltveit, *Odda, Ullensvang og Kinsarvik i gamal og ny tid*, 2 vols. (Odda, Ullensvang og Kinsarvik bygdeboknemnd, 1963), pp. 420-21.
31. Rolv Straume, *Bø bygdebok*, 3 vols. (Tromsø: Bø kommune, 1964), vol. 3, pp. 351-52.
32. Hans-Jørgen Dokka, *Fra allmueskole til folkeskole: Studier i den Norske folkeskoles historie i det 19. hundreåret* (Oslo: Universitetsforlaget, 1967), p. 210.
33. Sturla Brørs, *Namdalseid* (Namdalseid: Beitstaden historielag, 1974), p. 93.
34. Hartvig Nissen, "The School System of Norway," *Journal of the Society of Arts*, vol. 2, no. 98 (October 6, 1854), p. 766.
35. Asbjørn Øverås, A. E. Erichsen, and Johan Due, *Trondheim katedralskoles historie: 1152-1952* (Trondheim: F. Bruns bokhandel, 1952), p. 338.
36. Marcus Jacob Monrad, *Om de klassiske studiers betydning for den høiere almendannelse* (Christiania: J. Dyhwad, 1857).
37. Dahl, pp. 61-7.
38. Fredrik Ording, *Henrik Ibsens vennekreds: Det lærde Holland: Et kapitel av Norsk kulturliv* (Oslo: Grøndahl & søn, 1927).
39. Dahl, p. 68.
40. Outlined in Odelsting proposition no. 44 (1857).
41. Dahl, p 90.
42. *Statistiske tabeller vedkommende undervisningsvæsenets tilstand i Norge i 1853* (Christiania: 1857/58).
43. Hartvig Nissen, "Om ordningen af vort høiere skolevæsen," *Morgenbladet* (1865) no. 21, 24, 25, & 26; a booklet having the same title was also published (Christiania: P. T. Mallings forlagsboghandel, 1865).
44. Ibid., p. 31.
45. Ibid., pp. 35-38.
46. Ibid., p. 39.
47. *Forslag til en forandret ordning af det høiere skolevæsen* (Christiania: P. T. Mallings bogtrykkeri, 1867).
48. Ibid., p. 2.
49. Ibid., p. 7.
50. Ibid., p. 320.
51. Ibid., p. 325.
52. Ibid.

53. Reactions of faculty group included in *Forslag til en forandret ordning*, 1867, pp. 76-80.
54. Ibid., pp. 80-82.
55. Ibid., pp. 475-77.
56. *Forslag til en forandret ordning*, vol. 3.
57. For a full discussion of Aars and Voss, see Bjarne Bjørndal, *P. Voss og hans samtid* (Oslo: Universitetsforlaget, 1959); for a specific treatment of the proposal, see "I anledning af kommitte-instillinge i skolesagen," Christiania, den 11. Marts, 1869.
58. Tønnes Sirevåg, "Utsyn over Norsk videregående skole i 175 år," draft manuscript.
59. For a full discussion of the men and their positions, see Victor Hellern, *Den Norske skoles idegrunnlag* (Oslo: Universitetesforlaget, 1968), pp. 57-68.
60. Sigmund Skard, *Classical Tradition in Norway* (Oslo: Universitetsforlaget, 1980), p. 115; *Lov om offentlige skoler for en høiere almendannelse* (Christiania: Grøndahl & søn, 1869), Article 3.
61. Hartvig Nissen, *Skolevæsenets ordning Massachusetts* (Christiania: P. T. Mallings bogtrykkeri, 1868).
62. Jansen, vol. 10, p. 155.

Chapter Eight: A Common Foundation School
1. Theodore Jorgenson, *History of Norwegian Literature* (New York: Haskell House, 1970), p. 273.
2. Johan Ernst Sars, *Udsigt over den Norske historie*, 4 vols. (Christiania: A. Cammermeyer, 1873-91).
3. Karen Larsen, *A History of Norway* (Princeton: Princeton University Press, 1974), p. 455.
4. James A. Storing, *Norwegian Democracy* (Boston: Houghton Mifflin, 1963), pp. 59-63; Stein Kuhnle, *Patterns of Social and Political Mobilization: A Historical Analysis of Nordic Countries* (London: Sage, 1975), p. 22.
5. Camilla Collett, *Amtmandens Døtre* (Christiania: A. Cammermeyer, 1855).
6. Henrik Ibsen, *A Doll's House*, translated by William Archer (London: W. Heinemann, 1879).
7. Betty Selid, *Women in Norway: Their Position in Family Life, Employment and Society* (Oslo: Department of Cultural Relations, Royal Ministry of Foreign Affairs, 1970), p. 12.
8. Norges Offisielle Statistikk, *Historisk statistikk 1978* (Oslo: Statistisk Sentralbyrå, 1978), p. 643.
9. "Reform i vort folkeskolevæsen," *Dagbladet*, Oct. 8, 1884.
10. Ibid., p. 1.
11. "Folkeoplysningen," *Dagbladet*, Nov. 15, 1869, p. 1.
12. For a brief overview of the events, see *Udkast til love*, (1880), pp. 8-18.
13. *Stortings-tidende*, Okt., 1880, p. 149.
14. *Stortings-efterretninger*, (1880), p. 227.

15. "Statsminister Sverdrup," *Morgenbladet*, Okt., 1884, p. 211, and reprinted in *Statsminister Sverdrups forslag til reform i vort folkeskolevæsen og forhv. Statsraad N. Hertzbergs bemærkninger til dette forslag* (Oslo: Konservative foreningers centralstyrelse (1885), p. 47.

16. Examples of Hertzberg's activities may be: *Om skolelov-kommissions udkast til love om folkeskolen* (Christiania: Alb. Cammermeyer, 1888); *Om forslagene til nye love for folkeskolen* (Christiania: Alb. Cammermeyer, 1888); "Om det forhold, hvori forslagene til nye love for folkeskolen sætern folkeskolen til kirken," *Kirkelige tidspørsmaal* (Christiania: Lutherstiftelsen, 1888). For a discussion of the debate, see Victor Hellern, *Den Norske skoles idegrunnlag* (Oslo: Universitetsforlaget, 1968), pp. 108-114.

17. For a full account of the consideration of the Sverdrup proposal until it became law, see Hans-Jørgen Dokka, *Fra allmueskole til folkeskole: Studier i den Norske folkeskoles historie i det 19. hundreåret* (Oslo: Universitetsforlaget, 1967).

18. *Udkast til love om folkeskolen* (Christiania: W. C. Fabritius & sønner, 1887).

19. J. A. Bonnevie, "Skoledirektør Bonnevies foredrag," a separately published copy of a lecture given to the *Studentersamfundet* in Christiania in 1896.

20. *Innstilling fra kirke komiteen angaaende den kongelige proposition til lov om folkeskolen paa landet* (Christiania: W. C. Fabritius & sønner, 1887).

21. See *Lov om folkeskolen i byene* and *Lov om folkeskolen paa landet*, 26 Juni 1889 (Christiania: Grøndahl & søn, 1889).

22. *Historisk statistikk 1978*, p. 642.

23. For a historical overview of age grading practices in Europe, see Val D. Rust, *Alternatives in Education: Theoretical and Historical Perspectives* (London: Sage, 1977), pp. 166-180.

24. Dokka, p. 213.

25. *Lov om folkeskolen paa landet*, 1889, Articles 2, 4.

26. Dokka, p. 219.

27. Einar Høigård og Herman Ruge, *Den Norske skoles historie: En oversikt* (Oslo: J. W. Cappelens forlag, 1947), pp. 173-74.

28. U.S. Bureau of the Census, *Historical Statistics of the United Sates: Colonial Times to 1957* (Washington, D.C.: U.S. Government Printing Office, 1960).

29. *Lov om folkeskolen paa landet*, 1889, Article 16.

30. Ibid., Article 3.

31. Reidar Myhre, *Den Norske skoles utvikling: Ide og virkelighet* (Oslo: Fabritius forlag, 1976), p. 58.

32. The best classical study of nationalism and education in these countries is found in Edward Reisner, *Nationalism and Education since 1879* (New York: Macmillan, 1922).

33. Quoted in Knut Gjerset, *History of the Norwegian People*, 2 vols. (New York: Macmillan, 1915), vol. 2, p. 594.

34. Quoted in Ibid., p. 594.

35. *Lov om folkeskolen paa landet*, 1889, Article 47.

36. Ibid., Article 52.

Chapter Nine: Education Beyond the Folk School

1. Ingeborg Lyche, *Adult Education in Norway* (Oslo: Universitetsforlaget, 1964), P. 12.
2. Kaare Fostervoll (ed.), *Mot rikare mål: Den Norske folkhøgskulen 1864-1964* (Oslo: Noregs Høgskulelærerlag, 1964).
3. Alv. H. Helland, *De hundre år: Fortellinger fra Norges historie: 1814-1914* (Oslo: J. W. Cappelens forlag, 1947), pp. 241-42.
4. Hilmar Rormark, *Skolen som lever: Tradisjon og samtid i folkehøskolen* (Skien: Noregs boklag, 1972), pp. 20-25.
5. Karen Larsen, *A History of Norway* (Princeton: Princeton University Press, 1974), p. 453.
6. Christopher Bruun, *Folkelige grundtanker* (Hamar: 0. Arvesen, 1878).
7. Gunnar Lande, "Menn og meiningar i folkehøgskolen," in Fostervoll, p. 24.
8. Helland, p. 242.
9. Olav Kolltveit, *Odda, Ullensvang og Kinsarvik i gamal og ny tid, 2 vols.* (Odda Ullensvang og Kinsarvik bygdeboknemnd, 1963), p. 458.
10. Ibid., p. 462.
11. Ibid., p. 463.
12. Peter Kolberg, "Den kristelege folkehøgskolerørslen, kristelege ungdomsskolen in Noreg," in Fostervoll, p. 133.
13. *Historisk statistikk 1978*, p. 621.
14. Anders Ohnstad, *Aurland bygdebok: Fram til om lag 1920* (Aurland: Aurland sogelag, 1962), p. 404.
15. Ibid.
16. Kolltveit, p. 435.
17. Ola Høyland, *Stord bygdebok: Stord i gamal og ny tid* (Bergen: boktrykk, 1973), p. 120.
18. Nils Hjelmtveit, *Education in Norway* (Oslo: Royal Norwegian Information Service, 1946), p. 18.
19. Edgar B. Wesley, *NEA: The First Hundred Years* (New York: Harper Brothers, 1957), p. 65.
20. *Lov om folkeskolen paa landet* (Chrisiania: Grøndahl & søn, 1889), Article 3.
21. Thomas Drag, "Jørgen Dam, Philologist," translated by Anders Ørbeck and found in Hanna Astrup Larsen (ed.), *Norway's Best Stories* (New York: Books for Libraries Press, 1971), pp. 137-152.
22. Høigård og Ruge, p. 187.
23. Ibid., p. 187.
24. Georg Klem, "Politiske forutsetninger for skoleloven av 1896," *Avhandlinger fra universitetets historiske seminar*, vol. 8, no. 1 (1931).
25. *Stortings-efterretninger*, 1871, p. 207.
26. *Stortings-tidende*, 1871, p. 542.
27. *Stortings-tidende*, 1862/63, p. 594.
28. *Stortings-forhandlinger*, 1889, nr. 101, pp. 785-87.
29. Ibid., pp. 787-831.
30. *Lov om høiere almenskoler af 27de Juli 1896*. Kapitel B.
31. Ibid., Article 72.

310   Notes

32. *Stortings-tidende*, 1896, p. 954.
33. Kemp, p. 56.
34. *Stortings-tidende*, 1891, pp. 401-405.
35. *Stortings-forhandlinger*, 1889, no. 3, pp. 948-973.
36. Ibid., pp. 58-59.
37. Ibid., p. 68.
38. For a full account, see Raymond E. Lindgren, *Norway-Sweden: Union, Disunion, and Scandinavian Integration* (Princeton: Princeton University Press, 1959).
39. *Stortings-tidende*, Okt. 1869.
40. Herbert Spencer, *Education* (New York: Appleton, 1897).
41. Science Commission, "Sixth Science Commission Report," *Nature*, vol. 12 (1875), p. 594.
42. *Historisk statistikk 1978*, p. 623.
43. *Stortings-forhandlinger*, 18 June 1896, pp. 980-84.
44. Ibid., pp. 1007-1008.
45. Olav Sunnana, *Johannes Steen: Statsminister og parlamentarisk førar* (Oslo: Norske samlaget, 1967), pp. 200-201.
46. Addendum number 10; for a discussion see *Stortings-forhandlinger*, 10 July 1889, no. 10, pp. 349-54.
47. Klem, p. 83.
48. *Schools Public and Private in the North of Europe*, Special Reports on Educational Subjects, volume 17 (London: Printed for His Majesty's Stationary Office, 1907), p. 37.
49. Ibid.

Chapter Ten: Extension of Participation in Education
1. Bjørnstjerne Bjørnson, *Arne*, translated by Rasmus B. Anderson and printed in the Patriots Edition (New York: Doubleday, Page & Co., 1881), pp. 36 & 44.
2. Norges Offisielle Statistikk, *Historisk statistikk, 1978*, (Oslo: Statistisk Sentralbyrå, 1978), pp. 619-21.
3. Hans-Jørgen Dokka, *Fra allmueskole til folkeskole: Studier i den Norske folkeskoles historie i det 19. hundreåret* (Oslo: Universitetsforlaget, 1967), p. 279.
4. Ibid., p. 279.
5. Table 10.2 taken from Dokka, pp. 280-81.
6. *Historisk statistikk 1978*, p. 33.
7. Tore Lindbekk, "Education in Norway," in Natalie Rogoff Ramsøy (ed.), *Norwegian Society* (Oslo: Universitetsforlaget, 1968), p. 183.
8. Arne Garborg, *Bondestudentar* (Oslo: H. Aschehoug & Co., 1955).
9. Dokka, p. 281.
10. J. Gude-Smith, et al., *Den kvindelige industriskole i Kristiania* (Kristiania: Det mallingske bogtrykkeri, 1895), pp. 1-4.
11. Georg Klem, "Politiske forutsetninger for skoleloven av 1896," *Avhandlinger fra universitetets historiske seminar*, vol. 8, no. 1 (1931), p. 64.

12. Otto Anderssen, "Norwegisches Schulwesen," in Wilhelm Rein (ed.), *Encyklopädisches Handbuch der Pädagogik*, 2. Aufl., 10 vols. (Langensalza, 1902-11), vol. 6, p. 311.
13. *Stortings-forhandlinger*, Ot. prp. nr. 23, (1878).
14. *Stortings-tidende* (13 Mai 1878), p. 298.
15. Ibid., p. 305.
16. Ibid., p. 299.
17. Edvard Bull, Wilhelm Keilhau, Haakon Shetelig, og Sverre Steen, *Det Norske folks liv og historie: Gjennem tidene*, 11 vols. (Oslo: H. Aschehoug & Co., 1929-38), vol. 10, p. 244.
18. He had written a series of articles on women in the *Dagbladet* in 1882.
19. Karen Larsen, *A History of Norway* (Princeton: Princeton University Press, 1974), p. 472.
20. Betty Selid, *Women in Norway: Their Position in Family Life, Employment and Society* (Oslo: Department of Cultural Relations, Royal Ministry of Foreign Affairs, 1970), p. 11.
21. Kristine Bonnevie, "Kvinderne ved universitetet," in Marie Høgh (ed.) *Norske kvinder: En oversikt over deres stilling og livsvilkaar i hunredeaaret 1814-1914* (Kristiania: Berg & Høghs forlag, 1914), pp. 130-35.
22. Ibid.
23. *Lov om almueskolesvæsenet paa landet*, 16. Mai 1860, Article 11.
24. For a full discussion see Helge Dahl, *Norsk lærerutdanning fra 1814 til i dag* (Oslo: Universitetsforlaget, 1959), pp. 157-171.
25. Called *Reglement for lærerindeprøver*, and it was changed somewhat in a further ruling in November, 1872, labelled *Nærmere bestemmelser*.
26. *Historisk statistikk 1978*, p. 619.
27. Reidar Myhre, *Den Norske skoles utvikling: Ide og virkelighet* (Oslo: Fabritius forlag, 1976), p. 61.
28. Ibid., p. 61.
29. *Dagbladet*, Okt. 8, 1884.
30. Dahl, p. 173.
31. The development of this decision is traced in Dahl, pp. 171-197.
32. Myhre, p, 61.
33. *Historisk statistikk 1978*, p. 626.
34. Anderssen, p. 112.
35. Article 9.
36. Marit Dahl, Hans Tangerud and Lise Vislie, *Integration of Handicapped Pupils in Compulsory Education in Norway* (Oslo: Universitetsforlaget, 1982), p. 17.
37. *Lov om almueskolevæsent paa landet*, 1860, Article 51; *Lov om almueskole i kjøbstæderne*, 1848, Article 16.
38. Johannes Moldenhower, *Det kongelige blindeinstituts historie* (Kjøbenhavn: Holger Meyer, 1905).
39. H. M. Hauge, *Kristiania offentlige blindeskole: 1861-1911* (Kristiania: Centraltrykkeriet, 1911), p. 19.

40. Ruth E. Bender, *The Conquest of Deafness* (Cleveland: Case Western Reserve University, 1970), p. 81.
41. C. Goos. *Det kongelige døvstumme-institut i Kjøbenhavn* (Kjøbenhavn: H. Meyers, 1907), p. 426.
42. *Historisk statistikk 1978*, p. 620.
43. *Stortings-forhandlinger*, 1882, vol 6a, Indst. s. nr. 70, pp. 257-64.
44. R. C. Scheerenberger, *History of Mental Retardation* (London: Brookes Publishing, 1983), p. 73.
45. Ibid., p. 83.
46. *Sophies Minde: Beretning fra stiftelsens styre for årene 1913-1932* (Oslo: 0. Fredr. Arnesen, 1933).
47. Ibid.
48. "Vanføreforsorgen i Norge," Innstilling fra socialdepartement av 21. Sept. 1922.
49. Isabel Ross, *Journey into Light: The Story of the Education of the Blind* (New York: Appleton-Century Croft, 1951), pp. 5-6.

Chapter 11: Workers and Their Education

1. Edvard Bull, *Sozialgeschichte der norwegischen Demokratie* (Stuttgart: Ernst Klett, 1969), p. 49.
2. Ibid., p. 50.
3. Ibid., p. 52.
4. Henry Valen and Daniel Katz, *Political Parties in Norway* (Oslo: Universitetsforlaget, 1964), p. 23.
5. Karen Larsen, *A History of Norway* (Princeton: Princeton University Press, 1974), p. 498.
6. Per Kviberg (ed.), *Kristiania og skibsfarten* (Kristiania: Alb. Cammermeyer, 1917), p. 126.
7. Ibid., p. 126.
8. Ibid., pp. 126-27.
9. Ibid., pp. 116-25.
10. Ibid., pp. 134-35.
11. Ibid., pp. 120-24.
12. Chr. Rømming, "Yrkesskoler for håndverk og industri," in *Det Norske yrkeskolestellet for håndverk og industri* (Oslo: Yrkesopplæringsrådet for håndverk og industri, 1949), p. 6.
13. P. A. R. Sollied, "Den lavere tekniske undervisning i Norge: 1814-1914," in Sem Sæland, Andor Hoel og P. A. R. Sollied, *Norges tekniske undervisningsvæsen: 1814-1914* (Kristiania: J. M. Stenersens forlag, 1914), p. 23.
14. Ingrid Pedersen, *Litt om tegne- og arkitektundervisning i Norge før høiskolens tid* (Trondheim: F. Brun forlag, 1935), p. 33.
15. Sollied, pp. 24-5.
16. Joh. K. Bergwitz, *Hortens tekniske skole: 1855-1905* (Kristiania: Fred. B. Dahl, 1906).
17. *Stortings-forhandlinger*, 1868/69, vol. 4, no. 22, pp. 1-85.

Notes   313

18. E. A. H. Sinding, et al., *Kristiania tekniske skoles 25 aars jubilæum* (Kristiania: J. Chr. Gundersen, 1898).
19. F. Arentz, *Bergens tekniske skole: 1875-1900* (Bergen: John Grieg, 1900).
20. *Stortings-forhandlinger*, 1879, vol. 1, St. prp. no. IA.
21. Departementet for kirke- og undervisningsvæsenet, *Beretning om skolevæsenets tilstand: 1878* (Kristiania: Det steenske bogtrykkeri, 1880), p. 77.
22. Andor Hoel, "De tekniske læreanstalter i Trondhjem, Kristiania og Bergen," in Sem Sæland, Andor Hoel og P. A. R. Sollied, *Norges tekniske undervisningsvæsen: 1814-1914* (Kristiania: J. M. Stenersens forlag, 1914).
23. Sollied, pp. 29-32.
24. Hoel, pp. 14-20.
25. Holtsmark, p. 9.
26. *Otto Treiders Handelsskole: 1882-1982* (Oslo: S. Hammerstads boktrykkeri, 1982).
27. Øvind Stav, *Bergens handelsgymnasium: 1904-1929* (Bergen: A. S. John Grieg, 1929); Ole Lind, *Sandefjord: Kommunale handelsgymnasium og handelsskole: 1904-1954* (Sandefjord: Skolens forlag, 1954).
28. Sigvald Hasund og Ivar Nesheim, *Landbruks undervisningen i Norge gjennem hundre år: 1825-1925* (Oslo: J. W. Cappelens forlag, 1926), p. 34.
29. Ibid.
30. Hasund and Nesheim, for a full account see pp. 34-36.
31. Hasund and Nesheim, pp. 36-40.
32. *Stortings-forhandlinger*, 1893, 7.IIm s, 1397-1426, "Landbrugsbudgettet."
33. *Stortings-forhandlinger*, 1914, vol. 2a, 7.IIm s, 1397-1426, "Landbrugsbudgettet."
34. *Stortings-tidende*, 1871, p. 542.
35. Kviberg, pp. 76-9.
36. Herman Nohl, *Die pädagogische Bewegung in Deutschland und ihre Theorie* (Frankfurt: Schulte-Bulmke, 1963).
37. For a general discussion of the Norwegian movement see Einar Høigård and Herman Ruge, *Den Norske skoles historie: En oversikt* (Oslo: J. W. Cappelens forlag, 1947), pp. 201-211.
38. Anna Holsen, *Fortsettelsesskoler i Tyskland, Schweiz, og Østerrige* (Kristiania: J. Chr. Gundersens bog- og nodetrykkeri, 1898).
39. Karen Grinaker, Elise Lunder, and Christiane W. Sønsteby, *Framhaldsskolen for jenter: Gjennom 50 år* (Oslo: Merkur boktrykkeri, 1950), pp. 16-17.
40. Norges Offisielle Statistikk, *Beretning om skolevæsenets tilstand: 1900* (Kristiania: H. Aschehoug & Co., 1904), pp. 160-61.
41. Ibid., 1920, p. 59.
42. Ibid., 1910, pp. 98-99.
43. Kirke- og undervisningsdepartementet, *Innstilling fra 31. Jan. 1919*, "Om fortsettelsesskoler og fagskoler."
44. Ibid.
45. *Innstilling fra 31. Jan. 1919.*

314   Notes

46. We are unable to go into detail about this part of Norway's story. No full account of developments is available, but some sense of the activities can be gained from works such as Johan Hertzberg, "Den Norske skole i dag," *Særtryk av Kirke og Kultur*, vol. 37 (1930), pp. 257-275; *Den nye barneskole: Festskrift til overlærer Anna Sethne* (Oslo: Steen, 1937); Karl Falk, et al., *Vårt arbetssätt: Aktivitetspedagogik i praktisk utforming* (Stockholm: Kooperativa förbundets bokförlag, 1947).

Chapter Twelve: Education in a Free Norway: 1905 and Beyond

1. Einar Høigård og Herman Ruge, *Den Norske skoles historie: En oversikt* (Oslo: J. W. Cappelens forlag, 1947), p. 182.
2. Hans-Jørgen Dokka, "Enhetsskole-vedtaket av 1920: Den historiske og politiske bakgrunn," *Skolen 1983: Årbok for Norsk Skolehistorie*, 2. Årgang (1983), p. 30.
3. *Schools Public and Private in the North of Europe*, Special Reports on Educational Subjects Presented to both Houses of Parliament (London: HMSO, 1907), p. 59.
4. Ibid.
5. *Indstilling om en nærmere tilknytning mellem folkeskolen og den høiere almenskole* (Kristiania: J. Fredr. Arnesen, 1913), pp., 12-13.
6. *Beretningen om Kristiania folkeskolevæsen før 1900* (Kristiania: J. Chr. Gundersen, 1901), p. 69.
7. *Stortings-forhandlinger*, 1908, Indst. ov., vol. 66.
8. *Aschehougs Konversasjons-leksikon* (Oslo: H. Aschehoug & Co., 1971), vol. 14, p. 633.
9. Høigård og Ruge, pp. 183-86.
10. *Innstilling om forandringer i loven om folkeskolen paa landet*. Ot. prp. nr. 37 (1914); see also Indst. o. XII, (1914).
11. Bjarne Svare, Edvard Brakstad, og Eirik Sundli, *Eidsvoll offentlige landsgymnas gjennom 25 år* (Eidsvoll: F. Memmy, 1947), p. 6.
12. Ola Nordsletten, et al., *Rogaland landsgymnas: 1924-1949* (Bryne: Jæprent, 1949), p. 6.
13. Helge Sivertsen, *Demokratisk og national oppseding i Norsk skole* (Bergen: Johan Grieg, 1946), p. 57.
14. Knud Knudsen, *Latinskole uten latin* (Kristiania: Cammermeyer, 1884).
15. Sivertsen, p. 57.
16. Norges Offisielle Statistikk, *Historisk statistikk 1978*, (Oslo: Statistisk Sentralbyrå, 1978), p. 623.
17. Sigmund Skard, *Classical Tradition in Norway* (Oslo: Universitetsforlaget, 1980), p. 130.
18. Ibid., p. 129.
19. Høigård og Ruge, p. 281.
20. Skard, Chapter 12.
21. Quoted in Skard, p. 133.
22. Val D. Rust, *Alternatives in Education: Theoretical and Historical Perspectives* (London: Sage, 1977), pp. 63-83.

23. *Historisk statistikk 1978*, p. 623.
24. The committee was not given that name, but the name quickly became attached to it.
25. Magnus Alfsen, *Enhetsskolekomiteens indstilling* (Kristiania: J. Chr. Gundersen, 1913), p. 4.
26. *Indstilling om en nærmere tilknytning*, Bilag 1.
27. Tønnes Sirevåg, "Utsyn over Norsk videregående skole i 175 år," draft manuscript, pp. 101-102.
28. Enhetsskolekomiteen, *Uttalelser fra høiere almenskoler, skolestyre, skoleraadene og skoledirektørene om en nærmere tilknytning mellem folkeskolen og den høiere almenskole* (Bergen: Johan Grieg, 1915).
29. Høigård og Ruge, p. 189.
30. Dokka, p. 21.
31. Ibid.
32. See a full statement by Gjøstein in *Om en nærmere tilknytning mellem folkeskolen og den høiere almenskole*, Bilag 2., St. meld. nr. 8 (1917).
33. Ibid.
34. *Stortings-forhandlinger*, (1920), vol. 7a, p. 972.
35. Dokka, pp. 18-19.

Chapter Thirteen: The Labor Party Takes Command
1. Harry Eckstein, *Division and Cohesion in Democracy: A Study of Norway* (Princeton: Princeton University Press, 1966), p. 207.
2. Karen Larsen, *A History of Norway* (Princeton: Princeton University Press, 1974), p. 524.
3. Neil Elder, Alastair H. Thomas, and David Arter, *The Consensual Democracies? The Government and Politics of the Scandinavian States* (Oxford: Martin Robertson, 1982).
4. *Dokumenter vedkommende skole kommisjon av 1920* (Kristiania: Steenske boktrykkeri, 1922), pp. 52-53.
5. Ibid.
6. Den parlamentariske skolekommisjon, *I: Kommisjonens nedsettlse og enhetsskolen* (Oslo: Det mallingske bogtrykkeri, 1927), p. 3.
7. Ibid., p. 5.; Den parlamentariske skolekommisjon, *I. Kommisjonens nedsettelse og enhetsskolen, II. Utkast til lov om folkeskolen på landet; III. Utkast til lov om folkeskolen i kjøpstædene; IV. Utkast til lov om framhaldsskoler på landet og fortsettelsesskoler i byene; V. Utkast til lov om høiere skoler* (Oslo: Det mallingske bogtrykkeri, 1927), p. 3.
8. Einar Jansen, *Norsk biografisk leksikon*, 18 vols (Oslo: H. Aschehoug & Co., 1934), vol. 12, pp. 109-110.
9. Ibid., 110.
10. Norges Offisielle Statistikk, *Historisk statistikk 1978* (Oslo: Statistisk Sentralbyrå, 1978), pp. 619 & 626.
11. Den parlamentariske skolekommisjon, "Innstilling om lærerskolen," p. 2.
12. Edvard Bull. "Den store Norske skolekommisjon," *Nordisk Tidskrift*, 4. Årgang (1928), p. 579.

316   Notes

13. Vilhelm Bjerknes, *Falsk og ekte enhetsskole* (Oslo: Steenske forlag, 1928).
14. Ibid., p. 38.
15. *Stortings-forhandlinger*, Besl. o. nr. 100, 1930, vol. 6b, pp. 167-173.
16. *Stortings-forhandlinger*, 1931, vol. 8, pp. 406-26.
17. Ibid., p. 425.
18. *I. Kommisjoners nedsettelse og enhetsskolen*, "Instrument maker Gjøsteins dissens," pp. 32-50.
19. Thorleif Øisang, *Fra almueskole til enhetsskole* (Oslo: Arbeidernes opplysningsforbund, 1953).
20. Bull, p. 581.
21. Ibid., p. 581.
22. *II. Utkast til lov om folkeskolen på landet*, pp. 35-48.
23. *III. Utkast til lov om folkeskolen i kjøpstædene.*
24. Bull, p. 587.
25. Ibid., *V. Utkast til lov om høiere skoler*, pp. 208-09.
26. Ibid; Bull, p. 585.
27. *V. Utkast til lov om høiere skoler*, pp. 208-09.
28. Ibid., p. 209.
29. Ibid., pp. 104-06.
30. Bull, p. 590.
31. *V. Utkast til lov om høiere skoler*, pp. 108-10.
32. Ibid., p. 209.
33. Ibid., pp. 114-28.
34. Kirke-og undervisningsdepartement, *Om fortsettelsesskoler og fagskoler* (Kristiania: Arbeidernes Aktietrykkeri, 1921).
35. *Videregående undervisning for landsungdom*, pp. 3-29.
36. *Lov om norrøn artiumslinje*, Ot. prp. nr. 13, 1930. The law actually took effect on 19 June 1931.
37. *Innstilling fra lærerorganisasjonernes skolene* (Oslo: 0. Fredr. Arnesen, 1933), p. 5.
38. Ibid., p. 19.
39. Kirke og undervisningsdepartementet, Ot. prp. nr. 19, "Om utferdigelse av ny lov om høiere almenskoler," 1934.
40. *Lov av 10 Mai 1935 om høiere almenskoler*, kapittel 1.
41. *II. Utkast til lov om folkeskolen på landet*, Article 65.
42. *I. Kommisjonsnedsettelse og enhetsskolen*, pp. 44-45.
43. *Lov om folkeskolen på landet*, kapittel 5.
44. Kirke og undervisningsdepartement, *Innstilling til lov om framhaldsskoler* (Oslo: J. Chr. Gundersens boktrykkeri, 1937), p. 3.
45. Norges Offisielle Statistikk, *Skolestatistikk 1936-37* (Oslo: H. Aschehoug & Co., 1940).
46. It had actually reached the point where the *Storting* was moving to pass the law; see *Lov om framhaldsskoler*, Ot. prp. nr. 34, 1939.
47. *Vedtak til lov om framhaldsskoler*, Besl. o. nr. 225, 1946.
48. *Historisk statistikk 1978*, p. 621.

49. Kirke-og undervisningsdepartement, *Innstilling om lov om yrkesundervisning for håndverk og industri* (Oslo: Kirster boktrykkeri, 1937).
50. Ibid., p. 4; see also *Innstilling fra 31 Jan. 1919*.
51. Ibid., p. 4.
52. Yrkesopplåringsrådet for håndverk og industri, *Det Norske yrkesskolestellet for håndverk og industri* (Oslo: Yrkesopplæringsrådet for håndverk og industri, 1949), p. 10.
53. *Innstilling om yrkesundervisning*.
54. *Lov av 1 mars 1940 Nr. 1 om yrkeskoler for håndverk og industri*.
55. Article 50.
56. Matias Skarb, *Undervisningsplan for folkeskoler paa landet: Et udkast* (Lillehammer: Framgang bogtrykkeri, 1890).
57. Olav Lund, "Skolens arbeid og oppgaver gjennom 50 år," *Norsk Pedagogisk Årbok*, (1950/51), p. 43.
58. *Normalplan for landsfolkeskolen* (Kristiania: J. M. Stenersens forlag, 1922).
59. Ibid., p. 59.
60. The plan was actually separated into a town and a countryside version: *Normalplan for byfolkeskolen* and *Normalplan for landsfolkeskolen* (Oslo: H. Aschehoug & Co., 1939).
61. B. Ribsskog, "De nye normalplaner," *Vår Skole*, vol. 28, nr. 33 (19 Aug. 1939), p. 403.

Chapter Fourteen: Education during World War II and Its Aftermath

1. Education in this period has been treated in two different ways by scholars. First, it is treated as if the war never existed. For example, Einar Høigård and Herman Ruge, *Den Norske skoles historie: En oversikt* (Oslo: J. W. Cappelens forlag, 1947), gives four words, "then came the war" to the five years, this coming in the middle of sentence about a law on continuation schools that had been recommended to the *Storting* a month before the invasion, but which had to wait until 1946 to be passed, without amendments (p. 249). Reidar Myhre, *Den Norske skoles utvikling: Ide og virkelighet* (Oslo: Fabritius forlag, 1976), does not even mention the war. Alfred Oftedal Telhaug, *Norsk skoleutvikling etter 1945* (Oslo: Didakta Norsk forlag, 1982), begins his study with 1945, but makes a number of references to the past, jumping conveniently over the war years. The other way the war years have been treated has been to glorify the role of school people in the resistance movement. See, for example, Magnus Jensen, "Kampen om skolen," in Sverre Steen (ed.), *Norges krig: 1940-1945* (Oslo: Gyldendal Norsk forlag, 1950), bd. 3, pp. 73-110; Helga Steene, "Den Norske læreraksjonen for 20 år siden," *Aftenposten*, 19 Feb. 1962, pp. 3 & 9, 20 Feb. 1962, p. 3; or Hans-Jørgen Dokka, *En skole gjennom 250 år* (Oslo: NKS-forlaget, 1988).
2. Per Røssum, *Skolepolitikk og lærerstrid*, mimeographed Senior Thesis from the History Department, University of Oslo, 1981, p. 171.

3. The general events described here are drawn mainly from Tore Gjelsvik, *Norwegian Resistance: 1940-1945*, translated from the Norwegian by Thomas K. Derry (Montreal: McGill-Queens University Press, 1977); Ralph Hewins, *Quisling: Prophet without Honour* (London: W. H. Allen, 1965), and Ibid.
4. Tønnes Sirevåg, "Utsyn over Norsk videregående skole i 175 år," draft manuscript, p. 162.
5. From a notice circulated by the newly created Department of Culture and Folk-Enlightenment, "Den nye skolen og lærerstanden," *Vår Skole*, vol. 29, nr. 49 (14 Dec. 1940), p. 545.
6. Jensen, p. 76.
7. Notice by R. Skancke reprinted in the *Norsk Skuleblad*, vol. 8, nr. 7 (1941), p. 106.
8. Notice to various teacher organizations sent by the Department on 17 March, 1941 and reprinted in the *Norsk Skuleblad*, vol. 8, nr. 16 (1941), p. 239.
9. Helga Steene, see note 1 above.
10. "De 43 yrkesorganisasjoners skriv av 15. Mai 1941 til Reichskommissar für die besetzten norwegischen Gebiete," published in *Vår Skole*, vol. 31, nr. 1 (21 Juli 1945).
11. Steene, p. 80.
12. Proclamation of 7 Feb. 1942, published in many outlets including *Vår Skole*, vol. 31, no. 4 (21 Feb. 1942).
13. "Landsleder Orvar Sæther om Norges Lærersamband," *Norsk Skuleblad*, vol. 9, nr. 7 (14 Feb. 1942), pp. 98-101.
14. "Lærerfronten avslutter sit 'illegale' virke med landsmøte," published in several outlets including *Norsk Skuleblad*, vol. 9, no. 2 (14 Juli 1945), pp. 27-28.
15. An English translation found in Gjelsvik, p. 60.
16. Ibid., pp. 60-65.
17. Ibid.
18. Some account of those who remained in the classroom can be found in Hans Lødrup, *Læreraksjonenens sanne bakgrunn: Et tidsbilde* (Kristiansund: Eget forlag, 1948).
19. Røssum, p. 12.
20. Among those studies that prove helpful are Hallvard Røger, "Nationalismens pedagogiske teorier," *Magistergradsavhandling i pedagogik*, University of Oslo, 1961; Geir Oddmund Kragstad, "Nazistisk oppdragelses- og skoleideologi i Norge 1940-45," *Hovedfagsoppgave i pedagogik*, University of Oslo, 1980; and Per Røssum.
21. Sirevåg, pp. 181-186.
22. Ordinance of 14 July 1941 reprinted in *Norsk Skuleblad*, vol. 8, nr. 33 (1941), p. 502.
23. Reprinted in *Norsk Skuleblad*, vol. 1, nr. 47 (1941), pp. 707 & 708.
24. Erling Kokkersvold and Liv Mjelde, *Yrkeskolen som forsvant* (Oslo: Gyldendal, 1982), p. 72.
25. Telhaug, p. 21.

26. Notice found in *Den Norske Skole*, vol. 1 (1942), p. 47.

27. Article 9.

28. Department of Church and Education notice reprinted in *Vår Skole*, vol. 30, nr. 12 (22 Mar. 1941), p. 155.

29. Orvar Sæther, "Grunnsyn i oppdragelsen," *Den Norske Skole* vol. 1 (1942), p. 53.

30. J. Eldal, "Normalplanen av 1939 og nasjonalsosialismen," *Norsk Skuleblad*, vol. 8, nr. 5 (1941), p. 68.

31. Ibid., pp. 68-69.

32. J. Eldal, "Normalplan av 1939 og nasjonalsosialismen," *Norsk Skuleblad*, vol. 9, nr. 7 (14 Feb. 1942), pp. 102-04.

33. Ibid., p. 102.

34. Kirke-og undervisningsdepartementet, *Normalplan for byfolkeskolen* (Oslo: H. Aschehoug & Co., 1939), p. 62.

35. Ibid., 64.

36. Ibid.

37. Eldal, p. 103.

38. *Normalplan*, pp. 64-65.

39. Announcement printed in *Vår Skole*, vol. 30, nr. 19 (3 May 1941), p. 236.

40. Sirevåg gives an expanded account of these developments, pp. 170-174.

41. The increase appears to be more for bookkeeping purposes than learning, *Den Norske Skole*, vol. 2 (1943), p. 23.

42. H. C. Roti, "Larvik under og etter okkupasjonen," *Norsk Pedagogisk Tidskrift*, vol. 30 (1946), pp. 249-256.

43. Olav Barstad, "Skulane på Hadeland under og etter okkupasjonstida," *Norsk Pedagogisk Tidskrift, vol. 30 (1946), pp. 212-216*.

44. For an account of treatment given to supporters of National Unification, see Marta Steinsvik, *Frimodige ytringer* (Oslo: Eget forlag, 1946).

45. Kaare Fostervoll, "Suspensjon av lærere p.g.a. uverdig holdning," *Den Høgre Skolen*, vol. 44, nr. 2 (1945), pp. 70-71.

46. Ibid.

47. *Fellesprogrammet. De politiske partienes samarbeidsprogram for gjenreisningen.*

48. Kay Piene, "Forhåndskarakterer — eksamenskarakterer," *Den Høgre Skolen*, vol. 44, nr. 2 (1945), pp. 36-52.

49. Notice sent on 12 June 1945 by the Department of Church and Education, "Tyskens stilling i gymnaset som hovedfag eller bifag," *Den Høgre Skolen*, vol. 44, nr. 2 (1945), p. 60.

50. Notice sent on 20 June 1945 by the Department of Church and Education, "Tyskens stilling i gymnaset som hovedfag eller bifag," *Den høyre skolen*, vol. 44, nr. 2 (1945), pp. 62-66.

51. Samordningsnemnda for skoleverket, *I. Tilrådning om lov om folkehøgskolar* (Oslo: Brødrene Tengs, 1948), p. 4.

52. Samordningsnemnda for skoleverket, *XIX. Sammenfatning om utsyn* (Mysen: Indre smaalenenes trykkeri, 1952), p. 17.

Chapter Fifteen: Experimenting with New School Forms

1. Thomas K. Derry, *A History of Modern Norway: 1814-1972* (Oxford: Clarendon Press, 1973), p. 410.
2. Sigmund Skard, *Classical Tradition in Norway* (Oslo: Universitetsforlaget, 1980), p. 152.
3. Norges Offisielle Statistikk, *Historisk statistikk 1978* (Oslo: Statistisk Sentralbyrå, 1978), p. 33.
4. Derry, p. 412.
5. *Historisk statistikk 1978*, p. 22.
6. *Om lov om forsøk i skolen*, Ot. prp. nr. 40, 1954.
7. A number of materials exist on the work of the National Council for Innovation in Education. We shall mention a small eight page pamphlet put out by the Council itself, Forsøksrådet for Skoleverk, "The National Council for Innovation in Education: Its Structure and Work," (undated); another book of over 100 pages was written by two Swedish experts for OECD, Sixten marklund og Eskil Bjørklund, *Forsøksråd for skoleverket*, in the series "Forsøk og reform i skolen," nr. 24 (Oslo: Universitetsforlaget, 1971); and another valuable study by a Norwegian historian, Alfred Oftedal Telhaug, with Ove Kristian Haugaløkken, *Forsøksrådet-fornyer i Norsk skole: Historisk beskrivelse* (Oslo: Gyldendal Norsk forlag, 1984).
8. Samordningsnemnda for skoleverket, *XIX. Sammenfatning om utsyn* (Mysen: Indre smaalenenes trykkeri, 1952), pp. 12-13.
9. Tønnes Sirevåg, "Utsyn over Norsk videregående skole i 175 år," draft manuscript.
10. Samordningsnemnda for skoleverket, pp. 12-13.
11. A copy of a letter sent to the Department on 28 June 1952 by the Norwegian Secondary Teachers Association, "Forsøksommeren i den høgre skolen," *Den Høgre Skolen*, vol. 51 (1 Nov. 1952), pp. 7-8.
12. *Om tiltak til styrking av skoleverket*, St. meld. nr. 9 (1954).
13. Hans-Jørgen Dokka, "Enhetsproblemet i den Norske skoles historie," *Kirke og Kultur*, vol. 79, nr. 10 (1974), pp. 587-88.
14. Tønnes Sirevåg, "Ten Years of Norwegian School Experimentation," mimeographed copy of an unpublished report written in 1964, p. 10.
15. Ibid., p. 11.
16. Forsøksrådet, "Konstituerende møte 29. og 30. Nov. 1954," p. 12.
17. *Lov om folkeskolen*, Ot. prp. nr. 30 (1958).
18. Einar Høigård and Herman Ruge, *Den Norske skoles historie: En oversikt*, third edition (Oslo: J. W. Cappelens forlag, 1963), p. 269.
19. *Lov om folkeskolen fra 10 April 1959*.
20. Ibid., Article 1.
21. Ibid., Article 6.
22. Francis Sejersted, *Høyres historie: III. Opposisjon og posisjon* (Oslo: J. W. Cappelens forlag, 1984), p. 274.
23. Ibid., Article 1.
24. Article 2.
25. *Ot. prp. nr. 30*, p. 1.

26. *Lov om folkeskolen*, Regulation 1, p. 31.
27. Ibid., Article 3.
28. Ibid., Article 24.
29. Ibid., Article 29.
30. Ibid., Article 27.
31. Ibid., Article 28.
32. Ibid., Article 29.
33. Ibid., Article 10.
34. *Ot. prp. nr. 30*, Article 10.
35. *Lov om folkeskolen*. Article 10.
36. Notes under Ibid., Article 2.
37. Hans-Jørgen Dokka, *Reformarbeid i Norsk skole: 1950-årene - 1980* (Oslo: NKS-forlaget, 1981), p. 60.
38. Sejersted, p. 273.

Chapter Sixteen: The Nine Year Basic School

1. Forsøksrådet for skoleverket, *Læreplan for forsøk med 9-årig skole*, 1960, in the series published by the National Council for Innovation in Education, "Forsøk og reform i skolen" - nr. 5.
2. These issues are fully discussed by Hans-Jørgen Dokka, *Reformarbeid i Norsk skole: 1950-årene - 1980* (Oslo: NKS-forlaget, 1981), pp. 35-67.
3. *St. meld. nr. 75* (1959/60), p. 27.
4. Forsøksrådet for skoleverket, *Læreplan for forsøk med 9-årig skole*, 1963, revision in the series published by the National Council for Innovation in Education, "Forsøk og reform i skolen" - nr. 5.
5. Dokka, p. 49.
6. Forsøksrådet for skoleverket, *Læreplan for forsøk med 9-årig skole*. 1964, 2. utgave, in the series published by the National Council for Innovation in Education, "Forsøk og reform i skolen" - nr. 7.
7. Ibid., 3. opplag, 1965.
8. Dokka, p. 50.
9. *Ot. prp. nr. 59* (1966/67).
10. *Lov av 13 Juni 1969 om grunnskolen*, with an English translation, *Act of 13 June 1969, no. 24, Concerning the Basic School*.
11. Article 1.
12. Article 7.
13. Article 5.
14. Ibid.
15. Article 9.
16. Chapter 4, Articles 26-36.
17. Chapter 5, Articles 37-38.
18. Grunnskolerådet, *Mønsterplan for Grunnskolen* (Oslo: Universitetsforlaget, 1974), Article 7.
19. Article 7.
20. Ibid.

21. Torstein Harbo, Reidar Myhre, Per Solberg, *Kampen om mønsterplanen: Språk og sak* (Oslo: Universitetsforlaget, 1982), p. 19.
22. The relationship is fully outlined in Ibid., Chapter 4.
23. *Læreplan for forsøk*, 1960.
24. Hans-Jørgen Dokka, "Hvordan mønsterplanen ble til," *Norsk Pedagogisk Tidskrift*, vol. 63, nr. 9 (1979), p. 338.
25. Ibid.
26. Ibid., p. 343.
27. *Lov av 13 Juni 1969*, Article 7.
28. Dokka, 1979, pp. 344-45.
29. Ibid.
30. See Harbo, Myhre and Solberg in note 21, above, for a conservative interpretation, and Hans Tangerud, "Mønsterplanen - Ideologi og realitet," *Norsk Pedagogisk Tidskrift*, vol. 56, no. 4-5 (1972), for a liberal interpretation.
31. *St. meld. nr. 46* (1971/72).
32. *Lov av 13 Juni 1969*, Article 7.
33. *Mønsterplan for Grunnskole*, 1974, Article 7.
34. Ibid.
35. Per Dalin, "Innovation in Education: Norway," OECD/CERI publication of 8 June 1971, p. 14.
36. Ibid., p. 22.
37. Einar Høigård and Herman Ruge, *Den Norske skoles historie: En oversikt*, third edition (Oslo: J. W. Cappelens forlag, 1963), pp. 299-302.
38. *Mellombels lov av 16. Juni 1961 om utdanningskrav for lærerar i skulen*. Ot. prp. nr. 20 (1960/61).
39. Dalin, p. 14.
40. Alfred Oftedal Telhaug, *Norsk skoleutvikling etter 1945* (Oslo: Didakta Norsk forlag, 1982), pp. 98-99.
41. *Innstilling om lov om lærerutdanning fra Lærerutdanningsrådet*, 19. Desember 1968.
42. Printed in *Den Høgre Skolen*, nr. IB (1970).
43. *Ot. prp. nr. 51*, (1971/72).
44. *Ot. prp. nr. 36*, (1972/73).
45. *Lov av 8 Juni 1973 om lærerutdanning*, with an English translation, *Act of 8 June 1973, no. 49, Concerning the Training of Teachers*.

Chapter Seventeen: Reform at the Upper Secondary School

1. *Lov av 28. Juli 1949 om folkehøgskolar*.
2. Samordningsnemnda for skoleverket, *XIII: Den høgre skolen*, pp. 413-452.
3. A more limited law was passed in 1964, *Lov av 12. Juni 1964 om realskoler og gymnas*.
4. Samlegymnaskomiteen, *Innstilling fra komiteen til å utrede behovet for samlegymnas*, Oslo, 1960.
5. Gjelsvikutvalget, *Tilrådning om reform av gymnaset fra utvalet til å vudere reform av fagleg innhald og indre oppbygning i gymnaset*, Oslo, 1960.

6. Skolekomiteen av 1965, *Innstilling om det videregående skoleverket*, Kirke-og undervisningsdepartementet, avgitt 30. Mars 1967.
7. Ibid.
8. Skolekomiteen av 1965, *Innstilling II om det videregående skoleverket (den høgre skolen)*. *Forsøksplaner for studieretningene håndverk og industri, handel og kontor, husholdningsfag, sjøfart, estetiske fag og kunstutdanning, fysisk fostring og idrettsutdanning og allmenn studieretning*, Kirke- og undervisningsdepartementet, avgitt 1969.
9. Skolekomiteen av 1965, *Innstilling II om det videregående skoleverket (den høgre skolen)*. *Forsøksplaner for studieretningene landbruk, fiske, fisketilvirking og fiskeindustri m.v., lærlingeordning og lærlingeskole, høgre skole for funksjonshemmede og voksenopplæring. Det videre utviklingsarbeid i den høgre skolen*, Kirke- og undervisningsdepartementet, avgitt 3. april 1970.
10. Reidar Myhre, *Den Norske skoles utvikling: Ide og virkelighet* (Oslo: Fabritius forlag, 1976), p. 174.
11. Hans-Jørgen Dokka, *Reformarbeid i Norsk skole: 1950-årene - 1980* (Oslo: NKS-forlaget, 1981), p. 182.
12. *Om lov om gymnaset*, Ot. prp. nr. 5, 1972/73, pp. 5-6.
13. Myhre, p. 177.
14. Ibid.
15. Norges Offisielle Statistikk, *Historisk statistikk 1978* (Oslo: Statistisk Sentralbyrå, 1978), p. 645.
16. John Lyng served as Prime Minister for one month in 1963, and Per Borton served for six years between 1965 and 1971.
17. Myhre, pp. 177-200.
18. Gudmund Hernes og Knud Knudsen, *Utdanning og ulikhet*, NOU (Oslo: Universitetsforlaget, 1976), no. 46, p. X.
19. There had been a few early social studies on attendance ratios and social class. For example, Arne Skaug, "Fra hvilke befolkningsklasser kommer gymnasiaster og lærerskoleelever?" *Socialt Arbeid*, vol. 8, no. 4 (1934), pp. 138-146.
20. Vidkunn Coucheron Jarl, "De unge menns utdanning," *Norsk Pedagogisk Tidskrift*, vol. 37 (1953), pp. 67-93.
21. *Historisk statistikk 1978*, p. 623.
22. Coucheron Jarl.
23. Ibid., p. 88.
24. Natalie Rogoff Ramsøy, "Evner, utdannelse og yrkesvalg i Norsk samfunnsstruktur," *Tidsskrift for Samfunnsforskning* vol. 3 (August, 1961), p. 223.
25. Ibid., p. 225.
26. Reported in Alfred Oftedal Telhaug, *Norsk skoleutvikling etter 1945* (Oslo: Didakta Norsk forlag, 1982), p. 63.
27. *Historisk statistikk 1978*, p. 622.
28. Val D. Rust, "Private Schooling Arrangements in Europe," *Private School Quarterly*, vol. 1 (1984), p. 7.
29. Ibid.

30. Dokka, p. 197.
31. Privatskoleutvalget, *Innstilling om støtte til private skoler: Innstilling 1:* 31. Januar 1967, behandler videregående private skoler med paralleller i statlige, fylkeskommunale eller kommunale skoler, samlet antall, i alt 77 skoler; *Innstilling 2:* 10. oktober 1967, behandler videregående private skoler uten paralleller i tilsvarende statlige, fylkeskommunale eller kommunale skoler; *Innstilling 3:* 22. Desember 1967, behandler brevskolene, i alt 22 skoler; *Innstilling 4:* 22. Desember 1967, behandler private folkeskoler i Norge og for Norske barn i utlandet, i alt 43 skoler.
32. *Lov om tilskudd til private skoler*, Ot. prp, nr. 61, 1968/69.
33. *Lov av 6. mars 1970 om tilskudd til private skoler.*
34. *Innstilling I*, pp. 11-12.
35. Reidar Myhre, "Den videregående skole: Debatt og situasjon."
36. *Innstilling I*, p. 15.
37. Høyres landstyre, "Høyres hovedprogram og arbeidsprogram 1969-73," pamphlet published in Oslo in 1969.
38. *Om reform av gymnaset og forsøk med utbygging av det videregående skoleverk*, St. meld. nr. 91, 1969/70.
39. Kirke- og undervisningskomite, *Innstilling S*, nr. 293, 1970/71.
40. Dokka, p. 587.
41. *Lov av 21. Juni 1974 om videregående opplæring.*

Chapter Eighteen: Equality of Educational Opportunity
1. James Coleman, "The Concept of Equality of Educational Opportunity," *Harvard Educational Review*, vol. 38, no. 1 (Winter, 1968), pp. 7-22.
2. Torsten Husen, *Social Background and Educational Career* (Paris: OECD, 1972).
3. Henry Levin, "Educational Opportunity and Social Inequality in Western Europe," *Social Problems*, vol. 24, no. 2 (Dec., 1976), pp. 148-172.
4. Hans-Jørgen Dokka, *Reformarbeid i Norsk skole: 1950-årene - 1980* (Oslo: NKS-forlaget, 1981), p. 11.
5. OECD, *Development of Secondary Education: Trends and Implications* (Paris: OECD, 1969), p. 37.
6. Tore Lindbekk, *Skolesosiologi* (Theim: Tapir, 1977).
7. Liv Mjelde, "Education, Labor Force, Family: The Connection," in a collection of "Resources for Feminist Research," Toronto, 1984, p. 15.
8. Per O. Aamodt, *Utdanning og sosial bakgrunn*, Samfunnsøkonomiske Studier no. 51 (Oslo: Statistisk Sentralbyrå, 1982), p. 39.
9. Aamodt, p. 30.
10. Gudmund Hernes og Knud Knudsen, *Utdanning og ulikhet*, NOU, (Oslo: Universitetsforlaget, 1976), no. 46, p. viii.
11. For example, see ILO, *Teachers' Pay* (Geneva: International Labour Office, 1978), p. 82.
12. Hernes og Knudsen, p. viii.
13. *Utdanningsstatistikk: Videregående skoler, 1. Oktober 1982*, (Oslo: Statistisk Sentralbyrå, 1982), pp. 31-32.

14. Aamodt, p. 132.
15. Ibid.
16. Aamodt, p. 81.
17. Aamodt, p. 39.
18. Aamodt, p. 126.
19. Norges Offisielle Statistikk, *Historisk statistisk 1978* (Oslo: Statistisk Sentralbyrå, 1978), p. 623.
20. Gunnar Heckscher, *The Welfare State and Beyond: Success and Problems in Scandinavia* (Minneapolis: University of Minnesota Press, 1984), p. 173.
21. *Law of Equality between the Sexes*, passed June 9, 1978.
22. Mjelde, p. 15.
23. Ibid., p. 16.
24. *Statistisk årbok 1984*, pp. 92-93.
25. Mjelde, p. 16.
26. Val D. Rust, "Norwegian Secondary Education: Reflections on a Revolution," *Comparative Education*, vol. 15 (1985), p. 212.
27. T. Gakkestad, interview in June 1984.
28. Rust, p. 212.
29. T. Green, D. P. Ericson, and R. H. Seidman, *Predicting the Behavior of the Educational System* (Syracuse: Syracuse University Press, 1980).
30. *The Unfinished Agenda: The Role of Vocational Education in the High School*, a policy statement of the National Commission on Secondary Vocational Education, 1985.
31. Article 8.
32. *Lov av 23. november 1951 om spesialskoler.*
33. Marit Dahl, Hans Tangerud, and Lise Vislie, *Integration of Handicapped Pupils in Compulsory Education in Norway* (Oslo: Universitetsforlaget, 1982), p. 24.
34. Quoted in Ibid., p. 23.
35. Kjell Skogen, interview in August, 1986.
36. Dahl, et al., p. 19.
37. Telhaug, p. 232.
38. *Utvalg for yrkesopplæring av psykisk handikappede*, named by the Department of Church and Education in 1966.
39. *Komite til å utrede spørsmål som knytter seg til organisering av innhold av videregående opplæring med nødvendinge støttetiltak for evneveik ungdom*, a committee by the Council of Special Education in conjunction with the Department of Church and Education.
40. *Utvalget til å utarbeide nye lovregler for spesialundervisning*, named in 1969.
41. Skogen.
42. *Statistisk årbok 1984*, p. 382, and *Historisk statistikk 1978*, p. 620.
43. Skogen.
44. Skogen.
45. Samordningsnemnda for skoleverket 1947, *III, Samiske skole- og opplysningsspørsmål*, pp. 47-70.

46. Vilhelm Aubert, "Stratification," in Natalie Rogoff Ramsøy, *Norwegian Society* (Oslo: Universitetsforlaget, 1968), p. 154.
47. Article 66.
48. Samordningsnemnda, Nr. III.
49. *Law of April 10, 1959 Concerning the Elementary School*, Article 37, no. 1.
50. For example, Anton Hoem, "Samer, skole og samfunn," *Tidskrift for Samfunnsforskning* (1968).
51. OECD, *Reviews of National Policies for Education: Norway* (Paris: Organisation for Economic Co-Operation and Development, 1976), p. 185.
52. *Lov av 13. juni 1969, nr. 24 om Grunnskolen med tilleggslov av 13 juni 1975*, Article 40, nr. 7.
53. OECD, p. 189.
54. *Statistisk årbok 1984*, p. 56.
55. Mohammed D. Awan, "Socialization of Pakistani Children in Norway," paper delivered to the VI World Congress of Comparative Education in Rio de Janeiro from 6-10 July, 1987, p. 2.
56. *St. meld. nr. 74*, 1979-80, p. 29.
57. Awan, p. 13.

Chapter Nineteen: Control Issues in Education
1. For a discussion of Labor Party domination, see Bryron J. Nordstrom (ed.), *Dictionary of Scandinavian History* (Westport, Conn.: Greenwood press, 1986), pp. 424-427.
2. Neil Elder, Alastair H. Thomas, and David Arter, *The Consensual Democracies? The Government and Politics of the Scandinavian States* (Oxford: Martin Robertsen, 1982).
3. Alfred Oftedal Telhaug, *Norsk skoleutvikling etter 1945* (Oslo: Didakta Norsk forlag, 1982), p. 282.
4. Ibid.
5. Article 47.
6. Article 28.
7. Article 30.
8. Article 33.
9. For a full discussion of the issue, see Hans Tangerud, *Mønsterplanen i søkelyset* (Oslo: Universitetsforlaget, 1980), Chapter 3.
10. Article 31.
11. R. Gross and P. Gross, *Radical School Reform* (Boston: Simon and Schuster, 1969).
12. Val D. Rust, "Anti-Authoritarian Education in West Germany," *Intellect* (November, 1972), pp. 130-133.
13. T. Hague, "The Experimental Gymnas, Norway," in Per Dalin (ed.), *Case Studies of Educational Innovation: At the School Level*, 3 vols. (Paris: OECD, 1973), vol. 3.
14. Per Dalin and Val D. Rust, *Can Schools Learn?* (London: NFER- Nelson, 1983).
15. Jon Frode Blichfeldt, *Skole møter skole* (Oslo: Tanum-Norli, 1975).

16. Dalin and Rust.
17. Torleiv Teitan, "Åpne skoler i Norge," IMTEC Management Analysis Paper, undated.
18. *Om det pedagogiske utviklingsarbeidet i skolane og om forsøksverksemda i skoleverket i 1980-81*, St. meld. nr. 76.
19. Per Dalin, "Innovation in Education: Norway," a technical report by CERI for OECD, Paris, 1969.
20. "Partiene om skolepolitikken," *Norsk Skoleblad*, vol. 27 (5 September 1981), pp. 4-5.
21. "National Development of Norwegian Education, 1981-84," a working document prepared for an ICE-Conference in Feb., 1984.
22. Ministry of Church and Education, "Computer Technology in School," Report to the *Storting*, no. 39 (1983-84).
23. Val D. Rust and Per Dalin, "Computer Education Norwegian Style: A Comprehensive Approach," *Educational Technology*, vol. 25, no. 6 (1985), pp. 17-20.
24. "National Development of Norwegian Education," pp. 7-8.
25. Ibid.
26. "Nytt inntektssystem for fylkeskommunene," NOU (Oslo: Universitetsforlaget, 1979), p. 44.
27. "Nytt inntektssystem for kommunene," NOU (Oslo: Universitetsforlaget, 1982), p. 15.
28. *Om et nytt inntektssystem for kommunene og fylkeskommunene*, St. meld. nr. 26 (1983-84), p. 39.
29. Ibid., p. 39.
30. *Om endringer i lover vedrørende inntektssystemet for kommunene og fylkeskommunene*, Ot. prp. nr. 48 (1984-85).

Chapter Twenty: Educational Reform in Norway
1. Stein Kuhnle, *Patterns of Social and Political Mobilization: A Historical Analysis of the Nordic Countries* (London: Sage, 1975).
2. For an elaboration of this assumption, see Martin Carnoy and Henry M. Levin, *The Limits of Educational Reform* (New York: McKay, 1976), pp. 26-29.
3. For a description of political corporatism in Norway, see Stein Rokkan, "Numerical Democracy and Corporate Pluralism," in Robert A. Dahl (ed.), *Political Oppositions in Western Democracies* (New Haven: Yale University Press, 1966).
4. The term was coined by Per Dalin, in his studies of school renewal. See Per Dalin, *Limits to Educational Change* (London: Macmillan Press, 1978).
5. Neil Elder, Alastair H. Thomas, and David Arter, *The Consensual Democracies? The Government and Politics of the Scandinavian States* (Oxford: Martin Robertson, 1982).
6. Sixten Marklund, "The Post-Compulsory Era of Swedish Education," *Compare*, vol. 2, no. 2 (1981), pp. 185-190.

7. Gunnar Heckscher, *The Welfare State and Beyond: Success and Problems in Scandinavia* (Minneapolis: University of Minnesota Press, 1984).
8. Steinar Riksaasen, *Grunnskolen - Et system i krise* (Oslo: Gyldendal Norsk forlag, 1988).

Index